OKANAGAN UNIV/COLLEGE LIBRARY

P9-DUJ-442

Autism and Blindness
Research and Reflections

Dedication

To my children Ellie, Ben, Daniel and Jed

OKANAGAN UNIVERSITY COLLEGE
LIBRARY
BRITISH COLUMBIA

Autism
and
Blindness

Research and Reflections

Edited by

LINDA PRING PhD, CPSYCHOL, AFBPsS

Professor of Psychology, Goldsmiths College,
University of London

Consulting Editor in Psychology and Education
MARGARET SNOWLING
University of York

W
WHURR PUBLISHERS
LONDON AND PHILADELPHIA

© 2005 Whurr Publishers Ltd
First published 2005
by Whurr Publishers Ltd
19b Compton Terrace
London N1 2UN England and
325 Chestnut Street, Philadelphia PA 19106 USA

All rights reserved. No part of this publication may be
reproduced, stored in a retrieval system, or transmitted
in any form or by any means, electronic, mechanical,
photocopying, recording or otherwise, without the prior
permission of Whurr Publishers Limited.

This publication is sold subject to the conditions that it shall not, by
way of trade or otherwise, be lent, resold, hired out, or otherwise
circulated without the publisher's prior consent in any form of
binding or cover other than that in which it is published and
without a similar condition including this condition being imposed
upon any subsequent purchaser.

British Library Cataloguing in Publication Data

A catalogue record for this book
is available from the British Library.

ISBN 1 86156 444 9

Typeset by Adrian McLaughlin, a@microguides.net
Printed and bound in the UK by Athenæum Press Ltd, Gateshead,
Tyne & Wear.

Contents

Preface

When I set out on this venture I had no idea how generous my colleagues would be. This has provided me with a sense of tremendous optimism, not only about the people who have dedicated so much effort in trying to understand autism and blindness, but also in the outcome of their endeavour. This volume is the result of becoming acutely aware that there was a debate about the connections between autism and blindness that had very important practical and theoretical implications, and which as yet had not been voiced in one forum. I highlighted certain aspects that these two had in common in my inaugural lecture and I knew well that the whole picture could only be effectively painted if many authors could be brought together to provide their diverse perspectives. I was delighted to find that leaders in the field generously agreed to contribute to this work.

There is no doubt in my mind that the objective of trying to interpret and summarise the most current research reflecting the relationship between autism and blindness has been achieved. By providing in one volume a range of viewpoints, each bringing their own unique insights, a truly special text has been created, one that reflects in its variety the true nature of scientific enquiry and how that leads us to a better understanding of the subject matter. In Chapter 1, I have attempted to provide an overview of the different contributions that are to follow, and in the commentary at the end Helen Tager-Flusberg has provided her own reflections on those accounts.

Linda Pring
September 2004

Contributors

Glyn Collis PhD is a senior lecturer at Warwick University. Following a PhD at Leicester University, Glyn worked as a research fellow at the University of Strathclyde in Rudolph Schaffer's group studying social development in infancy. In addition to children with visual impairment and autism, Glyn's research interests include social and cognitive development in young children, language development and children's social relationships.

Gina Conti-Ramsden PhD, FRCSLT is Professor of Child Language and Learning at the University of Manchester. Her research interests focus on language disorders and development from preschool age to adolescence. She is the author of several books and a number of academic articles in this area, including a book on language development and social interaction in blind children.

Naomi Dale PhD is a consultant clinical psychologist specializing in childhood disability. She qualified at Nottingham University and gained her doctorate in infant child development at Cambridge University. She has worked in community-based child disability and family support services and has developed training programmes for working with families of children with disabilities. Since 1995 she has worked at Great Ormond Street Hospital for Children, London, specializing in clinical and research work with children with congenital visual impairment and at the Neuroscience Unit of the Institute of Child Health (UCL). She is also joint head of the psychology services of the hospital.

Ros Gibbons BA(Hons), MEd has been involved with the teaching of children with visual impairment for over 20 years, both in special and in mainstream schools. She has also been a Regional Tutor on the distance learning course for teachers of children with visual impairments at the

University of Birmingham, where she has studied the education of children with autism and applied it to the teaching of children with autistic spectrum disorders. She is now Deputy Head of Services for Visual Disability in Wandsworth, London.

R. Peter Hobson PhD, FRCPsych, CPsychol is Tavistock Professor of Developmental Psychopathology in the University of London, based at the Tavistock Clinic and the Institute of Child Health, UCL. He is an experimental psychologist with a PhD from the University of Cambridge, a psychiatrist and a psychoanalyst. His interest in the significance of interpersonal relations for human social and cognitive development has led him to conduct psychological studies of mothers and babies, children with autism and/or congenital blindness, and adults with personality disorder. The aim of his most recent book, *The Cradle of Thought* (2002, Macmillan), is to integrate these strands of work.

Rita Jordan PhD, CPsychol After a degree in psychology, Rita became a teacher in nursery and primary mainstream and took a Master's in Child Development researching curriculum development and parent training for those with profound and multiple difficulties. She taught children with severe learning difficulties, and then children with autistic spectrum disorders, for nine years, some of whom also had a visual impairment. Currently, Rita is Reader in Autism Studies at the University of Birmingham where she runs programmes of study for professionals and parents working with individuals with autistic spectrum disorders (including a web-based programme for carers and practitioners and a module for educational psychologists) and supervises research. She has written and researched on many aspects of autistic spectrum disorders.

Susan Leekam PhD is a reader in developmental psychology at the University of Durham. After completing postdoctoral research fellowships at the University of Sussex and in Melbourne, she took up a lectureship at the University of Kent in 1991 and subsequently a readership at Durham in 2000. Her research into the impairments of children with autism reflects a particular interest in the developmental changes that occur in social interaction and cognition. She has recently directed an NHS-funded research project on the pattern of behaviours in autistic spectrum disorders, involving a 10-year collaboration with colleagues Dr Lorna Wing and Dr Judith Gould at the National Autistic Society.

Vicky Lewis MA, DPhil Vicky Lewis's research interest in disabled children began with her DPhil at Oxford University in which she studied the visual and tactual development of young children with Down syndrome.

In 1976 she moved to Warwick University as a lecturer in Developmental Psychology. For many years she taught a third year option on the psychological consequences of disability, which led to the publication of her book *Development and Handicap* in 1987, the second edition of which was published as *Development and Disability* by Blackwell in 2003. Her main research interests remain with the consequences of disability for development, focusing on children with autism and, most recently, blind children. In 1996 she moved to the Open University as Professor of Education.

Miguel Pérez-Pereira PhD is Professor of Developmental and Educational Psychology at the University of Santiago de Compostela. His main research interests concern language acquisition in non-handicapped and in blind children. He has published several books and book chapters on developmental psychology, language acquisition in Spanish-speaking and Galician-speaking children, psychological development in blind children and language acquisition by congenitally blind children, as well as a number of papers on these topics in academic journals. He is co-author of *Language Development and Social Interaction in Blind Children* (1999, Psychology Press).

Linda Pring PhD, CPsychol, AFBPsS, Professor of Psychology at Goldsmiths College, London, studied at the University of Newcastle and later at Birkbeck College, University of London. She joined the Medical Research Council Developmental Psychology Unit in 1980 and it was here that she began research with children who were blind and children with dyslexia. In 1985 she took up a post as a lecturer in the Psychology Department, Goldsmiths College, University of London. There she continued to do research and in 1989 Professor Beate Hermelin joined her and their collaboration on 'savant' syndrome began. She was awarded a Chair in Psychology in 2000. She recently headed an international team looking at the uses of tactile graphics in a project funded by the European Science Foundation.

Valerie Tadic BSc(Hons) obtained her undergraduate degree at Goldsmiths College, University of London. Since completing her degree in 2002, Valerie has carried out a variety of research in the area of musical talent in adults with visual impairment and also explored the incidence of autism in children with congenital blindness. She continues to research language and memory in children with congenital blindness in collaboration with Professor Linda Pring at Goldsmiths College, where she is currently studying for an MSc in Research Methods in Psychology.

Helen Tager-Flusberg PhD is Professor of Anatomy and Neurobiology and Director of the Laboratory of Developmental Cognitive Neuroscience at Boston University School of Medicine. Helen has conducted research on autism for over 25 years, and is internationally recognized for her work on language and social–cognitive impairments in this population. Her research also focuses on children with other genetically based developmental disorders, with special emphasis on specific language impairment, Down syndrome and Williams syndrome. Her research explores the connections of genes, brain pathology, and cognitive and language impairments in these populations, as well as in autism. Her most recent research award is for an NIH Autism Research Center of Excellence established at Boston University School of Medicine. She has edited four books and authored over 120 articles and book chapters.

Shirley Wyver PhD is a senior lecturer at the Institute of Early Childhood, Macquarie University. Before joining the Institute in 1993, Shirley worked as a psychologist with the Child and Adolescent Section of the Royal Blind Society, New South Wales. Her research has been presented in publications such as *Journal of Visual Impairment and Blindness* and *British Journal of Visual Impairment*. In addition to working in the area of blindness and visual impairment, her research interests include pretend play and cognitive development.

Acknowledgements

I would like to thank Clive and Maggie for their support.

CHAPTER 1

Autism and blindness: building on the sum of their parts

LINDA PRING

The aim of this collection of contributions is to provide new insights into the relationship between autism and blindness – a relationship that is illuminating but certainly complex and from some perspectives debatable. The book offers a set of chapters by leading researchers and clinicians who have characterized significant features associated with both types of impairment and the parallels between them. Its primary focus is on social–cognitive development and to some extent this provides an extension of the work begun by Neil O'Connor and Beate Hermelin (1978). In their book *Hearing and Seeing and Space and Time*, they describe studies with children with sensory loss and cognitive impairments, comparing children who are congenitally blind and deaf with those suffering from autism. Their studies are considered now to be classic not only because of a new methodology, comparing groups of children with impairments, but also for the inventive nature of the studies. Their focus was on explaining the different cognitive styles that the children presented, and their findings reveal important evidence from which many current perspectives begin.

Autism considered by itself has been the subject of increasing interest both to specialists and to the general public. Since Kanner first described the syndrome in the mid-twentieth century, the understanding of autism has come a long way. The abnormal developmental pattern observed in autism has highlighted the key significance of certain features of typical development. Thus psychological explanations of autism not only may provide insights into the disorder itself but may, by comparison, significantly elucidate cognitive and social development in typically developing children. Autism is now understood to be a neurodevelopmental condition sensitive to genetic and other organic disruptions influencing brain development (Lord and Bailey, 2002). There is also an increasing recognition of a broader spectrum of autistic disorders (ASD), and the current prevalence rate of approximately 6.0/1000 (Charman, 2002) suggests that the disorder is far from rare. Psychological research has helped by describing the behaviours that characterize individuals with autism, and it is useful to remember that the diagnosis has no medical test but relies on the behavioural and developmental picture observed. For example, a distinctive feature of the diagnosis is the impaired development of 'theory of mind', i.e. the 'everyday' ability to understand other people's beliefs, thoughts and desires in order to explain and predict their behaviour. With the ability to infer mental states, like the true and false beliefs of oneself and others, children become more capable of participating in a wide range of conversational and social interactions.

There is a contrast between the impetus for research on children with autism and that for research on children who are blind. The loss of a sensory channel has not been considered to provide unique insights into typical development in the way that has been true of autism. Instead, the significance of the loss of the visual channel has informed reflections about issues such as cross-modal integration, plasticity, imagery and differential cognitive styles. Moreover, the challenges to experimental studies with this group are associated with many features unrelated to psychological questions but fundamental to good research. Many of these are mentioned in the following chapters; among them are: difficulties associated with diagnosis resulting in difficulties with inclusion and exclusion criteria, frequent co-morbidity with other disabilities, low incidence rates, geographical dispersion and within-group heterogeneity. Despite these problems, interest in the development of children who are blind has been the subject of important theoretical and experimental research and these are also referred to in the chapters that follow. Perhaps the insightful work of Selma Fraiberg stands out as providing a foundation for future research. Since Fraiberg's classic descriptions (Fraiberg, 1977), researchers have increasingly noted the commonalities between children with autism and those with severe and profound visual impairment. At about the same time the pivotal role of joint attention in typical development and its impairment in children with autism was being recognized. Joint attention behaviours involve the triadic coordination or sharing of attention among the infant, another person and an object or event. The critical medium of attention might be vision and, if so, might help to explain the increasing number of associations being drawn between autism and blindness.

Our understanding of joint attention and its association with later social and language development has proved to be a key component in predicting trajectories in typical children as well as development in autism, and certainly in the developmental pattern of children with visual disabilities. Yet questions remain as to the significance of shared behaviours between the groups, and indeed as to whether, on closer inspection, these will still be considered 'shared' behaviours. Such considerations are important, for the answers provide the context for parental support, educational programmes and therapeutic interventions. Thinking about autism and blindness, and delineating clearly the variety of research avenues explored to date, are objectives of the current volume. Hopefully, it will act as a catalyst for reflection and progress in the field.

In his books *Autism and the Development of Mind* (1993) and *The Cradle of Thought* (2002), Peter Hobson develops his unique and philosophical thesis on human thought and mind. In these he suggests that by exploring our earliest beginnings we might try to understand our mental life. His starting points concern *thought*, *will* and *feelings*. We are fortunate to have, in Chapter 2 of this book, an essay by him which clarifies particular elements of his thinking and, in so doing, brings out important distinctions relevant to his empirical approach. He makes the point that there is no clear boundary between blind children with the syndrome of autism and those with some 'autistic features', yet such a distinction may have methodological merit. Commonalities between autism and blindness are suggested to be related not simply to co-morbidity but to the determining role of vision in the development of mind. He outlines the potential alternative pathways that blind children might take to 'circumvent the vision-dependent handicaps', leading us through a variety of original and influential studies of children with autism and with congenital and total sight loss. These studies by necessity provide but a sample of the data on which so many of his ideas rest; nevertheless this is a useful beginning to a set of chapters that offer both similar and contrasting interpretations of the same data. It is the nature of the best academic research and debate that there should be a diversity of views.

Susan Leekam has worked with children with autism and Shirley Wyver with blind children. In Chapter 3, they use their understanding and knowledge of the behaviour of these children to highlight important theoretical distinctions that need to be made clear to understand cognition and to see the framework into which to place the empirical evidence. At the heart of their chapter are their efforts to bring more attention to the nature of sensation and its relationship to cognition. Starting with the debate concerning sensation and cognition they make a case for the importance of 'modalarity' to understand critical constructs, such as innateness or the nature of internal mental representations and their role in development. They highlight some recent changes in our understanding of cross-modal integration and the increasing evidence for subtle and complex alternative sensory processing pathways that may serve as a substrate for compensatory mechanisms.

In an important way they continue to explore some of the propositions made by O'Connor and Hermelin (1978) a quarter of a century ago. The reference to sensory difficulties in children with autism and the implications of this are interesting and may help to determine some new routes for research. The role of low-level sensory processes and possibly adaptive cross-modal integration is seen as being an important contributor to development not just for blind children but for those with autism as well. They also suggest how this can link to social interaction and symbolic development. Their contribution highlights the need, when exploring child development, to remain open to different interpretations and to consider how restrictions in sensation and perception may provide new insights by which to understand development.

The chapter that Valerie Tadic and I contributed to this book (Chapter 4) explores associations between autism and blindness partly by focusing on early childhood behaviour in children who are blind. The chapter provides a brief overview of theoretical considerations arising from our understanding of theory of mind. It refers in particular to longitudinal research on three blind children from a corpus collected as part of a research project at Goldsmiths College. The need for longitudinal designs becomes increasingly important if we are to understand this group, and the data presented refer to changes over 14 months. The single case studies presented essentially represent 'still photos' from which to understand more general developmental growth patterns in such children (e.g. Hatton et al., 1997). We draw out the relevance of the cases against the theoretical backdrop and emphasize the need to try to combine traditional, carefully designed experimental studies with 'real life evaluations' provided by caregivers and/or teachers with everyday experience of the child and their context. Further, we report the use of the Autistic Screening Questionnaire (ASQ) completed by carers/teachers on behalf of 18 children born blind.

The second focus of the chapter presents evidence for a distinctive pattern of memory performance in individuals who are blind, and we go on to link this pattern with 'weak coherence', a cognitive style or architecture described by Uta Frith (2003) in the context of autism. Pitch processing and the musical abilities of people with visual impairments are considered within this context as is its relevance to autism and talent. We argue that certain forms of talent may be associated with a cognitive style suggestive of weak coherence. Studies with savant artists, and savant musicians who are congenitally blind, are described, exploring the associations of talent, autism and blindness.

The work of the Developmental Vision Team at Great Ormond Street Hospital and the allied research at the Institute of Child Health are given excellent representation by the exceptionally informative contribution by Naomi Dale (Chapter 5). The clarity of the reasoning behind the research and the implementation of the retrospective studies are very illuminating.

The chapter tackles the increasingly prevalent problem for clinicians in understanding why a substantial minority of infants with severe visual impairment experience developmental setback or regression. The need, in the case of blind children, to understand the typical and atypical trajectories of development is highlighted from different perspectives. Despite support for parents and children based on the available knowledge about the impact of blindness, many infants in their sample failed to progress or even regressed and lost skills that had earlier been acquired. A database set up in 1977 allowed for comparisons between blind infants visiting the clinic and typical infant development, as well as that seen in autism. Charted trajectories of development and detailed analysis of behaviour on developmental tests provided the evidence. The setback phenomenon is described in detail and the problems of setting up the research and the inclusion of groups with differential sight status are considered.

Categorization of congenital visual disorders has already been mentioned in this introduction and is notoriously difficult. Dale gives us the benefit of the most recent research studies relating to issues of sampling and classification based on the site of origin of the disorder. She describes other, related, issues such as the impact of level of vision, age, cognitive and language development, joint attention, and familial and psychosocial environment among others. Risk factors associated with setback are described as accumulating, and Dale is understandably reluctant to be definitive about the relationship between setback and autism. The validity of using tools designed to assess autism for assessment in the case of blindness is a problem, and so is assessing development in children who are blind with tools developed for the sighted. The nature of the subgroup of children who suffer this setback is still uncertain with respect to autism and blindness. Indeed, it is argued that it is still unproven whether it is a neurodevelopmental condition that occurs independently of the visual disorder or whether it is secondary to visual disorder and associated with the disruption of vision; however, the latter interpretation is, on the balance of evidence at this time, preferred. The chapter also considers future directions with regard to intervention and the need for developing suitable assessment instruments is considered. Dale shows the balance that needs to be struck by clinicians among scientific investigations, applications for remediation, and an involvement at the more immediate level of the child and his or her parents. Here we are offered the opportunity to see all three approaches providing an optimistic vision for the future.

Language has many functions: communication, social interaction, categorization and, related to this, the organization of thought. The authors of Chapter 6, Miguel Pérez-Pereira and Gina Conti-Ramsden, have spent much of their considerable research efforts exploring language in children and in particular in children with significant challenges to overcome such as language disorder itself or blindness. Their research has breathed life into an area that had been somewhat neglected. The chapter provides a lively account that explains and describes their perspective on the cognitive characteristics of blind children and why the authors would like to play down a relationship with autism. A critical review of the literature is presented making many points about the methodological problems in this area of research and certainly there are problems of the kind identified. On the other hand, as Hobson suggests in his chapter, there are sometimes valid reasons for adopting designs that may be questioned.

Be that as it may, Pérez-Pereira and Conti-Ramsden raise and review many important issues, including symbolic play, pronoun reversal, theory of mind development, along with careful and detailed psycholinguistic studies of the constructs involved in the initiation of dyadic conversations and formulaic and imitative speech. Generally, they suggest that blind children do not share very many features or intentions or behaviours with children who are autistic or, if they do, these are superficial. The careful observation of children's language, they argue, may be understood in its own terms and related to the logical consequences of lack of vision.

Vicky Lewis and Glyn Collis have made very significant contributions to both theory and practice, with regard to education as well as to psychological development. In Chapter 7, they reflect the complexity of the issues by drawing on many different studies in which they have been directly involved, comparing their conclusions with those drawn by others. In particular, their chapter allows us to reflect on the potential hazards of dealing with negative results. For example, when observing infants, whose behaviour is often enigmatic and difficult to interpret, most researchers when reporting their findings are careful to reflect on the inherent problems. Yet in the case of children who are blind, who may pose similar difficulties of interpretation, not least because the observers have sight and the observed do not, researchers may jump to conclusions too readily or over-generalize, thereby misunderstanding the significance of the behaviours seen. Though some children with disabilities may lack certain abilities, others from the same group may not.

Among the research themes examined by Lewis and Collis are symbolic play and also the Euclidean properties of space. The former considers young people with autism as well as children who are blind and the latter refers in particular to issues raised specifically in the context of those born without vision. The authors show that, with different tasks and different underlying methods, competence may be revealed where previously it was considered non-existent or impaired. Moreover, they argue that, simply because researchers have studied individual cases of talent (for example, as described by Pring and Tadic in Chapter 4) in regard to autism, it would be wrong to assume the general prevalence of such cases. They argue that the majority of children and young people with autism simply do not show associations with particular competencies, and in the same way myths – such as people with blindness benefiting from a 'sixth sense' – may be just that. The studies they describe are original and inventive, illustrating the sensitivity that is needed to explore child development.

The educational implications of research in this area are drawn most emphatically by Rita Jordan in Chapter 8; it is fortunate to have a contribution from someone who has already published extensively on many of the issues raised in this book. Her focus is on those children who are blind and also suffer from autistic spectrum disorders. She underlines the complexity of the condition and the multiplicity of factors that will affect development and the congruence between the two groups in these respects. Collections of behaviours seen may or may not reflect autistic spectrum disorders. Normal development in children who are blind may include some 'autistic' behaviours, but, equally, some autistic behaviours may be understood through visual disturbances. Clinical judgement is at the heart of her contribution, which is a telling insight in a chapter about educational implications. It has a wealth of references to the responses of the individuals, whose own introspections and interpretations are the focus of her research. They offer fascinating insights and speak for Jordan's whole approach, where she refers to the importance of looking at special educational needs at the level of the individual child. What is critical is to contextualize this within the knowledge structure developed about the diagnoses.

She considers similarities and differences in development between the groups of children and the analysis leads naturally on to the topic of effective educational strategies. By focusing on the dual disability, Jordan has taken best practice in relation to the needs of children with autistic spectrum disorders and adapted it to what we already understand of the needs of children with visual disabilities. Here there is no room for ambiguity or uncertainty; children at home or in the classroom demand education and intervention now, and so the contribution speaks unequivocally and from the current state of understanding. The difficulties that arise because of the rarity of the condition, and the consequences for service provision, are also considered. The field benefits from specialists like Jordan to interpret and formulate strategies for dealing with these children both at home and at school.

Chapter 9, by Ros Gibbons, could very well have been the first chapter in the book. For one thing, it starts with thumbnail sketches of two children who have complex needs involving visual impairment and autistic spectrum disorders. The immediacy of these descriptions will be important to the reader whose first-hand experience with children with special needs is limited. They also serve to illustrate the perspective that Ros Gibbons takes in this chapter – that is, a commitment to address the practical needs of the children and discuss how research with other groups of children with special needs can help inform us. In the section on therapies and the section on teaching programmes, we are given a review of current techniques along with a critical commentary. This serves to put into context the implications of each therapy or teaching plan and considers when and where a programme might be appropriate. Those considered are: sensory integration therapies, auditory integration training, touch therapy, holding therapy, behaviour optometry and tinted glasses. Among the teaching programmes referred to are: behaviour modification programmes (e.g. Lovaas) and TEACCH. Apart from considering teaching and intervention therapy models, Gibbons also emphasizes the impact of the environment and curriculum issues.

The last section of the chapter is perhaps symbolic in that it refers to communication. Here the key role that communication plays is recognized and the reader is given a brief survey of different techniques that can be taught, such as the Picture Exchange Communication System (PECS), signing and augmented speech, as well as techniques that support communication like social stories and objects of reference. The commitment of the author to teaching and intervention that is sensitive to the needs of the client emerges from the review that is offered, and the final sentence serves to give a flavour of this: 'In this way we can establish communication and devise teaching programmes which are helpful rather than intrusive.'

Finally, I am grateful to Helen Tager-Flusberg for contributing an especially insightful and illuminating commentary on the overall picture that the book represents. It is no surprise to find that she starts from her own experiences both inside and outside the research laboratory, and her clarity and vision help the reader to understand why differing viewpoints may present an encouraging sign of progress in research with autism and blindness.

Progress in research needs to be informed not only by past research findings but also by the reflections of people who have taken the time to accept the challenges inherent in this area of research. This volume represents precisely that mix of perspectives, and in doing so it hopefully will stimulate further creative reflections that will enhance our understanding of both autism and blindness.

References

Charman T (2002) The prevalence of autism spectrum disorders: Recent evidence and future challenges. European Child Adolescent Psychiatry 11: 249–56.

Fraiberg S (1977) Insights from the Blind: Comparative studies of blind and sighted infants. New York: Basic Books.

Frith U (2003) Autism: Explaining the enigma, 2nd edn. Oxford: Blackwell.

Hatton DE, Bailey DB, Burchinall MR, Ferrell KA (1997) Developmental growth curves of pre-school children with vision impairments Child Development 68: 788–806.

Hobson RP (1993) Autism and the Development of Mind. Hove: Erlbaum.

Hobson RP (2002) The Cradle of Thought. London: Macmillan.

Kanner L (1943) Autistic disturbances of affective contact. Nervous Child 2: 217–50.

Lord C, Bailey A (2002) Autism spectrum disorders. In: Rutter M, Taylor E (eds) Child and Adolescent Psychiatry: Modern approaches, 4th edn. Oxford: Blackwell.

O'Connor N, Hermelin B (1978) Seeing and Hearing and Space and Time. London: Academic Press.

CHAPTER 2

Why connect? On the relation between autism and blindness

R. PETER HOBSON

Introduction

If one adopts the perspective of developmental psychopathology and seeks to discover how psychological abnormalities arise through deficits or deviations in the processes and patterning of typical development – and if one welcomes the challenge to revise our view of 'normality' when no developmental processes present themselves as candidates for derailment to explain the atypical case – then one is faced with a recurrent problem. The problem is to decide at what points and in which respects it is appropriate to map a given phenomenon or psychological process in the psychopathological case on to a set of phenomena or psychological processes that occupy a corresponding place in typical development. When one gets this mapping right, then the yield in theoretical and practical understanding may be immense; but when one gets it wrong, it may take a long while to see that the relation between typical and atypical development is not at all what one had supposed.

To express this position in less abstract terms: if you want to learn more about something, see where and how it can go wrong. But do not be misled into thinking that the way it goes wrong indicates in any direct way what normal functioning means, nor that it is easy to be sure when you have identified the 'it' that is out of sorts. Or if you want to see how malfunction has arisen, try to figure out what adequate functioning looks like, and what component processes are necessary and sufficient for its operation. But do not jump to the conclusion that these processes reveal where pathology lies. All depends on the validity and fit of the correspondences one chooses to make.

In the hope that these introductory remarks may have established my credentials for reasonableness and self-critical reflection, I am now going to jump straight in. I believe that there is an important – no, more than important – developmental connection between typically developing young children, children with autism and children with congenital blindness. I say more than important, because what forms the connection between these conditions is a developmental process both unique to and pivotal for human psychological growth. It is by mapping the three developmental trajectories on to one another that we bring into relief otherwise obscure and mostly unrecognized patterns that weave through early social and cognitive development.

So, before I say what I think these patterns are, and try to pursue my claim that they are more than important for understanding human development, I need to justify the enterprise on which I am embarked. As Simon Baron-Cohen has commented on the putative connection between autism and congenital blindness: '. . . might this be no more than a surface similarity? We should be careful not to assume that just because two church bells are ringing simultaneously they are causally connected by the same rope' (Baron-Cohen, 2002, p. 792). I think the appropriate metaphor would be to claim that two church bells are causally connected to ropes, not the same rope, but that too might be incorrect, especially since there are bells that sound like the work of bell-ringers, but are broadcast without such causative mechanisms in operation (or in the case of recordings of bell music, not directly).

So this is the problem to be faced: *is* there more than a surface similarity between autism and blindness, and *does* the pathogenesis of these two conditions have something essential in common? Unless one can make an adequate response to these questions, it seems premature not merely to draw parallels between the two conditions, but also to derive conclusions about each and about 'normal' development from the very atypicalities that each presents.

Why connect?

So why should we connect congenital blindness with the syndrome of autism? I can think of two ways to pick up the gauntlet. The first is to provide evidence that clinical features prevalent in blind children, either severally or packaged together as a syndrome, are strikingly similar to those of sighted children with autism, whether in origin or in quality or in associated clinical manifestations. The second way is to offer an explanatory account that encompasses the psychopathology of blindness and autism and provides a more plausible and satisfying – and hopefully, correct – integrative developmental perspective than anything else on offer.

From an historical perspective, these two kinds of response have not been so separate from each other. Early clinical, descriptive accounts of blind children not only portrayed elements of the clinical picture reminiscent of autism, but also suggested how deficits in interpersonal experience attributable to lack of vision might be responsible for these unusual clinical features. Perhaps most striking and potentially revealing were cases where 'autistic-like' phenomena presented in children who in other respects were not afflicted with the syndrome of autism. For example, why should blind children show echolalia and/or confusions in the use of personal pronouns, and why is their symbolic play so peculiarly restricted?

When researchers address such questions, they often treat single-case studies rather dismissively, on the grounds that particular circumstances might influence the clinical presentation of any given individual. Yet cohorts of single cases have cumulative force, and they provide penetrating detail that is missing from conventional research designs. Especially vivid accounts of blind children were published by Selma Fraiberg and by clinicians from what was the Hampstead Clinic (subsequently the Anna Freud Clinic) in London. For example, Fraiberg and Adelson (1977) described a manifestly non-autistic child, Kathie, who was congenitally totally blind from retrolental fibroplasia (retinopathy of prematurity). When Kathie was 2 years old, her language competence compared favourably with that of a sighted child of the same age, but between the ages of $2\frac{1}{2}$ and 3 years, it became evident that Kathie could not represent herself through a toy or doll. She could not recreate or invent a situation in play. For example, when Kathie was just over 3 years old she merely squeezed some 'play dough' she was given, and it made little difference when Fraiberg suggested that they make a cookie and guided Kathie's hands to this task. When Fraiberg asked: 'Can I have a bite of the cookie, Kathie?', Kathie said 'You have a bite!', put it in her own mouth, and said reflectively: 'This cookie different.' When she was provided with a small basin of water, a doll and a towel as play materials, and encouraged to give dolly a bath, Kathie showed little interest. Then as soon as she touched the water, she herself stepped into the tiny tub, and began to chant her own bath-time songs. Even when it was suggested that Kathie wash the dolly's hair and the doll was made to protest with 'No, no, I don't want a shampoo', Kathie failed to pick up the game. At the same time, Kathie would make frequent mistakes in the use of personal pronouns. 'Want me carry you?' she said to her mother when she herself wanted to be carried. It was only after she reached the age of 4 that Kathie began to represent herself in doll play and to master the use of personal pronouns.

When it came to offering an explanation for these observations, Fraiberg and Adelson wrote: 'Now we would like to suggest that the observations on subject–object in play and the problem of expressing subject and object in language have a unified core in the capacity for a certain level of mental representation. The capacity to represent oneself in play is a measure of the level of conceptual development in which the self can be taken as an object and other objects can be used for symbolic representation of the self' (1977, p. 261).

In the Hampstead Clinic, meanwhile, Wills (1979a, 1979b) also took the view that blind children are retarded in the ability to symbolize, and she pointed out how often their play is an exact repetition of some event. Sandler and Wills (1965) emphasized that, although blind children can often say what their caregivers or other people may say to them, they are less able to enact the role of someone else, and early attempts at role play lack the constant reversal of roles that is familiar in the play of sighted young children. In revisiting accounts of these children, Sandler and Hobson (2001) have highlighted how difficulties in appreciating flexible and coordinated, socially grounded perspectives, and in applying such perspectives in their own relations to the world, seemed to be characteristic of the children's psychological functioning.

Here there is reason to pause: for when interpreting the meaning of clinical features in blind children, one must be careful to consider how far these are attributable to visual impairment, or instead to coincidental neurological damage, social–emotional deprivation or other deficits in environmental provision (Warren, 1994). This applies to the range of psychological abnormalities in visually impaired children that resemble those seen in sighted children with autism, for example in social–communicative functioning (Curson, 1979; Rowland, 1983; Urwin, 1983; Preisler, 1991), in creative symbolic play and language (Andersen, Dunlea and Kekelis, 1984; Rogers and Pulchalski, 1984; Dunlea, 1989; Preisler, 1993), in stereotypies, mannerisms and ritualistic behaviour (Sandler, 1963; Chess, 1971; Jan, Freeman and Scott, 1977; Wills, 1979a, 1979b), or in their uneven profile of cognitive abilities, including difficulties with abstract thinking (Tillman, 1967; Wills, 1981) (see Green and Schecter, 1957; Elonen and Cain, 1964; McGuire, 1969; and Blank, 1975 for additional details).

Therefore it is helpful that studies with a primary focus on the concomitants of blindness per se have been complemented by research on children with specific medical diagnoses. For example, Keeler (1958) described five preschool children with retrolental fibroplasia who presented with a syndrome very much like that of early childhood autism, and a further 35 children with the same diagnosis who had similar but milder behavioural difficulties (see also Chase, 1972). Ten of the 18 rubella children in whom Chess (1971) identified full or partial autism suffered with visual as well as other defects. Rogers and Newhart-Larson (1989) described the syndrome of autism in five totally blind young children with Leber's amaurosis, and recorded autistic-like clinical features in a control group with congenital blindness from other causes (in the majority of cases, retrolental fibroplasia). From this vantage point, it is easy to appreciate the potential importance of interaction among multiple functional deficits that include but are by no means confined to the effects of visual deprivation (also Wing, 1969).

Making the case

The evidence considered thus far is certainly suggestive. At *some* level of description, there is impressive overlap between the clinical presentation of at least some blind children, and the features of early childhood autism in sighted children. And there are two levels at which this comparison may be drawn. First, one might consider the clinical features one by one: the children's impairments in social relations, their language abnormalities, their limited ability to engage in symbolic play, and so on. Here it remains to build a convincing case that the parallels between blind children and sighted children with autism are similar *enough* to posit a common underlying structure to the psychological deficits. There are other questions, too: how prevalent are such features in blind children, do they group with one another in such a way as to suggest common mechanisms in their development, and is there specificity to the association with blindness rather than with other conditions such as deafness? Secondly, one can focus upon autism as a syndrome, that is, the constellation of clinical features comprising the diagnostic criteria for the disorder. Here one can ask how prevalent is autism, rather than how commonplace are 'autistic features', among blind children – and again, just *how* similar is the syndrome in blind vis-à-vis sighted children?

Then there is the need for a theory to unite the observations. For the time being, we can work with a controversial proposal already on the table: that a major contribution to 'autistic-like' psychopathology, in blind and sighted children alike, is the children's difficulties in understanding the nature and implications of people's distinctive yet coordinated psychological relations with each other and with the world. If one adds to this the hypothesis that, in each condition, the principal obstacle to achieving such understanding is to be found in the children's deficient *experiences* of self-in-relation-to-others, and their limited awareness of self and other as individuated centres of consciousness vis-à-vis a shared world, then we have theoretical foundations for the studies that follow.

Questions and answers from recent research

I now turn to a programme of research into the relation between autism and congenital blindness conducted by colleagues and myself. We have not tackled head-on all the issues we have been considering, because this would have required – and still requires – methods beyond our scope. For example, the proper way to test for the prevalence of clinical features within a given disorder is to establish an appropriate epidemiological sample, and we were not in a position to gather data on blind children who were representative of all such individuals in the UK in terms of aetiologies, degrees of visual impairment, quality of social experience, and so on. Instead, we adopted the strategy of making comparisons between a number of matched groups.

In relation to visually impaired children, we confined ourselves to cases of profound congenital visual impairment, amounting to complete blindness or minimal light perception from birth. Our reason was partly that, as a number of workers (e.g. Preisler, 1991) have observed, children appear to benefit greatly from even small amounts of visual input, and we have been concerned to investigate how children are affected when they have a more or less total lack of visual experience. Unlike many other authors, therefore, when I refer to the 'blind children' in our studies, this is the group to which I am referring.

Secondly, we excluded cases where there were signs of coincidental neurologically based impairment – although of course this could not be excluded with certainty. Our aim was to reduce the likelihood that neurological dysfunction might have had a major role in causing the children's psychological abnormalities, independent of the children's lack of visual experience.

Thirdly, we employed a variety of control groups in order to determine specific associations between clinical features characteristic of blindness and those characteristic of autism, as well as to sharpen the focus on qualitative aspects of the clinical picture. This has sometimes meant having blind children serve as control participants for other blind children, so that we could establish whether blind children who differed in one critical respect – and here we were most interested in those who had severe social difficulties vis-à-vis children who were socially unimpaired – also differed in other respects relevant to the condition of autism.

Fourthly, and despite our own belief that there is not a clear boundary between blind children with the syndrome of autism and those with 'autistic features', we have adopted the methodological position that, for certain purposes, it is necessary to conduct separate studies of blind children who do and do not satisfy the diagnostic criteria for autism. Our reasoning is that, if in fact it were the case that 'autism' sometimes occurs in blind children coincidentally, in the sense that its pathogenesis is independent of the visual impairment and would have occurred in these children even if they had not been blind, then we need to avoid conflating deficits that are a reflection of this kind of autism with deficits that are more plausibly explained as at least partly the developmental outcome of being blind.

So let me offer succinct summaries of some of our studies in relation to questions that are relevant for our overarching theme: why connect?

(i)   *Question: Is the syndrome of autism prevalent in blind children?*
       Answer: Yes.

In our first study (Brown et al., 1997), we selected 24 children from 6 schools for the blind, on the basis that they were aged between 3 and 9 years of age and satisfied the criteria already noted (total or near-total blindness from birth, absence of manifest neurological impairment, and so on). Each of the children was observed for at least three periods of 20 minutes at play, in the classroom during a lesson and in a session of language testing. We applied two systematic rating scales for clinical features of autism – the Childhood Autism Rating Scale (CARS: Schopler, Reichler and Renner, 1988) and the Behavior Checklist for Disordered Preschoolers (BCDP: Sherman, Shapiro and Glassman, 1983) – and also filled out a systematic checklist of DSM-IIIR (American Psychiatric Association, 1987) criteria for autism in conjunction with a teacher. Finally, our child psychiatrist investigator reflected upon her own observations of each of the children, and considered whether she would have given them the diagnosis of autism.

One of the findings was that 10 out of the 24 congenitally blind children satisfied DSM-IIIR criteria for autism, a proportion that is very similar to the 7 out of 27 which Fraiberg (1977) considered to represent the incidence of autism in the population of blind children she had encountered. The diagnosis was not restricted to any particular medical diagnosis. By and large, systematic observations of the children were congruent with the DSM diagnoses, and there was little to distinguish the blind children with autism from a group of sighted children with autism who were matched for age and IQ. The one suggestion of atypicality in the blind children's autism was that, in a number of cases, their social relations seemed to have a degree of affective engagement and communication with others that is very unusual in sighted children with autism.

The obvious limitation of this study was that, although it is very likely that most severely visually impaired children would have been attending schools of the kinds we visited, we do not know how many congenitally blind children without autism might have been at non-specialized schools. Although this might modify the estimate of the prevalence rate of autism, the condition was so common in the children we studied that it is safe to conclude that the coincidence is clinically significant.

(ii) *Question: Is this simply a matter of 'co-morbidity' between two potentially separable conditions, blindness on the one hand and autism on the other?*

Answer: No.

In the study already cited, we found that 'autistic-like' clinical features were distributed across the blind children, and were not confined to those with the full syndrome of autism. When the children who did not satisfy the criteria for autism were compared with matched (non-autistic) sighted children, a number were distinctive in showing such features as echolalia, a difficulty in making peer relationships and poor imaginative play, and a majority displayed stereotyped body movements.

(iii) *Question: Are the clinical features really like those of children with autism?*

Answer: More or less, yes.

We conducted a further study (Hobson, Lee and Brown, 1999) in which we constituted a new group of even more closely matched sighted children with autism, to compare with nine of the blind children with autism. Here we could dwell on the qualities of the clinical features, including the children's abnormalities in play. What we found was that, although all the children in each group satisfied the DSM-IIIR criteria for autism, observational measures suggested that when one considered *marked* abnormalities, for instance as reflected by CARS item scores greater than 2 out of 4, two-thirds of the sighted children but only one-third of the blind children with autism showed such severe impairments in relating to people, emotional response, abnormalities in taste, smell and touch responses, and 'general impressions' of the degree of autism. Almost half the sighted children with autism but none of the blind children were also markedly abnormal in their listening response, whereas a minority of the sighted but a majority of the blind participants were markedly abnormal in their body and object use. Or, again, on the BCDP ratings there was a relatively high proportion of blind children rated as having abnormalities in responses to objects, postural oddities and motor stereotypies, gross motor coordination, personal pronoun usage and immediate echolalia, but a relatively low proportion of the blind who were abnormal in the variety and depth of affect and modulation of affect. Finally, seven of the nine blind children showed some evidence of pretend acts, with or without symbolic props – although in only one child was this actively elaborated into a theme, and in no case was one object used to represent another – whereas this was the case for only two of the sighted children with autism.

(iv) Question: Are the associations among clinical features indicative of kinship in the pathogenesis of 'autistic features' and autism in blind and sighted children?

Answer: Probably yes.

This is a difficult question to address, for the reason that it depends on one's view of the pathogenic mechanisms. We take the view that the critical factor lies in the children's abnormal engagement with the attitudes of other people, both in one-to-one social exchanges and in mutual relations vis-à-vis a shared world. The idea is that blindness predisposes to – but does not itself amount to sufficient conditions for – a difficulty in responding to and identifying with the psychological orientation of other people towards the world (including the child's self), such that the child has difficulty in appreciating how objects and events can be construed differently by different individuals, from person-anchored perspectives. The children's confusions over the use of 'I' and 'you' would be a direct reflection of this difficulty, and their limitations in symbolic play would be expected from their relative inability to attribute novel person-anchored meanings to the materials of play. On the basis of this hypothesis, we predicted that, if one compared socially impaired blind children who did *not* have autism with socially able blind children who were matched *according to IQ as well as age*, then (1) the quality of the social impairment of the former group would be akin to that of sighted children with autism (albeit not so severe), and (2) the children would be more autistic-like in a number of respects, and not only in their social relations, according to ratings on the CARS. In other words, we tested whether, on a continuum of psychopathology, there are non-autistic blind children who have the *kind* of social impairment familiar from observations of sighted children with autism, and whether these same children are also those who have additional 'autistic-like' features.

In this study (Hobson and Bishop, 2003), therefore, we constituted two matched groups of non-autistic, congenitally blind children: one group of nine children was judged by their teachers to have the ability to establish mutual interpersonal contact with adults and peers, and the other group of nine children was substantially less able to do this. Then we rated their social engagement, emotional tone, play and language during three sessions of play in the school playground. It turned out that the qualities of social impairment in the more disabled children were indeed similar to those in sighted children with autism. They were more socially isolated than their peers, less likely to express pleasure, less likely to play or be involved in reciprocal play, and less likely to comment on things and events. Moreover, independent CARS ratings in a different play setting revealed that a substantial majority of the socially impaired group had elevated scores not only for their autistic-like quality of relating to people and 'general impressions' of autism, but also for relatively non-social features of autism such as body and object use.

In a more recent study (Bishop and Hobson, submitted), we have conducted a similar study that focuses upon the children's impairments in symbolic play. Once again, the blind children with marked social impairments and elevated CARS scores were those who also showed restricted symbolic play – and close examination of the play revealed abnormalities in role-taking that are compatible with deficits in applying different perspectives to the figures and events represented in play.

(v)   *Question: Is there evidence that the social–cognitive impairment (whether or not specifically delayed rather than 'deviant') that is claimed to be prevalent among blind children and pathognomic of sighted children with autism operates at different levels across the development of blind children?*

      Answer: Probably yes.

In addition to the above studies of the social relations of congenitally blind children, we investigated their 'theory of mind' abilities (Minter, Hobson and Bishop, 1998; see Pring, Dewart and Brockbank, 1998). The relevance of this is that difficulties in the kinds of perspective-taking we have been considering – that is, in adopting different psychological orientations to the world – would be expected to have implications for the children's ability to conceptualize what it means for different people to have different beliefs about a situation or event. In an early uncontrolled study, McAlpine and Moore (1995) had reported that visually impaired children found difficulty with a task in which they needed to predict what someone would expect to find in a familiar container (one for a hamburger, the other for milk) when the participants themselves knew these actually contained a sock and water, respectively. Only two out of seven children with severe visual impairment succeeded in this task, even though their mental ages were 4 years 6 months or above, a level at which sighted children would be expected to respond correctly. In our own study, we asked 21 blind and 21 matched sighted children aged between 5 and 9 years (mean verbal mental age of each group 6 years 10 months) to feel a warm teapot and guess its contents. They were then made aware that it contained sand, not liquid. The children were asked two questions, in counterbalanced order: what they first thought was in the teapot, before the contents were poured out, and what a peer who was coming in next would think was in the teapot when he or she felt it. The results were that nearly all the sighted children answered both questions correctly, but approximately half the blind children answered one or both of the questions incorrectly, basing their replies on their current awareness of the teapot's contents. A significant minority (20%) of the blind children also failed another test in which a pencil in a box was moved when a third person had absented herself from the room, and the question was where she would look to recover it when she returned.

(vi) Question: Is the natural history of autism in blind children expected to be the same as that in sighted children with autism?

Answer: Probably no.

We have a study in progress to investigate this question. We predict that congenitally blind children who receive the diagnosis of autism early in life will tend to 'grow out of' their autism to some degree – and whatever degree that is, it will be greater than is the case for matched sighted children with autism. In order to understand why we predict this, it is worth returning to our hypothesis: if the principal factor leading to blind children's autistic-like presentation is a certain quality of impairment in social engagement to which lack of vision makes a contribution, and if (this being so) blind children with autism may have a less severe *primary* social incapacity than that in sighted children with autism – and we have already seen evidence that this is indeed the case – then it may be that there are ways to circumvent the vision-dependent handicaps and to tap into the children's relatively intact potential for social engagement, to make progress that is denied to sighted children with autism.

In fact, the results of this study (which will not be available before 2005, given the time period that needs to elapse for the follow-up observations) will be important for seeing just how much of the clinical picture of autism in the blind children might have altered. We anticipate that there may be changes not only in the children's social impairment, but also in other domains of psychological functioning such as their performance on IQ tests – our reasoning being that, early on in life, the development of thinking is heavily dependent on a minimum level of social engagement with others (Hobson, 2002).

All this leads to the final question.

(vii) Question: If it is the case that autism in congenitally blind children is different as well as similar to autism in sighted children, then why is it not better to state that some blind children are 'autistic-like' or show 'quasi-autistic features' (Rutter et al., 1999; Frith, 2003)?

Answer: Because this begs the most interesting further questions, not only about the developmental psychopathology of blindness, but also about autism in sighted children.

In a way, of course, it is a matter of taste whether one wishes to stress the differences or the similarities between autism, or for that matter 'autistic features', in blind and in sighted children. But there is a good reason to accept that, if the standard diagnostic criteria for a given syndrome apply to a given case, then the corresponding diagnosis applies as well. This is not simply consistent and logical; it may also rescue us from the trap of feeling confident that we know what we mean when we apply the term 'autism' to what appear to be more typical cases among sighted children. The fact is that a syndrome is simply that, a constellation of clinical features, and there may well be a host of differences among individuals who manifest any given syndrome. If one chooses to exclude cases like those involving blind children (or, come to that, those with severe mental handicap or those with or without genetic predisposition), then one is likely to overlook how certain of the pathogenic mechanisms that apply to such cases *also* apply to more 'typically atypical' sighted children with autism. For example, if it proves that social–developmental factors are indeed pivotal for the pathogenesis of autism in blind children, and moreover that visual impairment is especially potent in predisposing to the kinds of social–developmental handicaps that lead to autism, then one might come to appreciate how related social–developmental handicaps are also critical for the pathogenesis of autism in sighted children. We may even come to discover that, much more than we have realized, the cognitive as well as social abnormalities of sighted children with autism are developmental sequelae to forms of impairment in interpersonal engagement to which blind children are especially prone – and discover, too, that some cases of autism in sighted children may show intellectual as well as social progress if their social engagement is facilitated. The pathogenesis of autism in blind children may prove to be invaluable for our understanding of 'autism' itself.

Why connect . . . with others, if you are a young child?

In this contribution, I have desisted from offering a detailed theoretical account of the connection between blindness and autism. This is partly because I have tried to formulate such an account elsewhere (e.g. Hobson, 1990, 1993, 2002; Hobson et al., 1997). Yet perhaps as a final flourish, I should clarify what is at stake for our view of psychological development. What is at stake seems to be something very basic: the degree to which we conceptualize both typical and atypical early mental development in a narrowly cognitive and in some ways individualistic framework, or as deeply embedded in affectively configured relations with the world, and especially a child's affective engagement with people and people's ways of relating to a shared environment.

If we begin with autism, it is commonly said that children with this disorder have a 'metarepresentational deficit'. They appear to have difficulty in what might variously be described as (a) representing their own representations, or (b) relating to their own psychological relations with the world, or (c) having awareness of their own ways of construing objects and events. The importance of this difficulty is that it might reflect or even explain the co-occurrence of deficits in interpersonal understanding ('theory of mind') and limitations of symbolic play in children with autism. The hypothesis is that each of these abnormalities arises on the basis of the children's inability to grasp how people (including themselves) mentally represent the world according to individual psychological perspectives, or descriptions-for-persons. In the case of symbolic play, the idea is that in order to attribute symbolic meanings to objects that do not usually have such meanings, or to pretend that an object exists when it does not, one needs to grasp that meanings are dissociable from the objects to which they normally apply. This entails that a child understands the meaning-conferring property of psychological relations between a person and the world. To put it simply, one could not pretend that a 'this' is a 'that' unless one grasped that, as a person, one can choose to represent 'this' as 'that'.

If all this is valid, then a question arises about the developmental sources of such understanding in typical development, and the reasons for its relative lack in autism. There are those who consider that the impairment in autism is 'cognitive' not simply in its effects – and limitations in thinking and in acquiring concepts about the mind are certainly part of the picture – but also in its origins. For example, Leslie (1987) argued that an innate 'decoupling mechanism' is malfunctioning in autism, whereas I have contended that, on the contrary, deficits in so-called 'theory of mind' are the developmental outcome of impairments in interpersonal relations that involve affective engagement with other people's attitudes towards the world (e.g. Hobson, 1990, 1993). The critical issue, then, is whether a young child's ability to relate to people's ways of construing the world – to think about thoughts, for example, whether these are the child's or those of others – is founded upon pre-reflective propensities to respond to and even assume aspects of what can be perceived to be the outer-directed psychological orientations of other people.

I shall not dwell on the ramifications of this issue for our theories about the origins of self-awareness and self-reflection, but I hope that the relevance for understanding the developmental psychology of blind children will be obvious. The fact is that blind children do have difficulties in perceiving and identifying with the attitudes of others, as these attitudes are directed to a shared world. I have alluded to how this might be relevant for their difficulties in pronoun usage, echolalia, limitations in symbolic play, and so on. I have not dealt with whether such abnormalities are specific to lack of vision rather than, for example, deafness or other cases of perceptual deprivation (e.g. Petersen and Siegal, 1995); nor have I dwelt on cases, and in particular children who had terrible social privation in the orphanages of Caucescu's Romania (e.g. Rutter et al., 1999), where again it is plausible that 'autistic-like' phenomena arise on the basis of profound lack of social engagement with others. Instead I have concentrated on the reasons for believing that there is far more than a surface similarity between 'autistic features' and the syndrome of autism in congenitally blind children, and the presentation of autism in sighted children. Once one accepts the validity of this mapping, then one needs to explain it: and in order to explain it, we may find that we need a more radically socially grounded account of early psychological development in both typically developing and 'atypical' children.

I shall conclude by stating the obvious. If there are good reasons why infants and young children need to connect with other people, reasons to do not only with having a social life but also with discovering what it is to have human mental perspectives, then there may also be good reasons for reviewing how the syndrome of autism reflects the developmental implications of impairments in interpersonal relatedness – and how kindred abnormalities in congenitally blind children might clarify what is essential to these impairments, and what makes their effects as serious as they are.

Acknowledgements

I thank my colleagues for their very substantial contributions to the collaborative studies described, and of course to the schools and pupils who have been willing to help us with our research.

References

American Psychiatric Association (APA) (1987) Diagnostic and Statistical Manual of Mental Disorders, 3rd edn, revised (DSM-IIIR). Washington, DC: APA.

Andersen ES, Dunlea A, Kekelis LS (1984) Blind children's language: Resolving some differences. Journal of Child Language 11: 645–64.

Baron-Cohen S (2002) I am loved, therefore I think. Book review of The Cradle of Thought by R. P. Hobson. Nature 416: 791–2.

Bishop M, Hobson RP (2004) Symbolic play in congenitally blind children. (Submitted for publication.)

Blank HR (1975) Reflections on the special senses in relation to the development of affect with special emphasis on blindness. Journal of the American Psychoanalytic Association 23: 32–50.

Brown R, Hobson RP, Lee A, Stevenson J (1997) Are there 'autistic-like' features in congenitally blind children? Journal of Child Psychology and Psychiatry 38: 693–703.

Chase JB (1972) Retrolental Fibroplasia and Autistic Symptomatology. New York: American Foundation for the Blind.

Chess S (1971) Autism in children with congenital rubella. Journal of Autism and Childhood Schizophrenia 1: 33–47.

Curson A (1979) The blind nursery school child. Psychoanalytic Study of the Child 34: 51–83.

Dunlea A (1989) Vision and the Emergence of Meaning. Cambridge: Cambridge University Press.

Elonen AS, Cain AC (1964) Diagnostic evaluation and treatment of deviant blind children. American Journal of Orthopsychiatry 34: 625–33.

Fraiberg S (1977) Insights from the Blind. London: Souvenir Press.

Fraiberg S, Adelson E (1977) Self-representation in language and play. In: Fraiberg S (ed.) Insights from the Blind. London: Souvenir Press, pp. 248–70.

Frith U (2003) Autism: Explaining the enigma, 2nd edn. Oxford: Blackwell Science.

Green MR, Schecter DE (1957) Autistic and symbiotic disorders in three blind children. Psychiatric Quarterly 31: 628–46.

Hobson RP (1990) On acquiring knowledge about people and the capacity to pretend: A response to Leslie. Psychological Review 97: 114–21.

Hobson RP (1993) Autism and the Development of Mind. Hillsdale, NJ: Lawrence Erlbaum Associates.

Hobson RP (2002) The Cradle of Thought. London: Macmillan Press.

Hobson RP, Bishop M (2003) The pathogenesis of autism: insights from congenital blindness. Philosophical Transactions of the Royal Society 358: 335–44.

Hobson RP, Brown R, Minter ME, Lee A (1997) 'Autism' revisited: the case of congenital blindness. In: Lewis V, Collis GM (eds) Blindness and Psychological Development in Young Children. Leicester: British Psychological Society, pp. 99–115.

Hobson RP, Lee A, Brown R (1999) Autism and congenital blindness. Journal of Autism and Developmental Disorders 29: 45–56.

Jan JE, Freeman RD, Scott EP (1977) Visual Impairment in Children and Adolescents. New York: Grune & Stratton.

Keeler WR (1958) Autistic patterns and defective communication in blind children with retrolental fibroplasias. In: Hoch PH, Zubin J (eds) Psychopathology of Communication. New York: Grune & Stratton, pp. 64–83.

Leslie AM (1987) Pretense and representation: the origins of 'theory of mind'. Psychological Review 94: 412–26.

McAlpine LM, Moore C (1995) The development of social understanding in children with visual impairments. Journal of Visual Impairment and Blindness 89: 349–58.

McGuire LL (1969) Psycho-dynamic development problems in the congenitally blind. Ed.D. Thesis, University of Southern California.

Minter ME, Hobson RP, Bishop M (1998) Congenital visual impairment and 'theory of mind'. British Journal of Developmental Psychology 16: 183–96.

Peterson CC, Siegal M (1995) Deafness, conversation and theory of mind. Journal of Child Psychology and Psychiatry 36: 459–74.

Preisler GM (1991) Early patterns of interaction between blind infants and their sighted mothers. Child: Care, Health and Development 17: 65–90.

Preisler GM (1993) A descriptive study of blind children in nurseries with sighted children. Child: Care, Health and Development 19: 295–315.

Pring L, Dewart H, Brockbank M (1998) Social cognition in children with visual impairments. Journal of Visual Impairment and Blindness 92: 754–68.

Rogers SJ, Newhart-Larson S (1989) Characteristics of infantile autism in five children with Leber's congenital amaurosis. Developmental Medicine and Child Neurology 31: 598–608.

Rogers SJ, Puchalski CB (1984) Development of symbolic play in visually impaired young children. Topics in Early Childhood Special Education 3: 57–63.

Rowland C (1983) Patterns of interaction between three blind infants and their mothers. In: Mills AE (ed.) Language Acquisition in the Blind Child: Normal and deficient. London: Croom Helm, pp. 114–32.

Rutter M, Andersen-Wood L, Beckett C et al., and the English and Romanian adoptees' study team (1999) Quasi-autistic patterns following severe early global privation. Journal of Child Psychology and Psychiatry 40: 537–49.

Sandler A-M (1963) Aspects of passivity and ego development in the blind infant. Psychoanalytic Study of the Child 28: 343–60.

Sandler A-M, Hobson RP (2001) On engaging with people in early childhood: the case of congenital blindness. Clinical Child Psychology and Psychiatry 6: 205–22.

Sandler A-M, Wills DM (1965) Preliminary notes on play and mastery in the blind child. Journal of Child Psychotherapy 1:7–19.

Schopler E, Reichler RJ, Renner BR (1988) The Childhood Autism Rating Scale (CARS). Los Angeles: Western Psychological.

Sherman H, Shapiro T, Glassman M (1983) Play and language in developmentally disordered pre-schoolers: A new approach to classification. Journal of the American Academy of Child Psychiatry 22: 511–24.

Tillman MH (1967) The performance of blind and sighted children on the Wechsler Intelligence Scale for Children: Study II. International Journal for the Education of the Blind 16: 106–12.

Urwin C (1983) Dialogue and cognitive functioning in the early language development of three blind children. In: Mills AE (ed.) Language Acquisition in the Blind Child: Normal and deficient. London: Croom Helm, pp. 142–61.

Warren DH (1994) Blindness and Children: An individual differences approach. Cambridge: Cambridge University Press.

Wills DM (1979a) 'The ordinary devoted mother' and her blind baby. Psychoanalytic Study of the Child 34: 31–49.

Wills DM (1979b) Early speech development in blind children. Psychoanalytic Study of the Child 34: 85–117.

Wills DM (1981) Some notes on the application of the diagnostic profile to young blind children. Psychoanalytic Study of the Child 36: 217–37.

Wing L (1969) The handicaps of autistic children – a comparative study. Journal of Child Psychology and Psychiatry 10: 1–40.

CHAPTER 3

Beyond 'modalarity' and innateness: sensory experience, social interaction and symbolic development in children with autism and blindness

SUSAN LEEKAM AND SHIRLEY WYVER

As researchers working separately within the research traditions of autism and blindness, we have long been intrigued by the similarities and differences between children in each of these groups. Similarities are suggested by evidence that both groups experience sensory difficulties of some kind. Yet differences are also reported in terms of the quality of social interactions that blind and autistic children are able to achieve with other people. Then again, both similarities and differences are reported in relation to the higher-level cognitive and language skills of each group. The aim of the chapter is to explore these puzzling interconnections of sensory impairment, social interaction, and cognitive and linguistic development in both groups.

In exploring this puzzle we look at the possibility that sensory experiences are crucially linked to social experiences very early in development. We suggest that these interdependent experiences have an important role in both facilitating and constraining further social interaction and cognitive development. Two themes emerge from this discussion. The first is that sensory modalities are integrated rather than specialized, the second is that the effects of sensory and social experiences change with development.

The chapter starts by re-examining traditional theoretical debates about the link between sensation, perception and cognition. We then look at the evidence for sensory–perceptual abnormalities and the link between social interaction and perceptual–cognitive functioning in children with autism and blindness. Finally we look at the way in which sensory–social connections may be influenced by development.

From sensation to cognition: traditional theoretical debates

If you open any infant development textbook, you quickly become aware of an important theoretical debate. This debate is represented by the contrasting views of Piaget and Gibson about the nature of perception and cognition. Piaget's constructivist position is that the infant builds increasingly complex mental representations by exploring and acting on the world. In contrast, Gibson's direct perception position is that mental representations are unnecessary because the rich structure of the environment itself provides affordances for perception and action that the infant can discover. The question posed by Piaget and Gibson as to whether perception is either direct or mediated by mental representations is considered by some to be an epistemological issue that cannot be settled by empirical testing (see Loveland, 2001, for discussion). However there are two other issues central to the comparison of Piaget's and Gibson's theories that in principle may be studied independently of the directness issue. It is these issues that are the focus of this chapter. One is the issue of what we call 'modalarity'. Modalarity refers to the extent to which sensory information is either specialized or integrated and therefore apprehended in either an amodal or modality-specific way. This is distinguishable from the well-known issue of 'modularity' in cognitive science that relates to the modular organization of cognitive systems. The other issue is that of innateness – the extent to which percepts and concepts are either innately given from birth or depend on experience for their emergence.

By drawing attention to these issues of 'modalarity' and innateness, we want to highlight that each issue is potentially separate from the other. We also want to emphasize that research on autism and blindness needs to go beyond its current tendency for modal-specific explanations and traditional conceptions of nativism and empiricism. Instead we advocate a focus on intersensory functioning and on developmental explanations that take account of dynamic changes across time. First we explore the two issues of modalarity and innateness with respect to Piaget's and Gibson's theories and then we look at their relevance to the study of children with autism and blindness.

Piaget's position on the issues of modalarity and development was that infants begin life with only modal-specific sensory capacities that develop into higher-level cross-modal representations. Piaget argued that the newborn initially apprehends the world through separate senses of vision, hearing, touch, taste and smell. Through developmental processes of assimilation and accommodation during the sensorimotor period, cross-modal percepts and concepts are gradually constructed. Gibson's opposing position was that cross-modal perception is present from birth and the ability to extract structure from the environment simply improves with time and experience. Gibson argued that newborns are initially able to detect amodal properties, such as intensity, duration, temporal synchrony and co-location, from the complex information structure in the environment (Fenwick and Morrongiello, 1998). Through a process of perceptual learning, infants become increasingly able to discriminate relevant features in the perceptual field.

For Piaget and Gibson, therefore, the two issues of modalarity and development are closely related to each other. For Piaget the early capacity of the newborn is modality specific and non-representational but changes with development to become increasingly cross-modal and representational. For Gibson, on the other hand, the early perceptual capacity of the newborn begins as amodal and non-representational and remains the same way across time, with perception guiding the ability to detect and act on the affordances in the environment in increasingly efficient ways.

How can the issues about modalarity and development be applied to the case of blindness and autism? Taking first the case of blindness, much research has followed the Piagetian tradition. The prediction following Piaget's theory is that during early infancy perceptual abilities are quite limited, and regularities within the environment difficult to establish. This leads to delays in basic understandings about the physical world, such as object permanence (Rogers and Puchalski, 1988). Some researchers argue that delays are maintained until at least the end of the concrete operations period, although the empirical evidence supporting this view is conflicting and is often from studies with methodological problems (see Warren, 1994).

In contrast to Piaget's theory, Gibson would propose that the newborn blind infant's perception is not modality specific. The infant would be able to detect amodal properties allowing for auditory and tactile cross-modal perception. The evidence seems to support this view. Prenatally, both blind and sighted infants benefit from the same perceptual opportunities, given that visual stimulation is not available until after birth. *In utero* experience leads to some preferences for mother's voice (DeCasper and Fifer, 1980; DeCasper and Spence, 1986) and auditory patterns that may contribute to early speech perception (Lecanuet et al., 2000). Furthermore, stimulation received during the third trimester is concurrent and multimodal (somaesthetic, vestibular and auditory modalities) (Lewkowicz, 2000). Evidence for cross-modal perception is found in newborn sighted infants (Morrongiello, Fenwick and Chance, 1998) and in very young blind children (Landau, Spelke and Gleitman, 1984; Morrongiello et al., 1994). Unfortunately, though, little is known about intersensory integration and cross-modal perception in young blind infants (Warren, 1994) and most work with sighted children incorporates vision. It is important to note that Gibson does argue that vision has a specific role that cannot easily be replaced: 'a wider panorama of space and objects is available to vision' (1969, p. 229). In the absence of specific interventions to compensate for access to the broader external environment, it is likely that the blind infant will make more use of stimulation that is proximal rather than distal. If this is the case, it will, no doubt, have an impact on the way interactions with the physical and social environment occur. What needs to be considered is whether these altered interaction patterns are sufficient to enable the blind child to achieve the same developmental goals as normally developing sighted children.

While the evidence appears to support Gibson's case for amodality even before birth, the question of what is inbuilt and what is learned is still open (Lewkowicz, 2000). We know from research examining the entire DNA sequence of the human genome that there are not enough genes in the genome to fully specify the visual or any of the other sensory systems. Therefore in order to develop and specialize, the sensory systems must rely on experience and learning. Research using the sonic guide (binaural sensory aid) demonstrates that such learning does take place. The sonic guide is a head-mounted device which enables hearing to be substituted in place of vision. Information about visual distance is provided in terms of auditory pitch, enabling blind infants to extract abstract spatial information about objects (Aitken and Bower, 1982; Sampaio, 1989). Even when the information to be extracted from the senses is novel and does not follow an evolutionary path, learning occurs. Although the sonic guide has not been used with newborn blind human infants, research with neonate dark-reared macaques has demonstrated effective use of information obtained from the device during unstructured exploration (Strelow et al., 1987). Research with sighted infants and blind infants and children also shows rapid learning ability (Muir et al., 1985; Strelow and Warren, 1985).

In summary, the evidence from sighted infants and blind children points towards the possibility of an innate amodal bias. This innate bias may simply amount to a general predisposition to extract regularities from the environment while more specialized knowledge may depend on the actual experience that the infant receives. Therefore learning may be a central requirement of the innate capacity itself.

Despite theoretical and empirical challenges to Piaget's explanation, it is surprising that the influence of the Piagetian approach on blindness research has remained strong. Some researchers have moved away from this tradition (e.g. Millar, 1995; Ross and Tobin, 1997) yet Piaget's legacy remains, possibly due to significant work of Fraiberg (1977), who followed

Piagetian theory. On the other hand, Gibson's theory is not a theoretical approach favoured by researchers studying blindness, despite the compelling empirical support for an amodal approach. There may be several reasons for this situation. One is that the empirical evidence has not yet been successful in challenging predictions of delayed progress derived from Piagetian theory. Yet, as Warren (1994) and Perez-Pereira and Conti-Ramsden (1999) clearly demonstrate, when individual differences are considered, it is apparent that, in all major developmental areas examined by researchers, there are some blind children who exhibit equal if not better skills than their sighted peers. The heterogeneity of the population as well as other factors associated with many of the common causes of congenital blindness (e.g. prematurity, extended hospitalization) need to be accounted for when arguing a case for the relationship between blindness and cognitive delay. There are other possible reasons why Gibson's theory has received less support from blindness research than Piaget's theory. One is that conventional cognitive theoretical frameworks with their assumptions of indirect perception have tended to dominate the field, driving the direction of theoretical and empirical work in blindness. Another is that the issue of developmental change is not so well supported by research. One criticism is that Gibson's theory does not specify the developmental processes that enable the infant to become increasingly proficient at perceiving complex intersensory relations (Lewkowicz, 2000).

Turning now to the case of autism, how have the issues about modalarity and development been applied to this field? It has long been recognized that people with autism have atypical sensory and perceptual processing (Ornitz, 1989). Abnormalities have been reported in visual and auditory domains (see Mottron and Burack, 2001, for review) as well as in tactile and olfactory domains (Wing, 1969, 1971). Autobiographical accounts of adults with autism often describe their childhood as filled with fragmented, unpredictable, perceptual experiences, a description that would be consistent with either Piaget's or Gibson's analyses of crossmodal integration problems. Yet, unlike research in blindness, neither Piagetian nor Gibsonian theory provides a dominant theoretical framework for contemporary research.

Research in autism reflects the trend in developmental psychology of decline in influence of Piagetian theory due to lack of empirical and theoretical support. In addition, research in autism also pointed towards impairments in symbolic development rather than in object-based sensorimotor skills (Sigman and Ungerer, 1984). At the same time, the Gibsonian alternative has failed to be strongly represented in research on perceptual abnormalities in autism. An exception is the work of Loveland (1991, 2001). Loveland's basic proposal is that children with autism fail to perceive the affordances in the environment that are perceived by other children. Drawing on Gibson's concept of the perception–action cycle, she argues that children with autism fail to perceive the possibilities for action offered by other people. Loveland offers a unique analysis that connects concepts from Gibsonian theory to evidence from neurobiological development. Her proposal is that failure to perceive affordances, and particularly social affordances, has negative implications for 'sculpting' the neurons of the brain and for subsequent development. This approach has the potential to offer a powerful new framework for understanding the sensory–perceptual difficulties in autism.

While Piagetian and Gibsonian frameworks have had little recent influence on autism research, information processing and neuropsychological frameworks have come to dominate the field. These frameworks are based on adult models of psychological functioning and are rooted in a theoretical approach that assumes indirectness of perception and the presence of mental representations. Information processing accounts assume there are several subsystems that have different functions for manipulating, storing or transforming information from sensory input. Low-level information from one or more sensory inputs is interpreted and integrated by psychological processes at a higher level of cognitive analysis. Modular theories of neuropsychology make the added assumption that the perception and organization of information are directed by specialized cognitive mechanisms that drive perception in a 'top-down' way. These innate mechanisms are hard-wired to process knowledge in specialized cognitive domains such as knowledge of objects, language or theory of mind.

Recent explanations of perceptual and cognitive dysfunction in autism have tended to fall into two types. Research on perceptual processes and attention proposes that low-level and developmentally primitive capacities are impaired in autism often due to brain damage and that these have knock-on effects for higher-level cognitive abilities and for development. Recent research on higher-level cognitive processes (e.g. language, memory, theory of mind, reasoning) in contrast proposes that there is selective damage to central processing or domain-specific mechanisms while more general low-level sensory and perceptual processing abilities remain intact. Evidence showing fast-acting, automatic responding to human stimuli is attributed to the existence of these innate hard-wired cognitive mechanisms.

How do the issues of modalarity and innateness apply to these information processing explanations of autism? With respect to modalarity, information processing explanations do not make special claims about the amodal or modality-specific nature of information. However, research based on low-level information processing (attention, perception) is traditionally carried out within single-modality specific areas of vision and hearing, with the majority of studies focusing on visual impairment. Where auditory processing is tested, it tends to provide parallel findings rather than specifically focusing on the integration of information across sensory domains. Accounts based on higher-level cognitive processes in principle could offer an amodal approach – as domain-specific information about objects, language, etc. may be picked up from different sensory receptors involving integration across sensory modalities. However, in practice, this research does not address the possibility of whether coordination of information across the senses may be particularly problematic in either very young or older children.

With respect to the issue of innateness, two approaches are apparent. Among researchers studying low-level sensory or attentional difficulties, the view is that these basic impairments may be either innate or present early in infancy and have implications for the onset and development of subsequent higher mental functions. According to this account, both timing and experiences may be important. In practice, however, research tends to be carried out with older children or adolescents and there is little focus on the developmental process or the specific role of experience. Among researchers studying higher-level cognitive processes, some take a more nativist approach. The developmental process is seen in maturational terms and the role of experience and learning is not made explicit.

In summary, evidence indicates that children with autism have abnormalities in different sensory modalities but we know very little about the multimodal or cross-modal nature of these difficulties across development. Recent research on perceptual abilities in autism tends to be confined to the study of specific sensory domains, particularly vision. Research also generally tends to avoid investigating how experience actually works to facilitate learning, with certain dominant 'top-down' explanations of autism taking strongly nativist assumptions. Both these top-down accounts and the alternative 'bottom-up' low-level perceptual processing accounts may have difficulties accounting for developmental change (see Bishop, 1997, for discussion). More recent formulations of these accounts have become more bi-directional, suggesting interplay between bottom-up and top-down processes (Frith, 2003); yet theories in autism have not yet embraced a dynamic account of developmental process that takes account of the changes that occur with timing. The specification of developmental process therefore remains a missing dimension in research in autism.

From sensation to cognition: evidence from autism and blindness

So far we have considered traditional theoretical debates about the link between sensation, perception and cognition. We have also looked at the theoretical influences on research in autism and blindness. Our conclusion so far is that research needs to focus not only on the effect of modal-specific impairment but also on sensory integration across modalities. We also suggest that research needs to consider the developmental changes in the effects of sensory difficulties across time. In this section we develop these ideas further by reviewing evidence from autism and blindness.

First we describe evidence from blindness research. This research makes a relatively strong case for the importance of sensory integration in children's cognitive development. There is plenty of evidence to suggest that loss of vision can be compensated for by other senses. For example, research from Morrongiello et al. (1994) found that tactual exploration and object recognition did not differ for blind and sighted children, arguing that visual experience is not necessary for object representation. Blind individuals have also been found to outperform sighted controls in sound localization tasks (Lessard et al., 1998). The evidence that the visual cortex of blind adults has a role in processing of tactile and auditory information (Kujala et al., 1997) provides further support for the case that alternative sensory processing allows blind individuals to achieve similar levels of understanding of their physical and social world as sighted individuals.

However, in order to understand the nature of this compensatory process, there are various considerations that need to be made. First, we need to consider the nature of the sensory stimulus. It would trivialize the severity of the disability to argue that early cross-modal perception enables total compensation for absence of vision. As noted earlier, Gibson considered vision to have a special role in making available the wider or distal environment and therefore we need to make a distinction between proximal and distal information sources. This suggests that, for the blind infant, cross-modal perception and learning are therefore mainly confined to relations between proximal non-visual stimuli and that lack of integration of auditory and visual information is also likely to lead to greater difficulties in processing distal than proximal stimuli. In addition, the compensation possible through cross-modal perception will also be limited by special modal-specific properties of information processing. Each of the sensory modalities allows for the processing of different stimulus features, with vision enabling better processing of spatial information and audition enabling better processing of temporal information (O'Connor and Hermelin, 1978). Evidence of delays, such as in sound localization of blind infants (Bigelow, 1986), is consistent with the types of early difficulties we would expect. These kinds of difficulties would diminish in later years, as research with older individuals demonstrates (Lessard et al., 1998). With time, blind infants may achieve similar levels of understanding of their physical and social world, but with a developmental pathway that is more difficult, particularly if other risk factors are involved.

A second consideration is to take account of developmental differences between blind and sighted children. A common error in speculating about development of perception and cognition in blindness is to use the sighted infant as a model. Although empirical evidence of intersensory integration from sighted infants can provide some insight into the processes that may occur, it is otherwise limited. Intersensory perception research in sighted infants has almost always included vision as one of the modalities (usually auditory–visual), making comparisons difficult. More importantly, it is unlikely that the developmental pathway for the blind child is the same as it is for the sighted infant, but without access to visual information. To argue this is to ignore processes such as inhibition, where stimulation of one sensory modality leads to decreased responsiveness in another sensory modality (Lewkowicz, 2000), or modality switching, which seems to be enhanced in blind adults (Kujala et al., 1995). It also fails to take into account brain plasticity (Kujala et al., 1997).

In summary, evidence suggests that the blind infant has the same perceptual experiences before birth and exhibits the same potentials at birth as the sighted infant. The blind infant can extract information from amodal invariants, which enables an integrated perception of objects and events. Lack of vision results in a different developmental pathway for blind infants, with some information being much more difficult to extract, or less available through different mechanisms, than is the case for sighted infants.

Turning now to the case of autism, how do children with autism compare with blind children in terms of their capacity for integrated sensation/perception and for achieving an alternative cognitive developmental pathway? In looking at the research, the view we are beginning to develop is that children with autism are inefficient at both sensory–perceptual integration and modal-specific processing. Evidence for this proposal comes from several different sources. First, clinical studies suggest that children with autism have low-level sensory difficulties that resemble the problems of blind and deaf children. Wing (1969) compared children with autism and partially blind and deaf children and found remarkable similarities in behaviours. Her study compared auditory perception, skilled movements, visual perception and social behaviour in children with autism and children with partial deaf–blindness, as well as children in other clinical groups (Down syndrome, receptive aphasia, executive aphasia). The results showed that children with autism differed significantly from children in other clinical groups but when compared with partially deaf–blind children the differences were minimal. Similarities were found in odd reactions to sound and visual stimuli and in responses to proximal (including tactile and olfactory) stimuli.

While the conclusions from Wing's study are limited by the fact that the IQ level of the comparison groups was not matched, more recent research (Nieto and Leekam, 2002) also found that sensory difficulties were reported significantly more by parents of children with autism than in control groups of children with a language impairment and learning disability regardless of IQ and age levels. Indeed, 85% of autistic individuals with high IQ were found to have sensory abnormalities. In their study, details were collected of three domains of sensory abnormalities – proximal, visual and auditory. Proximal abnormalities included a range of different tactile and olfactory behaviours, auditory abnormalities included unusual responses to or fascination with particular sounds, and visual abnormalities included unusual attention to specific aspects of visual stimuli such as their brightness or movement. The autism group was more likely to have multimodal abnormalities, that is, they were likely to have abnormalities in more than one sensory domain while comparison groups of learning disability or language impairment did not. Among the autism group, by far the most common abnormality was the proximal class.

The multimodal nature of the sensory difficulty in autism and the preponderance of proximal abnormalities suggest that the sensory abnormalities of children with autism may be more similar to deaf–blind children than to children who have sensory loss in only one sensory domain. Able blind children appear able to compensate for this loss by relying on cross-modal perception at least from proximal information sources. Individuals with autism, however, seem to have very basic abnormalities in their proximal processing. Whether this is a cause, consequence or by-product of autism, such difficulty may create limitations for their capacity for sensory–perceptual integration.

Early information processing accounts also suggested that children with autism resembled deaf and blind children. These modality-specific accounts suggested that the problem in autism lay not at the level of the sensory receptors but with processing the information at a cognitive level. In contrast to the Gibsonian view, for example, the modality-specific account proposed by O'Connor and Hermelin (1978) proposed that sensory codes are, to some extent, determined by the modality from which they originated, with vision being associated with spatial codes and hearing being more closely linked with temporal codes. They suggested that individuals with sight and hearing are able to use a wider range of codes, but this is restricted if the child is blind or deaf. Although the autistic children in their sample did not have visual or hearing loss, O'Connor and Hermelin found that these children did have difficulty in using sensory stimulation to assist them to develop associated internal representations.

More recent modality-specific accounts suggest a neurobiological problem. A recent study by Milne et al. (2002) suggests that children with autism have a specific visual deficit. High functioning children with autism had difficulties in detecting coherent motion from an array of moving dots, a finding they related to the hypothesis that children with autism may have an impairment in the magnocellular pathway which processes the global nature of visual stimuli.

There is abundant support for the view that children with autism have fundamental difficulties with sensory processing (Ornitz, 1989). Shapiro and Hertzig (1991) described integrative deficits as central to these sensory and perceptual problems. At least three current theories support this view. Each gives a different explanation for the integration difficulty pitched at either a cognitive level or at a lower level of perception or attention. Frith (2003), for example, argues that children with autism lack central coherence. Central coherence is considered to be a central cohesive force that is a natural characteristic of the cognitive system. Evidence for weak central coherence is suggested by autistic children's enhanced piecemeal processing on block design and embedded figures tasks (Shah and Frith, 1993) and by their inability to make meaningful connections between stimuli (Frith and Snowling, 1983).

While Frith's explanation assumes that there is a central cognitive device that deals with the drive for meaning and cohesion, other explanations deal with the problem of integration as a low-level attentional or perceptual difficulty. Plaisted (2001), for example, argues that children with autism cannot integrate or draw together information because of an inability to recognize similarities between stimuli or situations. Evidence for this is indicated by poor performance on tasks that involve extracting common features of stimuli and particularly good performance on tasks that require discriminating different stimuli (Plaisted, O'Riordan and Baron-Cohen, 1998). Mottron and Burack (2001) provide another explanation that is consistent with Plaisted's. Essentially their proposal is that people with autism have enhanced low-level processing. They argue that individuals with autism cannot escape from detecting and attending to very specific sensory visual and auditory stimuli because their perceptual thresholds are lower than normal and low-level perceptual information dominates their attention. They suggest that an initial cognitive deficit is followed by compensation in terms of overtraining of another function and this overtraining then becomes maladaptive. This explanation provides a comparison with blindness. As Mottron points out, the outcome might be maladaptive for people with autism whereas, for people with blindness, such enhanced functioning (e.g. increased sensitivity to sounds and odours) may be adaptive.

The research by Plaisted et al. and by Mottron et al. raises a number of interesting questions for our developing argument. Could the failure of generalization that Plaisted proposes be the outcome of failure to integrate information across modalities very early in development? Could the enhanced low-level processing that Mottron proposes equate to more specialized processing, maybe because from the beginning children with autism have difficulty integrating sensory information? Why should compensation become adaptive for blind children and maladaptive for children with autism? There may be several explanations. Perhaps, for the blind, the sensory damage is more selective so there can be compensatory takeover by other functions, whereas for people with autism, multimodal sensory abnormalities push towards a different developmental pathway. Another possibility discussed in the next section is that social experience interacts with sensory experience in a different way for autistic than for blind children.

To summarize, while children with autism show some similarities with blind children at both a behavioural and a cognitive level, they are more likely to resemble children with multisensory impairments rather than children with only blindness. Research suggests that problems for children with autism may be magnified because unlike blind children they may not be able to make use of proximal stimuli for adaptive cross-modal integration. They fail to detect the similarities across stimuli and cannot use alternative sensory input to provide equivalent information, as blind children may be able to do. Instead, enhanced low-level processing and a tendency to separate and discriminate stimuli dominate. While we suggest that this problem might start with basic sensory–perceptual abilities early in infancy, developmental difficulties may continue to create problems at higher levels as perceptual and cognitive development proceeds over time.

From social interaction to cognition: traditional theoretical debates

So far we have been arguing that both children with autism and children with blindness are affected by their early sensory difficulties. Children with blindness may compensate with the use of other senses but there are some limitations and developmental delays in some aspects of functioning as a result. Children with autism may have more pervasive difficulties that might prevent them compensating with other senses. Where does the development of social interaction fit into this picture? How are social interactional difficulties related to sensory difficulties for children with autism and children with blindness? Our proposal is that sensory–perceptual and social experiences are interdependent for both groups and critically influence cognitive development. In this section we now turn to consider the importance of social interaction, presenting the traditional debates in the subject, and look at how this debate can be applied to the study of blindness and autism.

A traditional theoretical debate in the literature is whether social interaction emerges from particular mental processes or whether individual mental processes emerge from social interaction. Many developmental psychologists would argue that this is not a 'debate' at all but simply a description of an ongoing process because social interaction and individual mental processes must inevitably mutually influence each other across time. However, at present we do not have a clear theoretical account that can capture the transactional nature of the ongoing relationship between social interaction and cognitive development. Therefore it is helpful to consider explanations in terms of the relative weight they give to the role of either social interaction experience or individual cognition. In the discussion below, we focus on the link between social interaction and symbolic development in the domains of language and social cognition (theory of mind) to examine this further.

Starting with the proposal that social interaction emerges from particular mental processes, one view is that infants are born with innately specified cognitive mechanisms that determine subsequent cognitive development. For the development of symbolic functioning and theory of mind, for example, Baron-Cohen's (1995) mindreading system posits the existence of simple mechanisms that handle social–perceptual information (i.e. information about faces, eyes, body movement) received through visual and other senses, and more complex mechanisms that process inner representations of other people's perspectives and others' mental states (e.g. another person's focus of interest towards an object or another person's false belief about the world). Although each mechanism or module may need some minimal threshold of social experience to function, the existence or maintenance of each module is not in itself dependent on social interaction with others. However, the capacity to develop a theory of mind will affect social interaction. Therefore, children who have an impaired 'shared attention mechanism' or 'theory of mind mechanism' will have impaired social relationships and difficulties acquiring meanings in language.

Turning to the proposal that individual mental processes emerge from social interaction, Vygotsky (1934) considered that all mental processes have their origins in the social world, arguing that 'the very mechanism underlying higher mental functions is a copy from social interaction' (Vygotsky, 1934, p. 164). Cognitive and linguistic structures available within the social world become internal cognitive structures through a process of internalization. More recent social interactional and social cultural accounts of the developmental process suggest that processes of imitation and identification facilitate critical developments at the end of the first year (Tomasello, 1999; Hobson, 2002). This period of development is marked by the onset of triadic joint attention exchanges between self, another person and an object in which infants show awareness of others' perspectives. This onset is seen as marking a qualitatively new stage of development but also in terms of a developmental continuity from the earlier dyadic interpersonal and affect-sharing exchanges that are present in the early months of life

How does evidence from autism and blindness contribute to the debate about whether individual mental processes emerge from social interaction? The evidence from autism makes it difficult to settle the debate as both sides predict that children with autism will lack awareness of others' perspectives in triadic joint attention. Both views also predict that children with autism will have impaired social–perceptual ability to detect emotion and intention in others' faces, and will be poor at inferring representational mental states such as false belief. However, one difference between the accounts is that the mindreading account should not predict difficulties with aspects of dyadic interaction that do not involve perceiving or inferring another's inner state, interest or attention. Responses such as orienting to another's voice and positively responding to another's greeting are responses normally seen in infants in the first months of life and are even seen in animals. Recent evidence shows that children and adults with autism are impaired in these interpersonal interactions at a very basic dyadic level (Dawson et al., 1998; Hobson and Lee, 1998; Leekam, López and Moore, 2000).

As children with autism by definition have social interaction difficulties as part of their diagnosis, a more compelling case for the social interaction view is made in the case of the blind child who has normal IQ and language. The specific prediction made by Baron-Cohen's (1995) mindreading model was that blind children would have an intact 'theory of mind mechanism' and so would be able to infer inner states such as false belief. However, research evidence from several studies has since shown that blind children do indeed have impairments in theory of mind. This evidence has challenged traditional mindreading theory. In support of the social interactional view, it is argued that lack of vision prevents or minimizes opportunities to share others' experiences of the world or of themselves. The blind child is thus 'deprived of the experience of shifting perspectives on objects, events and themselves through identifying with the attitude of others' (Hobson, 2002, p. 191). This has implications for symbolic development and the development of social cognition. However, an interesting finding to emerge from studies showing theory of mind difficulties in children who are blind is that the children who were most impaired in theory of mind skills were those who had the greatest loss of vision and whose language was also delayed. Other children with less visual impairment were less delayed in theory of mind. These findings have led Garfield, Peterson and Perry (2001) to support an experiential account rather than a neurobiological account of theory of mind. Their view is that inferences about beliefs require exposure to propositional language. Garfield et al. argue that understanding of mind is built on the basis of social interaction and language acquisition and in particular on the basis of the richness of conversations in the family. Their view therefore takes a Vygotskian approach, supporting the developmental primacy of social interaction.

To summarize, research in autism and in blindness supports the case for the importance of social interaction in cognitive development. In the next section we consider how social interaction may be difficult for the blind child and for the child with autism and how these difficulties may be overcome to allow blind and autistic children to acquire language and theory of mind.

From social interaction to cognition: evidence from autism and blindness

A critical factor in symbolic development is the development of triadic joint attention, a capacity that facilitates perspective shifting and awareness of the perspectival nature of symbols (Tomasello, 1999). This is typically thought of as a visual capacity. The infant follows another person's gaze or points, or holds out an object, checking the other person's gaze toward it. A blind child's lack of sight might therefore provide a significant handicap in developing symbolic understanding. However, as Perez-Pereira and Conti-Ramsden (1999) point out, blind children can make use of hearing and touch to make contact with caregivers and draw attention to objects. Thus they do have the opportunity to shift perspectives in a similar way to sighted children.

What is the evidence for joint attention without vision? Unfortunately there is little systematic evidence on joint attention skills in blind children although two case studies have recently been published (Bigelow, 2003). Research on sighted children gives some indication about the way that non-visual cues are used in joint attention and symbol learning although, as mentioned earlier, comparisons with sighted children should be made cautiously. Research examining social referencing shows that multimodal cues from a mother's face plus her voice were the most effective type of cue in guiding an infant's behaviour in a potentially threatening situation but vocal cues alone were more effective than cues from the face alone. In our own work we have found that sighted children get better with age at using non-visual evidence such as the direction of another's voice to identify a referent in a word learning task (Leekam and Wyver, 1999). Evidence also suggests that, for sighted children, the ability to see the adult's face may be particularly important when learning novel signs or symbols but less important for using familiar signs as referents (Tomasello, Call and Gluckman, 1997; Leekam, 2003).

There is much evidence showing that sighted infants rely heavily on another person's direction of gaze when learning to name objects (Baldwin, 1991). If visual information from another's person's eyes and face facilitates word learning in sighted children, this may be partially compensated for by learning and touch when blind children learn words, as Perez-Pereira and Conti-Ramsden (1999) suggest. Nevertheless these opportunities will be restricted and ability to shift between perspectives when naming distal objects may be particularly affected. It is therefore not surprising that initial word learning may be delayed for children who are blind although evidence shows that subsequent lexical development and other pragmatic, semantic and syntactic speech functions are intact (Perez-Pereira and Conti-Ramsden, 1999). It may be that this relatively late onset of initial word learning and limited access to non-verbal conversational cues, rather than more general delays in language, create a specific subsequent delay in theory of mind. The risk of these kinds of delays may be even greater in children who are totally blind.

Research in blindness highlights the important role of the caregiver in symbolic development. It is likely that, in contrast to a sighted child, the caregiver engages in more 'follow-in' behaviours based around the child's focus of interest. By focusing on an object that the child is attending to, sharing attention by touch or sound, naming it and marking it in different context, the caregiver can assist the infant in language learning. However, the strategy differs from interaction with a sighted infant who also has at his or her disposal the opportunity to fast map words to objects by using the adult's line of sight (Baldwin, 1991). The fact that initial word learning of blind children is often delayed might suggest that those strategies available are not as fully effective in facilitating initial fast mapping of words. It also seems that the language used by mothers of blind infants may differ significantly from the language used by mothers of infants with vision. Although the use of directives in maternal speech was initially construed as negative, Conti-Ramsden and Pérez-Pereira (1999) have since demonstrated the functional nature of these directives, arguing that they contained more descriptions of objects and events compared with conversations between mothers and fully or partially sighted infants.

The pattern of development for children with autism may resemble that of blind children in certain ways. Children with autism may not make use of visual information from other people's faces or gestures although they do make use of visual information from objects. Extensive research on joint attention in autism shows that there are marked delays in joint attention skills. Although children with autism may acquire the ability to follow other people's pointing and requesting gestures at a later chronological and mental age than typically developing children, they fail to use or coordinate eye contact with these gestures (Mundy, Sigman and Kasari, 1994; Charman et al., 1997; Travis and Sigman, 2001). At an even more basic level, they orient less to another person's face in response to a vocalization although they have no difficulties in orienting their eyes to objects (Dawson et al., 1998; Leekam et al., 2000).

Children with autism are unlike many blind children in that, for many, language remains severely delayed or absent. However, those who do develop language have a similar pattern to blind children, in that they show delayed acquisition of first words but later stages of lexical and syntactic development are relatively unimpaired (Tager-Flusberg et al., 1990). For children with autism, however, there are marked difficulties with pragmatic and certain semantic aspects of language. How have these children first come to use language and how does their language ability relate to other aspects of development such as theory of mind? One hypothesis is that these higher functioning, more verbal children who acquire joint attention belong to a different diagnostic group that show milder symptoms from the start. This group could start with a greater capacity for dyadic orienting and hence show less impaired joint attention ability. This ability would in turn facilitate their language acquisition as it does for typically developing children. Parent reports, however, suggest that, even when joint attention does develop, it appears years later than normal (at 5 or 6 years) and for some children residual problems remain in the style of joint attention (Leekam, Hunnisett and Moore, 1998).

An alternative hypothesis, then, is that language acquisition itself facilitates joint attention. Evidence that children with autism might find a different route from other children is suggested by the findings of Carpenter, Pennington and Rogers (2002). In an observational study, Carpenter et al. found that children with autism appeared to show referential language without also showing gaze-following or communicative gestures. This was the opposite pattern to the one found for typically developing and learning-disabled children who engaged in joint attention before language. This finding might fit with Bigelow's (2003) observations that blind children's initiation of joint tactile attention becomes more effective as language develops. Perhaps, then, both children with autism and children who are blind develop an alternative strategy for word learning that avoids engagement with the other's face and gaze by using the sound directed away from the person and towards an object as the means of connecting the word with the object.

In summary, research on social interactions in autism and blindness may show that both groups are at a disadvantage compared with sighted children. Neither benefit from looking at the caregiver's face, a strategy much used by sighted children. Both groups of children may overcome this disadvantage when learning words and other symbols by making non-visual connections between the sounds of words and proximal objects. However, the child with blindness may rely more on parent input, though parental assistance may have limitations. In both cases, then, they may rely less on communicative intentions and use other ways of working out the relation between sign and referent, creating a different path to language development (Travis and Sigman, 2001).

Sensation, social interaction and cognition: the importance of development

Until now we have been making two rather separate points. The first is that, while both children with autism and children with blindness experience sensory difficulties of some kind, their capacity for cross-modal compensation might be different. The second is that, while both groups experience limitations in social interactions, their capacity to benefit from opportunities for interpersonal contact might differ. Now we want to put these two points together, by looking at the process by which sensory experiences and social interactions may depend on each other across development. Our thoughts on this are speculative. There is little research on this topic although, within the autism literature, theoretical links have been proposed between difficulties in sensory orienting and social interaction (Dawson and Lewy, 1989).

Starting from conception, the blind child before birth has the same perceptual experience as the sighted child. This would include the important prenatal foundations for social responsiveness such as recognition of maternal voice and differentiation of speech patterns. Whether this is also the case for the child with autism is difficult to determine but it is possible that there is a lowered threshold of sensitivity to social stimuli in particular or to auditory stimuli in general even before birth. At birth, the experiences available to blind and sighted infants are dramatically different. The same may be said for the difference between typically developing children and children with autism, if it is assumed that their sensory difficulties are present early in development and affect responsiveness across different modalities. However, this is difficult to assume given that difficulties are often not reported in the first year of life.

In the early months, there is a dynamic relationship between sensory experience and social interaction; each facilitates the other. For the typical sighted infant, the sensation of hearing a voice leads to the act of orienting by looking towards the sound. This brings the infant into visual contact with that person, improves the opportunity for further engagement and thereby provides further sensation that is socially modulated. Social interaction with caregivers brings the infant into focus with an array of sensory stimulation, strengthening sight–sound and sound–touch pairings as the infant learns what co-locates in the social domain. This might provide an important basis for strengthening the capacity for intersensory coordination.

Given the importance of the visual world and coordination of auditory and visual information in sighted infants, development in the first few years of life will be inevitably different for the child with blindness and the child with autism. In the case of blindness, we propose that, if an amodal approach to perception was adopted coupled with the assumption that infants are motivated to learn about and engage with their social world, a clearer framework emerges for understanding how the blind infant and his or her carers can compensate for lack of vision. In the case of autism we speculate that, if their problems of engaging with the social world can be seen alongside early problems in sensory and perceptual integration, we gain a clearer understanding of a compensatory pathway leading to narrowly focused, domain-specific, special skills.

Throughout this chapter we have treated children with autism and children with blindness as two separate, homogeneous groups. While this categorization works at some level, it is does not give an accurate portrayal of two groups. Both groups demonstrate wide variation of disability and the degree of visual impairment and degree of autism play an important role in the developmental trajectories of blind and autistic children. However, individuals who have a high degree of impairment in either vision or autistic behaviour may also have a high degree of general impairment in mental age, language age and IQ. This is most clearly elucidated in the studies that examine the occurrence of autistic-type behaviours in blind children. We know from epidemiological research (Wing and Gould, 1979) that the more learning disabled a person is, the more likely they are to have autism and therefore in any population of blind children low IQ also creates an increased risk for autism. A study by Brown et al. (1997), for example, found that all but two of the blind children they studied who had IQs below 70 and/or retinopathy of prematurity also had autistic-like features.

While research designs need to carefully control for the effect of mental age, language and IQ, and the effect of degree of impairment, it is also important to design studies that help us understand how each of these effects interacts with blindness or autism. For example, several studies show that certain precursor skills for theory of mind, such as gaze detection or joint attention, predict theory of mind performance in individuals with autism. However, the picture becomes clearer when IQ or language data are included in the analysis, by showing that these are the critical factors to predict theory of mind performance beyond precursor skills. Patterns like these, which differ from the patterns for typically developing children, give insights into potential compensatory strategies. Future research should therefore allow for a better understanding of how associated risk factors such as cognitive delay and language ability interact with blindness or autism. Such research also has important potential to assist in the development of intervention programmes.

To conclude, in considering the development in children with blindness and autism, it is important to note that many children with blindness achieve verbal intelligence scores within the normal range (Groenveld and Jan, 1992), and normal scores for language (Landau, 1983) and memory (Wyver and Markham, 1998). The same is true for high functioning individuals with autism, many of whom have extremely high IQ scores and language ability and achieve academically way beyond the level of their sighted peers. It seems more appropriate, then, for developmentalists to consider that cognitive and linguistic impairments are not a necessary consequence of blindness or autism. This changes the question to one of how development of high-level cognitive and linguistic skills can occur in the absence of either vision or social interactional skills. We believe that the comparison of children with autism and those who are blind will help researchers to move beyond traditional views of modalarity and innateness, by focusing on an approach to perception that takes account of the early impact of cross-modal integration and on an approach to development that takes account of alternative compensatory pathways.

References

Aitken S, Bower TGR (1982) Intersensory substitution in the blind. Journal of Experimental Child Psychology 33: 309–23.

Baldwin DA (1991) Infants' contribution to the achievement of joint reference. Child Development 63: 875–90.

Baron-Cohen S (1995) Mindblindness: An essay on autism and theory of mind. Cambridge, MA: MIT Press.

Bigelow AE (1986) The development of reaching in blind children. British Journal of Developmental Psychology 4: 355–66.

Bigelow A (2003) The development of joint attention in blind infants. Development and Psychopathology 15: 259–75.

Bishop DVM (1997) Cognitive neuropsychology and developmental disorders: uncomfortable bedfellows. Quarterly Journal of Experimental Psychology Section A 50: 899–923.

Brown R, Hobson RP, Lee A, Stevenson J (1997) Are there 'autistic-like' features in congenitally blind children? Journal of Child Psychology and Psychiatry 38: 693–703.

Carpenter M, Nagell K, Tomasello M (1998) Social cognition, joint attention and communicative competence from 9 to 15 months of age. Monographs of the Society for Research in Child Development 63 (4, Serial No. 255).

Carpenter M, Pennington BF, Rogers SJ (2002) Interrelations among social-cognitive skills in young children with autism and developmental delays. Journal of Autism and Developmental Disorders 32: 91–106.

Charman T, Swettenham J, Baron-Cohen S, Cox A, Baird G, Drew A (1997) Infants with autism: An investigation of empathy, pretend play, joint attention and imitation. Developmental Psychology 33: 781–9.

Conti-Ramsden G, Pérez-Pereira M (1999) Conversational interactions between mothers and their infants who are congenitally blind, have low vision or are sighted. Journal of Vision Impairment and Blindness 93: 691–703.

Dawson G, Lewy A (1989) Arousal, attention, and the social-emotional impairments of individuals with autism. In: Dawson G (ed.) Autism, Nature, Diagnosis, and Treatment. New York: Guilford Press, pp. 49–74.

Dawson G, Meltzoff A, Osterling J, Rinaldi J, Brown E (1998) Children with autism fail to orient to naturally occurring social stimuli. Journal of Autism and Developmental Disorders 28: 479–85.

DeCasper AJ, Fifer WP (1980) Of human bonding: Newborns prefer their mother's voice. Science 208: 1174–6.

DeCasper AJ, Spence MJ (1986) Prenatal maternal speech influences newborn's perception of speech sounds. Infant Behavior and Development 9:133–50.

Fenwick KD, Morrongiello BA (1998) Spatial co-location and infants' learning of auditory-visual associations. Infant Behavior and Development 21: 745–60.

Fraiberg S (1977) Insights From the Blind. New York: Basic Books.

Frith U (2003) Autism: Explaining the enigma. Oxford: Blackwell Publishing

Frith U, Snowling M (1983) Reading for meaning and reading for sound in autistic and dyslexic children. Journal of Developmental Psychology 1: 329–42.

Garfield J, Peterson CC, Perry T (2001) Social cognition, language acquisition and the development of theory of mind. Mind and Language 16: 494–541.

Gibson EJ (1969) Principles of Perceptual Learning and Development. Englewood Cliffs, NJ: Prentice Hall.

Groenveld M, Jan JE (1992) Intelligence profiles of low vision and blind children. Journal of Visual Impairment and Blindness 86: 68–71.

Hobson P (2002) The Cradle of Thought. London: Macmillan Press.

Hobson RP, Lee A (1998) Hello and goodbye: A study of social engagement in autism. Journal of Autism and Developmental Disorders 28: 117–26.

Kujala T, Alho K, Kekoni J, Hämäläinen H, Reinikainen K, Näätänen K (1995) Auditory and somatosensory event-related brain potentials in early blind humans. Experimental Brain Research 104: 519–26.

Kujala T, Lehtokosi A, Alho K, Kekoni J, Näätänen R (1997) Faster reaction times in the blind than sighted during bimodal divided attention. Acta Psychologica 96: 75–82.

Landau B (1983) Blind children's language is not meaningless. In: Mills AE (ed.) Language Acquisition in the Blind Child: Normal and deficient. London: Croom Helm.

Landau B, Spelke E, Gleitman H (1984) Spatial knowledge in a young blind child. Cognition 16: 225–60.

Lecanuet JP, Graniere-Defere C, Jacquet A-Y, DeCasper AJ (2000) Fetal discrimination of low-pitched musical notes. Developmental Psychobiology 36: 29–39.

Leekam SR (2003) Dyadic orienting and the problem of interpersonal engagement. Paper presented at Society for Research in Child Development, Tampa, FL.

Leekam SR, Wyver S (1999) Joint attention without vision. Paper presented at IXth European Conference on Developmental Psychology, Island of Spetses, Greece.

Leekam SR, Hunnisett E, Moore C (1998) Targets and cues: Gaze-following in children with autism. Journal of Child Psychology and Psychiatry 39: 951–62.

Leekam SR, López B, Moore C (2000) Attention and joint attention in preschool children with autism. Developmental Psychology 36: 261–73.

Lessard N, Paré M, Lepore F, Lassonde M (1998) Early-blind human subjects localize sound sources better than sighted subjects. Nature 395: 278–80.

Lewkowicz DJ (2000) The development of intersensory temporal perception: an epigenetic systems/limitations view. Psychological Bulletin 126: 281–308.

Loveland K (1991) Social affordances and interaction: Autism and the affordances of the human environment. Ecological Psychology 3: 99–119.

Loveland KA (2001) Toward an ecological theory of autism. In: Burack JA, Charman T, Yirmiya N, Zelazo PR (eds) The Development of Autism. Mahwah, NJ: Lawrence Erlbaum Associates, pp. 17–37.

Millar S (1995) Understanding and representing spatial information. British Journal of Visual Impairment 13: 8–11.

Milne E, Swettenham J, Hansen P, Campbell R, Jeffries H, Plaisted K (2002) High motion coherence thresholds in children with autism. Journal of Child Psychology and Psychiatry 43: 255–64.

Morrongiello BA, Humphrey GK, Timney B, Choi J, Rocca PT (1994) Tactual object exploration and recognition in blind and sighted children. Perception 23: 833–48.

Morrongiello BA, Fenwick KD, Chance G (1998) Crossmodal learning in newborn infants: Inferences about properties of auditory-visual events. Infant Behavior and Development 21: 543–53.

Mottron L, Burack JA (2001) Enhanced perceptual functioning in the development of autism. In: Burack JA, Charman T, Yirmiya N, Zelazo PR (eds) The Development of Autism. Mahwah, NJ: Lawrence Erlbaum Associates, pp. 131–48.

Muir DW, Humphrey GK, Dodwell PC, Humphrey DE (1985) Use of sonar sensors with human infants. In: Warren DH, Strelow ER (eds) Electronic Spatial Sensing for the Blind: Contributions from perception, rehabilitation, and computer vision. Dordrecht: Martinus Nijhoff Publishers.

Mundy P, Sigman M, Kasari C (1994) Joint attention, developmental level and symptom presentation. Development and Psychopathology 6: 389–401.

Nieto C, Leekam S (2002) Sensory impairments in children with autism. Poster presented at British Psychological Society Developmental Section Conference, Brighton.

O'Connor N, Hermelin B (1978) Seeing and Hearing in Space and Time. London: Academic Press.

Ornitz EM (1989) Autism at the interface between sensory and information processing. In: Dawson G (ed.) Autism, Nature, Diagnosis, and Treatment. New York: Guilford Press, pp. 174–207.

Pérez-Pereira M (1999) Deixis, personal reference, and the use of pronouns by blind children. Journal of Child Language 26: 655–80.

Pérez-Pereira M, Conti-Ramsden G (1999) Language Development and Social Interaction in Blind Children. Hove: Psychology Press.

Plaisted KC (2001) Reduced generalization in autism: An alternative to weak central coherence. In: Burack JA, Charman T, Yirmiya N, Zelazo PR (eds) The Development of Autism. Mahwah, NJ: Lawrence Erlbaum Associates, pp. 149–69.

Plaisted KC, O'Riordan MAF, Baron-Cohen S (1998) Enhanced visual search for a conjunctive target in autism: a research note. Journal of Child Psychology and Psychiatry 40: 733–42.

Rogers SJ, Puchalski CB (1988) Development of object permanence in visually impaired infants. Journal of Visual Impairment and Blindness 82: 137–42.

Ross S, Tobin MJ (1997) Object permanence, reaching, and locomotion in infants who are blind. Journal of Visual Impairment and Blindness 91: 25–32.

Sampaio E (1989) Is there a critical age for using the sonic guide with blind infants? Journal of Visual Impairment and Blindness 83: 105–8.

Shah A, Frith U (1993) Why do autistic children show superior performance on block design task? Journal of Child Psychology and Psychiatry 34: 1315–64.

Shapiro T, Hertzig ME (1991) Social deviance in autism: a central integrative failure as a model for social non engagement. Psychiatric Clinics of North America 14: 19–32.

Sigman M, Ungerer J (1984) Cognitive and language skills in autistic, mentally retarded and normal children. Developmental Psychology 20: 293–302.

Strelow ER, Warren DH (1985) Sensory substitution in blind children and neonates. In: Strelow ER, Warren DH (eds) Electronic Spatial Sensing for the Blind: Contributions from Perception, Rehabilitation, and Computer Vision. Dordrecht: Martinus Nijhoff Publishers.

Strelow ER, Warren DH, Sonnier BJ, Riesen AH (1987) Behavioral observations of sensory substitution in neonate macaques (*Macaca arctoides*). Behavioral Neuroscience 101: 738–41.

Tager-Flusberg H, Calkins S, Nolin T, Baumberger T, Anderson M, Chadwick-Dias A (1990) A longitudinal study of language acquisition in autistic and Down syndrome children. Journal of Autism and Developmental Disorders 20: 1–21.

Tomasello M (1999) The Cultural Origins of Human Cognition. Cambridge, MA: Harvard University Press.

Tomasello M, Call J, Gluckman A (1997) Comprehension of novel communicative signs by apes and human children. Child Development 68: 1067–80.

Travis LL, Sigman M (2001) Communicative intentions and symbols in autism: examining a case of altered development. In: Burack JA, Charman T, Yirmiya N, Zelazo PR (eds) The Development of Autism. Mahwah, NJ: Lawrence Erlbaum Associates, pp. 279–308.

Vygotsky LS (1934) Thought and Language. Cambridge, MA: MIT Press.

Warren DH (1994) Blindness and Children: An individual differences approach. Cambridge: Cambridge University Press.

Wing L (1969) The handicaps of autistic children: a comparative study. Journal of Child Psychology and Psychiatry 10: 1–40.

Wing L (1971) Perceptual and language development. In: Rutter M (ed.) Infantile Autism: Concepts, Characteristics and Treatment. Edinburgh: Churchill Livingstone, pp. 173–98.

Wing L, Gould J (1979) Severe impairments of social interaction and associated abnormalities in children: epidemiology and classification. Journal of Autism and Developmental Disorders 9: 11–29.

Wyver SR, Markham R (1998) Do children with visual impairments demonstrate superior short-term memory, memory strategies, and metamemory? Journal of Visual Impairment and Blindness 92: 799–811.

CHAPTER 4

More than meets the eye: blindness, talent and autism

LINDA PRING AND VALERIE TADIC

We have all come across blindness and for the most part think of it as a sensory–perceptual loss for which the remaining functional sensory channels like hearing or touch can provide some compensation. However, in the case of autism the impairments in communication, in social understanding and imagination, as well as in the ritualistic and obsessional behaviours seem to be features of a developmental disorder that cannot easily be compensated for. In certain respects these individuals are 'blind' to some aspects of the world around them, and this has consequences for their behaviour. In the first part of this chapter we explore some of the associations between autism and blindness by focusing on early childhood behaviour. Three single case studies are presented that illustrate important features discussed in the theoretical considerations. In the second part of the chapter the impact of blindness beyond the early developmental years is considered in the context of memory performance. One suggestion given prominence concerns the role of musical pitch memory and this links with the final section where talent is considered. Research with artists and musicians both with and without autism is used to illustrate a cognitive style that may be associated with the development of talents. The connections, with reference to the development of talent, autism and blindness, are examined. In the early 1980s there seemed no direct association between these, but as we will describe in this chapter it may be that there is more to this than meets the eye.

Research with early childhood behaviours

Theory of mind: theoretical considerations

Visual experience provides children and infants with a rich source of information about themselves and their surroundings. Through vision children are able to observe connections among other people's expressions of emotion and witness the context within which various feelings arise. For such reasons vision can be seen to play a critical role in the development of theory of mind.

Theory of mind refers to the 'everyday' ability to understand other people's beliefs, thoughts and desires in order to explain and predict their behaviour. With the ability to infer mental states, like the true and false beliefs of oneself and others, children become more capable of participating in a wide range of conversational and social interactions. Many studies now indicate that in almost all normally developing children theory of mind develops by the age of 4–5 years (Perner, Leekam and Wimmer, 1987).

With his modular account of mind Baron-Cohen (1995) has argued that the monitoring of others' eye direction and subsequent integration of this with a 'shared visual attention mechanism' play a key role in establishing a theory of mind module in the developing infant. Similarly, in the 'theory–theory' account originally offered by Meltzoff and Gopnik (1993), visual imitation provides the starting point for theory of mind development, requiring the child to map the seen movements of others onto the felt movements of self in order to produce an imitation. Furthermore, Hobson (1993) described foundations of theory of mind and interpersonal understanding in terms of a child taking part in triadic interactions, mainly visually based. Through joint attention behaviours (i.e. gaze monitoring, following points and producing proto-declarative points) that involve the child, an object or event and another person, the child is able to comprehend the attitude of the other person towards the object or event. These joint attention behaviours, which involve triadic coordination or sharing of attention, emerge in typical development between 6 and 12 months (Leekam and Moore, 2001) and are usually carried out in the visual modality (Hobson, 1993).

Significantly, disruption of joint attention behaviours has been given a central role in autism. More specifically, typical disturbances in social and communicative development seen in autism have been linked with impairment of theory of mind abilities, which is seen as the core deficit in autism (Happé, 1993). It is not surprising then that children who are autistic have consistently been found to perform poorly on so-called false belief tasks (e.g. Baron-Cohen, Leslie and Frith, 1985). Such tasks specifically require children to use their ability to infer mental states in order to predict other people's behaviours and beliefs.

Hobson (1993) was among the first to suggest a functional overlap in the developmental psychopathology of children who are congenitally blind and children who are autistic. In the case of children who are blind this is likely to be associated with the fact that without vision (and joint attention) they are denied the chance to associate emotional and mental states with their behavioural correlates. Brown et al. (1997) found that a lower ability group of children with visual impairment (verbal IQ < 70) could not be distinguished from children with autism by their scores on checklists of autistic-like behaviours, whereas a higher ability group (verbal IQ > 70) showed a higher level of these behaviours than normally developing children. Similarly, some children with profound congenital visual impairment (and no other impairments) have been found to have problems with false belief tasks at chronological and verbal mental ages older than 4 years, therefore demonstrating a delay in theory of mind development (Peterson, Peterson and Webb, 2000; Green, Pring and Swettenham, 2004).

Indeed, some children with profound visual impairment have been found to resemble sighted children who are autistic in various aspects. The similarities include abnormalities in social–communicative competence (Fraiberg, 1977), difficulty in emotional expressiveness and emotional recognition (Rogers and Puchalski, 1986; Minter, Hobson and Pring, 1991), a characteristic pattern in use of creative symbolic play and language (e.g. echolalia and pronoun reversal) (Andersen, Dunlea and Kekelis, 1984), mannerisms and stereotypical ritualistic behaviour (Chess, 1971), and impairments in cognitive abilities such as abstract thinking (Wills, 1981).

The development of social cognition in children who are blind

As a postgraduate student of Pring and Swettenham, Sarah Cupples (now Green) adopted the approach taken by Hobson (1993). She presented children with profound visual impairment with standard false belief tasks, such as the Sally-Anne Task (Wimmer and Perner, 1983), Containers Task and Boxes Task (Minter, Hobson and Bishop, 1998), as well as other tasks assessing the understanding of more advanced tests of theory of mind (e.g. Strange Stories Task by Happé, 1994; see also Pring, Dewart and Brockbank, 1999). These tasks involve second-order false belief understanding, such as 'I know that you know that I am not telling the truth', as well as the understanding of sarcasm and irony. Overall Cupples/Green's research (Green, 2001) supported Hobson's findings that children without vision appear to be at a significant disadvantage in understanding theory of mind, even when they are several years older than their sighted counterparts. On the other hand, even though the majority of children who are blind experience difficulties with false belief understanding and more advanced aspects of social cognition (Minter et al., 1998; Cupples, Pring and Swettenham, 1999), Cupples et al. observed that some children without vision show little or no difficulty at all in this area. More interestingly, those children with profound visual impairment who pass first-order false belief tasks have been found to be no different from sighted children in their performance on second-order false beliefs (Cupples et al., 1999). It seems that, once children who are visually impaired understood first-order false beliefs, their advanced understanding seems to 'catch up' with that of sighted children. On some occasions, however, a more profound deficit can be observed and such children will not be able to make up for this deficit (Cupples et al., 1999). Researchers in the area (e.g. Brown et al., 1997; Cupples et al., 1999; Hobson, Lee and Brown, 1999) agree that it is likely that verbal ability plays a very significant role in this process and subsequent outcome.

Three case studies – Katy, Robert and John

Some of the characteristics described above can perhaps best be illustrated by referring to individual case studies. The data were originally collected by Cupples and we present our interpretation of them below.

The three children described here were chosen because they exemplified three different ways in which theory of mind development may proceed in children with congenital and total sight loss. They were matched by chronological and mental age, which in all three children was within normal range (as assessed by WISC-R (Wechsler, 1976) and WPPSI (Wechsler, 1967)). The children were assessed on two occasions with approximately a year in between.

Katy was first assessed at 6 years 8 months, and was 7 years 11 months at the time of the second session. Her visual impairment is the result of Leber's amaurosis, a congenital retinal disorder (Good, 1993). Katy had been in a mainstream school setting since preschool. Her verbal skills were extremely good (IQ = 145) and she showed a consistently high ability pattern across the five WISC-R verbal subtests (Table 4.1). Katy was responsive and chatty during the testing sessions and told the researcher that she enjoyed activities such as playing 'schools' with her friends, playing hide and seek, making collages and pictures, and sometimes pretending to be other people.

The youngest of the children, Robert, was first assessed at the age of 6 years 6 months, and was 7 years 9 months at the time of the second session. His visual impairment is a result of an inherited syndrome called Norrie's disease (Webster and Roe, 1998). Robert, like Katy, attended a mainstream school at the time of the testing. His verbal IQ was found to fall within a normal range (IQ = 90) even though there were some inconsistencies in his verbal ability, with relative weakness on the Information and Comprehension subtests but strength on the Vocabulary subtests (WPPSI; Wechsler, 1967). At an informal interview Robert proved to be very good at imitating voices and said that he liked using cassette machines and making his friends laugh by telling them jokes. He also reported that he never pretended to be another person because he did not 'have any favourite characters'.

The oldest of the children, John, was 8 years 1 month at the time of the first session and 9 years old at the second session. His visual impairment was congenital but without a specific diagnosis. He attended a mainstream school at the time of the testing and even though his verbal IQ was within a normal range (IQ = 95) he showed an inconsistent pattern of verbal abilities with relative strength on Digit Span and weakness on Comprehension (WISC-R; Wechsler, 1976). John told the researcher that he likes playing on his computer and Brailler and making Lego/Duplo models with his friends but that he never engaged in pretend play.

Table 4.1 The three children's verbal IQ scores as measured by WISC-R (Wechsler, 1976) and WPPSI (Wechsler, 1967)

	Katy	Robert	John
Verbal IQ	145	90	95
Information	18	6	9
Similarities	18	10	9
Vocabulary	15	13	9
Comprehension	17	6	5
Digit span	17	7	14

The three children were initially assessed on first-order false belief tasks (i.e. Sally-Anne Task, Containers Task and Boxes Task) and some advanced theory of mind tasks (a modified version of Strange Stories Task by Happé, 1994). They were additionally assessed on second-order theory of mind understanding, the assessments being based on tasks devised by Baron-Cohen (1989). Finally we (Cupples, Pring, Swettenham and Tadic) examined the relationship between performance on assessments of theory of mind development and everyday social skills. We were interested to find out what patterns of 'real life' social competence could be found in children who are congenitally blind, regardless of their performance on standard theory of mind assessments.

Katy, Robert and John clearly exhibited a different pattern of performance on standardized assessments of theory of mind understanding as illustrated in Table 4.2. Katy showed extremely good understanding of theory of mind overall. Her performance on the assessment of false belief of first and second order is in line with the performance of sighted children of the same age (Cupples et al., 1999). Robert, on the other hand, showed a clear initial delay in theory of mind development relative to his verbal and mental age and the sighted pattern of development but over a period of 15 months had shown a dramatic improvement, passing the first- and second-order false belief tasks. John, however, showed an inconsistent pattern in theory of mind development in that he showed some understanding of first-order false belief tasks initially but failed to pass the theory of mind tasks overall when assessed again 11 months later, suggesting a longer-term delay in this area of development.

Table 4.2 The three children's performance on standard theory of mind (ToM) assessments

	Katy	Robert	John
First-order ToM task (max = 8)	8	1 (first session) 8 (second session)	5 (first session) 3 (second session)
Second-order ToM task (max = 4)	4	2	Fail
Advanced ToM task (max = 6)	5	Fail	Fail

The heterogeneity in development illustrated here confirms earlier findings that while some children with profound sight loss show good understanding of theory of mind, as shown in a false belief paradigm, some children who are blind experience a delay and some even a regression in this area of development (Cupples et al., 1999). This picture is in line with Fraiberg (1977) and many other clinicians who feel that children who are profoundly visually impaired are more heterogeneous in their developmental patterns than other groups of children with and without impairments. This may be related to the special role of the development of language in such children.

We suggest that the patterns in theory of mind development seen in our study may in turn reflect the patterns in language development in children who are blind. Indeed the development of theory of mind has been closely linked to language development, the implicit understanding being that a child's developing knowledge and appreciation of their own and others' mental states must be facilitated by language (Baron-Cohen, Tager-Flusberg and Cohen, 1993). A relationship between verbal IQ and theory of mind ability has already been observed in children with autism in whom language competence was found to make a significant, positive impact on their performance of theory of mind tasks (Happé, 1995). Can the performance of the children described here shed light on these issues?

Even though all three children had a verbal IQ within a normal range Katy, who showed a very good overall understanding of theory of mind, had a particularly high verbal IQ. More specifically, her verbal mental age at the time when she was 6 years 8 months old was 9 years 8 months (145 on WISC-R; Wechsler, 1976). It seems plausible to suggest that such high verbal ability may have helped Katy pass false belief and advanced theory of mind tasks all along. But what about children like Robert and John?

A number of developmental studies have shown that there are deviations and delays in language development and vocabulary acquisition in children who are blind (e.g. Andersen et al., 1984; Landau and Gleitman, 1985). These deviations and delays may be a consequence of a parent/child communication style where attention in a child without vision cannot be caught and directed by eye contact, leading to a more restricted and less rich language input (Andersen et al., 1984). However, it seems that this can, in the long run, be overcome and during the school years the language of children who are blind 'catches up' (Landau and Gleitman, 1985). Once a child with profound visual impairment achieves a certain competence in verbal ability they make a big leap in their social cognitive development. This might explain the initial delay in theory of mind development in children like Robert at the age when he was first tested.

However, the question remains why some children fail to progress and, in John's case, even regress in this area of development. Some clinicians (e.g. Dale and Sonksen, 2002) describe a phenomenon of serious developmental disruption or 'setback' which seems to occur between 15 and 27 months of age. One explanation for the setback occurring in the children with profound visual impairment is the notion of a sensitive or critical period of brain development in the first to second year of life that is dependent on the visual experience that would be expected at this age (see Dale and Sonksen, 2002). Another explanation is that development had not been 'normal' before the setback but that a change seems more apparent in older children because the tests and batteries assessing social and cognitive abilities may detect such changes better at this age.

Testing everyday social competence

To explore 'real life' social competence, we adapted the approach taken by Frith, Happé and Siddons (1994). Everyday social skills and adaptation were assessed through the reports of caregivers (i.e. teacher and/or learning support assistant) using the Vineland Adaptive Behaviour Scales (VABS: Sparrow, Balla and Cicchetti, 1984) and Active and Interactive Sociability Items (devised by Frith et al., 1994). The children's 'personal and social sufficiency' (Sparrow et al., 1984) was assessed on three out of nine subdomains of behaviour measured by VABS, namely: communication, social coping skills and interpersonal relationships. The additional items on Active and Interactive Sociability adapted from Frith et al. were used to assess behaviours that could be performed with (Interactive) and without (Active) ability to 'mentalize'.

Some of these items were of particular interest because of their possible connection to underlying theory of mind ability. For instance, social coping skills involve behaviours such as apologizing for mistakes and responding appropriately to meeting strangers, both of which require an awareness of other people's thoughts and feelings. Similarly, interpersonal relationships such as having friends and showing thoughtfulness in gifts also show awareness of other people's feelings and ideas.

In their study with 24 children with autism, Frith et al. (1994) found a relationship between performance on false belief tasks and the scores on the VABS and interactive sociability. More specifically, those children with autism who passed first-order theory of mind had higher scores on VABS communication domain and Interactive Sociability items than those who failed the tasks; notably our research yielded the same pattern. Katy, who showed extremely good performance on theory of mind assessment, received higher scores on Expressive Communication (VABS) and Interactive Sociability than Robert and John whose theory of mind understanding was delayed (Table 4.3 and see Table 4.2).

Table 4.3 The three children's performance on everyday assessment using Vineland Adaptive Behaviour Scale (Sparrow et al., 1984) and Active and Interactive Sociability items (Frith et al., 1994)

	Katy	Robert	John
Expressive Communication (max = 26)	22	12	13
Social Coping Skills (max = 32)	12	8	19
Interpersonal Relationships (max = 16)	8	0	3
Active Sociability* (max = 14)	5	1	5
Interactive Sociability* (max = 14)	5	3	3

*Active Sociability: independent of theory of mind (ToM) skills; Interactive Sociability: dependent on ToM skills.

However, on certain VABS items all three children, regardless of their IQ and theory of mind ability, showed unusual and perhaps limited social competence skills. All three were reported to have less than adequate social coping skills as assessed by VABS. Furthermore, all scored in the low range on the assessment of Active and Interactive Sociability (Table 4.3). In addition, the Active Sociability scores in this group were lower than the mean score gained by two groups of children with autism (those who passed and those who did not pass theory of mind tasks) studied by Frith and colleagues. We speculate that one explanation for this discrepancy is that specific Active Sociability items may assess behaviours that are likely to be particularly affected by lack of vision, in particular sharing of toys, initiating social contact and showing appropriate table manners. Nevertheless, the low scores were somewhat surprising and provide some insight into the way the parents and caregivers viewed the children (e.g. Robert's parents refer to his behaviour as 'being a bit of a handful').

The pattern of findings seen here reiterates the association between autism and blindness and ability level. Brown et al. (1997), for example, found that the children who were blind and obtained low IQ scores showed a tendency to score higher on the Childhood Autism Rating Scale (CARS: Schopler, Reichler and Renner, 1988) than those with high IQ scores, indicating a link between low mental ability and autistic-like features in children who are congenitally blind. Even though Katy, Robert and John were within the normal IQ range and none of the children were assessed for autistic-like features *per se*, some aspects of their everyday social skills bear resemblance to behaviours exhibited by children who are on the autistic spectrum. This is particularly true in the case of John whose assessments of both theory of mind understanding and everyday social competence were at a low level. John's difficulty in concentrating during the tasks may have had an adverse effect on his false belief task performance. Nevertheless, even though his real life social competence is better than his scores on theory of mind tasks, it still falls below the range expected for the sighted children and closely resembles that of children with autism who can master the first-order false belief. Similarly, in the case of Robert, catching up on delayed theory of mind development does not seem to lead to improvement in everyday skills and, on the contrary, his social competence seems to be on a level with children who are autistic.

In many respects Robert and John resemble sighted children who are autistic. But, if we are to draw comparison between autism and blindness based on these three cases, where does Katy fit in? Katy certainly provides a singular example of a very bright child with profound visual impairments. She has a robust understanding of theory of mind, at an equivalent level to that of older sighted children. Looking at her real life social competence, we observed earlier that some of her scores (i.e. Active Sociability and Social Coping) bore a resemblance to the scores of sighted children with autism studied by Frith et al. However, we think that a more rigorous assessment developed with children who do not have access to vision is essential in this regard. If a child who is blind resembles a child with autism on a measure not specifically devised with sightedness as a factor, assessing the cause of the child's performance is subsequently confounded.

Screening for autism in children with profound visual impairment

Research with children who are congenitally and totally blind is challenging and the relative rarity of occurrence contributes to this. Brown et al. (1997) carried out an extensive study with 43 children (24 of whom were children who were congenitally and totally blind) in order to consider the association with autism. They adopted the CARS (15 items) (Schopler et al., 1988) and Behaviours Checklist for Disordered Preschoolers – BCDP (Sherman, Shapiro and Glassman, 1983) – as screening instruments focusing on real-life social competence.

An interesting comparison can be drawn between their findings and our own (Tadic, Pring and Swettenham). We used a different instrument to screen for autism in a different group of children with congenital visual impairment, namely the Autistic Screening Questionnaire (ASQ) (Berument et al., 1999). The ASQ was developed and tested by Rutter and Lord as a reliable screening measure rather than a diagnostic instrument and was based on the current diagnostic criteria for autism. An aim of the test was to fulfil the needs of research in which the comparison of autism with other clinical groups (in terms of autistic-like features) is desired (Berument et al., 1999). It includes 40 items assessing behaviours such as pronoun reversal, eye gaze, compulsions and rituals, unusual attachment to objects, imaginative play, repetitive use of objects, offering to share, etc. According to Berument et al., a cut-off score of 15 or more provides the best differentiation of pervasive developmental disorder (PDD) (including autism) from other diagnoses for children aged at least 4 years. A much higher cut-off score of 22 or more would be required to separate autism from other PDDs (Berument et al., 1999).

In our study the ASQs were completed by the carers (teacher and/or learning support assistant) of 18 children who were congenitally and totally blind. There were a variety of aetiological causes for visual impairment in this group: Leber's amaurosis (4), retinopathy of prematurity (3), congenital microphthalmia (4), retrolental fibroplasia (1), congenital glaucoma (1), retinal dysplasia (1), retinal detachments (1), anophthalmia (1) and other unspecified causes (2). The children were between 8 and 15 years of age (mean age 8.67) with a male to female ratio of 2:1.

Three out of 18 children (approximately 17%) in our study received a score of 22 or over (mean score of 27.7) and 11 out of 18 (61%) received a score greater than 15 (mean score of 19.55). Even though a score of 22 or over is required to separate autism from other PDDs, the percentage of children who can be classified under the PDD (including autism) in this group was striking. This result provides strong and independent support for the findings by Hobson and his team (e.g. Brown et al., 1997; Hobson et al., 1999) who argued that there was a range of 'autistic-like' clinical features in children who are congenitally blind. In addition, in our study no clear relationship emerged between the IQ data and severity of autistic features but this is likely to be associated with the smaller sample. Nevertheless, our general conclusion from our group of children who are congenitally blind is that a high number met the criteria for autistic-like features. Hence we think blindness may predispose a child to autistic-like psychopathology.

Memory in individuals with profound visual impairments

We have noted that initial delays in development of a child with profound visual impairment can sometimes be overcome in later years. Nevertheless, without visual experience cognition is likely to retain some specific characteristics. It is interesting to ask whether the later cognitive characteristics of children and adults who were born blind can provide any evidence of such alternative learning strategies. In the section below we describe attempts to investigate this with school-aged children and adults with congenital and total blindness, and in particular refer to memory processes.

Memory can refer to many different aspects of mental processing including both content and recollection. In this section autobiographical memory studies are described along with memory in both the long and the short term. Additionally, memory for pitch is considered since it links with the following section on talent and exceptional abilities.

Autobiographical memory

This comprises biographical information and experienced events related to the self. Currently there is agreement on some of the broad cognitive features of this type of memory, in particular that autobiographical memories are mental constructions that very often feature imagery while simultaneously containing abstract personal knowledge (see Conway, Pleydell-Pearce and Whitecross, 2001, for a review). Conway and his colleagues have developed a strong theoretical formulation in which retrieval involves access to an autobiographical knowledge base that contains hierarchical layers ranging from conceptual and abstract memories to highly specific details of individual events. These memories have, for most people, a strong (visual) imagery component, giving the memory its sense of immediacy. This central role of visual imagery has been highlighted in both observation and research (Brewer, 1986; Williams, Healey and Ellis, 1999).

Surprisingly little is known about this type of memory in individuals who are born blind and it could be that, since visual images have traditionally been viewed as an integral part of remembering the past, visual impairment could have negative consequences on autobiographical memory. But our research (e.g. Goddard and Pring, 2001) revealed no evidence that visual impairment was associated with a deficient access to the past. Instead we found that individuals with total and congenital blindness even demonstrated a memory advantage in personal biographical/ semantic memory. This was tested using a fluency task where participants generated names of people (e.g. friends and teachers) associated with different periods in their life. When comparing the mean number of names produced in recall, a standard recency effect emerged; significantly fewer names were recalled from primary school compared with both secondary school and 3 years post school. Critically, participants who were blind showed an advantage over the sighted with an improved ability in recalling names from primary and secondary school. No group differences occurred in the more recent time frame. Of course this advantage, demonstrated by those who were visually impaired, could be due to an exposure effect rather than the effects of visual impairment on memory. It is not uncommon for children with a profound visual impairment to attend boarding school where teachers (and maybe also friends) are likely to have a greater impact on one's life experience. Thus the greater fluency observed in the visually impaired may be associated with a larger pool of possible names upon which to draw, which in turn are better remembered because of their greater emotional significance. Alternatively the advantage observed might be explained with a superior encoding process related to attentional strategies, which in turn could be directly related to a lack of vision and it is this interpretation that is supported by other findings outlined below.

Verbatim, long- and short-term recall

Bartlett wrote in his 1932 book on remembering that in the process of learning we tend to forget the exact material, the learning episode itself, but instead we remember the gist or the overall meaning of the material. It was of interest then that in some early studies on memory performance we found that children and adults who were blind did not forget their experience in quite the same way as their sighted counterparts. Their recall was remarkably accurate and often exceeded that of sighted individuals. Certainly in terms of short-term memory performance we have known for some time that children with visual impairments perform particularly well on 'digit span', i.e. accurately recalling the order of a string of numbers (e.g. Smits and Mommers, 1976). But we also found that this above-average performance extended to many types of material, not just number strings. For instance, in a study where blind children were asked to listen to a text and make inferences about the material, we found that they recalled the exact wording of sentences they heard (C Edmonds and L Pring, 1995, unpublished data) significantly better than closely matched sighted control children. Furthermore, adults and children who were born blind had superior recall for random word lists, presented both in Braille and on cassette tape (e.g. Pring, 1988; Pring and Painter, 2002). It was difficult to explain such superior 'verbatim' memory performance. Reference to the increased attention to the remaining channels of input when vision was not available, and the need for an extra or attenuated temporary storage buffer holding the contents of direct sensory experiences which could be 'read out' later, were proposed as explanations.

While it is the case then that, in terms of verbatim memory, recall is superior in people with visual impairment, no such superiority has been reported in connection with 'gist' memory, the type of conceptual, long-term memory mentioned by Bartlett. Indeed in our research, there have been a minority of studies where such conceptual or semantically based memories have been worse than those of the sighted (Pring, 1988; Pring and Painter, 2002). It is likely that differing attentional resource allocations will have both advantages and, under some circumstances, disadvantages.

This general pattern of increased memory performance, particularly for unassociated items, has been cited as a significant feature of autism (e.g. Frith, 1989). In autism, it has been shown that memory for unassociated items, such as words or colour sequences, is only marginally less accurate than memory for associated items. This is unusual since association generally predicts increased recall accuracy. Frith argues that in the case of autism the 'lack of preference for coherent over incoherent stimuli must be regarded as abnormal' and links it to her belief that, in autism, the inability to draw together information so as to derive coherent and meaningful ideas, and the failure of the mind to be predisposed to do so, explain the essential features of autism. This theory of autism referred to as 'weak central coherence' has received considerable support (Frith, 1989; Happé, 1999) and is elaborated upon in the context of talent.

Sensory memory: pitch processing

If it is true that people without vision do have a greater ability to retain sensory experience for longer periods than those who are sighted, then the result should extend from verbal material to pure sensory experience. It is hard to test this but in one attempt we prepared a cassette tape where approximately 20 words were presented one at a time and then participants were asked to recall them. But critically, in this study, we focused not on the memory for words but on the pitch of the voice that spoke the words on the tape (i.e. a low-pitched man's voice or a higher-pitched woman's voice). As predicted, what we found was that the individuals who were blind were significantly better at accurately recalling whether a man or woman had spoken the previously presented words (Pring and Painter, 2002). Their memory for the pitch of the voice speaking the words was clearly retained. It seems that paying increased attention to the available channels of the perceptual world, and perhaps retaining that material for longer, has real advantages not least in terms of pitch processing. Indeed, this may help to explain the fact that individuals without sight seem to have a higher occurrence of absolute pitch ability than is normally found in the population (Oakes, 1955). This ability is extremely rare in the general population, estimated to be around 1 in 10 000 (Takeuchi and Hulse, 1993). Remarkably, in our study using the ASQ described earlier we found that 8 out of 12 parents of blind children asked to comment on talent responded that their children had absolute pitch. This may be one explanation of why piano tuning has historically been a favoured occupation for people with visual difficulties. The nature of absolute pitch and the memory advantages outlined above have consequences for the understanding of both musical processing and exceptional ability. So we turn next to research with groups of individuals with exceptional abilities and ask if a predisposition to develop high-level skills could reside in individuals with autism as well, perhaps, as in blindness.

Talent

Research that is concerned with the question of exceptional ability is hampered by the fact that so little is known about the determinants of talent and the conditions for nurturing its manifestation. For example, there is an ongoing debate between those who argue in favour of practice as the key to skill acquisition (Ericsson, Krampe and Tesch-Romer, 1993) and those who see basic, possibly inherited, aptitude as critical (Gagné, 1998). Green and Gilhooly (1992) summarize the cognitive performance of experts in comparison with novices. They mention superior memory performance, more elaborated problem-solving strategies and knowledge structures but emphasize that rarely are there any differences in terms of basic memory capacity. Implicit learning plays a larger role in the development of expertise and is emphasized in many influential models of cognitive architecture such as Anderson's Active Control of Thought (ACT) model, developed over the last 20 years (e.g. Anderson, 1993). Implicit learning does not involve conscious, attention-demanding resources and has been linked to the notion of innate genius. The existence of child prodigies such as Mozart has been taken as evidence of this phenomenon, although challenged by Howe, Davidson and Sloboda (1998). These authors go on to stress the problems of defining terms such

as 'motivation', 'aptitude' or even 'talent' itself and have instead emphasized the important role of practice.

Research with individuals with autism and exceptional ability

Nevertheless whatever it is that determines talent with all that it entails, it is
natural to be astounded by cases of exceptional ability juxtaposed with low
cognitive functioning. Langdon Down in the late nineteenth century and
later Kanner in the context of autism provided the first reports of these
individuals. The savants described in the literature display conventional
talents in restricted domains. They generally fall within the spectrum of
autistic disorders and have been the subject of theoretical and empirical
investigations (e.g. Miller, 1989; Treffert, 1989; Hermelin, 2001). The types
of skills exhibited by savants include lightning and calendrical calculation
(Pring and Hermelin, 2002), drawing (Selfe, 1978; Pring, Hermelin and
Heavey, 1995), poetry (Dowker, Hermelin and Pring, 1996), hyperlexia
(Mehegan and Dreifuss, 1972; Frith and Snowling, 1983), linguistics
(Tsimpli and Smith, 1998) and music (Hermelin, O'Connor and Lee, 1987).

O'Connor and Hermelin designed the first empirical studies of groups
of savants and the empirical studies referred to in this section are nearly
all ones carried out by the first author together with Hermelin since 1990
(see also Hermelin, 2001). We explored savant cognition by using both
single case and group studies.

The question of why autism, in particular, seemed to be linked with
cases of savant talent was one line of research that we pursued (e.g. Pring
et al., 1995). The answer was indicated by the 'weak central coherence'
theory mentioned earlier. In one part of this theory it is argued that individuals with autism adopt a perceptual strategy where an interest and bias
towards the processing of segments of a display or experience take prece-
dence over the processing of the whole display or experience. Attention
is given to the local processing of individual parts rather than to the processing of the global or holistic display.

We have argued (e.g. Pring et al., 1995; Pring and Hermelin, 2002) that
there is a link between the expression of talent and this cognitive architecture characteristic of individuals with autism. The tendency to draw
away from the integration of information to form an overall contextually
meaningful and coherent representation may be a characteristic that is
unconventional and has certain properties that support talented thinking.
The extent to which an individual uses such a *segmentation* strategy, as
seen when perceptual coherence is weak, can be measured by their
performance on psychometric tasks such as the block design test or the
embedded figures task. Indeed Shah and Frith (1993) neatly demonstrated
that the superior performance by children with autism compared with

mental-age-matched controls, was due to an ability to *segment* the config-uration into its constituent parts and thus reconstruct the overall pattern, without the interference of the cohesive nature of the total gestalt.

The reasoning is the same for understanding the characteristic advan-tage shown by individuals with autism who speedily locate hidden or embedded figures in a display (e.g. Baron-Cohen, Jolliffe and Mortimer, 1997). When using the children's embedded figures test, Shah and Frith (1993) made the point that the participants' superiority in comparison with a mental-age-matched control group resulted from them being unhindered by the overall meaningful context, within which the simple figure was embedded.

From our perspective we wanted to ask if such a strong segmentation strategy, as has been seen in autism, would play an important role in the manifestation of talent among the autistic artists in particular, but, also, among individuals with talent but without impairments.

Autistic savant artists

Some of the most pertinent data we collected linking the ability to draw to weak coherence came from studies with a group of autistic artists who were at entry level to foundation art school (described in a paper by Pring et al., 1995). We found that in a block design test the artists who were autistic were significantly faster than their non-gifted, diagnosis- and IQ-matched controls. The savant artists seem to display *especially strong* segmentation skills that allow them to overcome the coherence of the visual displays even in comparison with their autistic counterparts with-out specific talent in drawing. Pring and Hermelin's postgraduate student Nicola Ryder (2003) tested a group of nine autistic artists with a similar task, the embedded figures test. Table 4.4 shows her results, namely that savant artists and art students were significantly quicker in locating a sim-ple pattern from a meaningful or abstract context when compared with a mental-age-matched autistic control group.

Table 4.4 The mean performance of artistic savants, art students and autistic controls on the embedded figures test

	Meaningful (children's embedded figures test)	**Abstract** (adult embedded figures test)
Savant artists	5.70 (3.54)	6.54 (5.37)
Autistic control group	11.29 (8.91)	10.42 (6.82)
Art students	4.71 (2.67)	4.43 (2.69)

Although the small numbers advise caution, our interpretation was that the group of savant artists fell at the extreme end of the continuum for showing the effects of a segmentation strategy. We hypothesized that the thinking style that emphasized segmentation, found in individuals with autism, supports or is a precursor of the manifestation of critical talented abilities. Perhaps the attention to detail, away from the context, affords a fresh access to visual ideas.

Segmentation style and talent

The work described briefly above with savant artists suggested to us that such segmentation processing not only might be the key to the prevalence of autistic individuals among savant artists, but could also link specific modular abilities to modular talents found in the general population. To test this we matched talented artistic children, selected by teachers, with a control group of children on age and verbal IQ. What we found was that, perhaps unsurprisingly, the children who could draw were also significantly faster at completing the block design test (Pring et al., 1995). Similarly, university art students were also significantly faster at finding embedded figures than were IQ-matched university psychology students (Ryder, Pring and Hermelin, 2002). These results with gifted children and adult artists echo earlier findings made in the context of creativity with students from the prestigious Chicago School of Art (Getzels and Csikszentmihalyi, 1976).

It seems that segmentation strategy as a cognitive style can be emphasized in those with artistic talent and perhaps this enables them to hold basic elements or parts of a visual display quite separately and uniquely protected from the context in which they appear. In this way the individuals can resist the integration with familiar and learnt associations that develop as a natural consequence of dealing with the whole. For some talented individuals *without* other impairments, it may be that segmentation strategies are simply an optional 'mind-set' by which to view and experience the world. Through practice or by natural inclination the ability to break conventional associations and gestalt processes through a characteristic cognitive style may be an important element in displaying talents, at least in some domains.

Absolute pitch abilities and musical savants

What would be the manifestation of such an enhanced segmentation strategy? One possibility would be the enhanced perception and retention of discrete auditory elements such as pitches or tones in music. One example of such a special type of processing with music is the ability to show absolute pitch. Absolute pitch (AP) is the ability to recognize, label and remember pitch information without reference to an external standard. To develop this ability you need to hold a single note in mind, associate it with a verbal label, and keep it separate from other musical representations. Normally we hold musical notes in a *relational* way so that if we are given an anchor note such as middle C we can then move up or down an octave. People with absolute pitch hold the musical notes independently and can therefore retrieve them directly from memory without referring to other notes. AP is not a necessary component of musical ability or talent and many professional musicians do not possess it. The separation of AP and musical ability has been confirmed in neurological terms by brain imaging studies that discriminate the brain structure of musicians with AP from musicians and non-musicians without AP (Schlaug et al., 1995).

Early musical instruction influences the development of AP (Takeuchi and Hulse, 1993) in certain individuals and is also associated with increased spatial abilities in adulthood (Eastlund-Gromko and Smith Poorman, 1998). In particular, people with AP perform better on the hidden figures test than those with relative pitch or non-musicians (Costa-Giomi et al., 2001). We reasoned that AP, in the same way as the good performance on the embedded figures test, was an index of weak coherence. If this were the case then children with autism might be predisposed to show exceptional AP abilities. In a series of studies on musical cognition in children with autism, Heaton (e.g. Heaton, 1998; Heaton, Hermelin and Pring, 1998) found support for this suggestion. She was the first to confirm that AP is prevalent among children with autism and is linked to special musical abilities. AP is universal to all musical savants (e.g. Miller, 1989) and is probably necessary for such individuals to implicitly learn, store and recall the use of the rules and patterns that govern music. Certainly Hermelin and O'Connor (1986) argued that implicit learning and the extraction of the rules and regularities of musical grammar allow savants to create accurate reproductions of musical pieces.

Recently, an undergraduate student, Katherine Woolf, examined the pitch and rhythm-processing abilities of five musical savants who were congenitally blind. They played a variety of musical instruments and had a varied cognitive profile ranging from severely to mildly retarded. Their performance confirmed their musical abilities and they all showed excellent AP. In addition, their performance on both a short-term memory for tone test and a more complex memory for rhythm test was either comparable or better than a group of sighted musicians without any cognitive impairment. Performance on the rhythm task in particular supported the notion that music processing is modular with some individual features, such as rhythm, developing independently (Woolf, Pring and Tadic, accepted, subject to revision).

Treffert (1989) commented on the relatively common triad of mental impairment, musical genius and congenital blindness, and Miller (1989) suggested that the linguistic and social problems associated with congenital blindness might be a contributing factor in the development of musical and, in particular, absolute pitch ability. However, for us the critical perspective is somewhat different. We suggest that children who are blind, perhaps because of their dominant available sensory channels and their lack of vision, begin to develop weak coherence and this may be the explanation for their AP abilities. In some rare individuals this provides the basis from which to develop exceptional musical talent.

In conclusion

In *Seeing and Hearing and Space and Time*, O'Connor and Hermelin (1978) concluded that the characteristic processing style of children with autism or those who were blind or deaf depended on their distinctive sensory input or their possibility for decoding it. Here we continue in their tradition and have tried to show how early childhood behaviour, memory performance and talent abilities in children and adults with visual impairments connect to the features of autism that have been described in the literature. The cognitive strategies imposed by the lack of sight, and the failure to 'see' as can be argued in autism, have some similar consequences. It is clear that many children who are blind show autistic-like psychopathology and a number of these children meet the full diagnosis of autism. This has been linked to the role of vision in the development of theory of mind, which in congenitally blind children, as we have shown (Green, Pring and Swettenham, 2004), is often delayed. We have illustrated this by describing research in socio-cognitive development in young children who are blind and most clearly through presenting three case studies of individual children with profound visual impairment. But what we have also understood is the crucial notion that not all blind children manifest autistic-like features. This we have shown by describing Katy who is an example of a congenitally blind child with a typical socio-cognitive development of a sighted child. If lack of vision predisposes a child to autistic-like psychopathology then it must be possible to intervene with this specific aspect of blind children's development. If we understand this, we can effectively circumvent delays/disturbances in development of a blind child and proceed to consider intervention studies.

The work described with talent and memory performance refers itself to the cognitive architecture that is likely to develop in a range of individuals both with talent and with impairments such as autism or blindness. First we noted that there were some similarities between the characteristic memory pattern found in children and adults who are blind and those with a diagnosis of autism. It is not certain whether the weak central coherence account helps to explain the memory advantages described for individuals who are blind but we would argue that it is likely. This was linked to the proposition that the strong perceptual segmentation strategy that follows from weak coherence is a characteristic of those individuals who display certain talents in general and autistic talent in particular.

We have tried to illustrate, with examples from our research, how the impairments in autism as well as congenital blindness may lead to the adoption of mental strategies that through shared characteristics have similar but not always the same consequences.

References

Andersen ES, Dunlea A, Kekelis LS (1984) Blind children's language: Resolving some differences. Journal of Child Language 11: 645–64.

Anderson JR (1993) Rules of the Mind. Hillsdale, NJ: Lawrence Erlbaum.

Baron-Cohen S (1989) The autistic child's theory of mind: A case of specific developmental delay. Journal of Child Psychology and Psychiatry and Allied Disciplines 30: 285–97.

Baron-Cohen S (1995) Mindblindedness: An essay on autism and theory of mind. Cambridge, MA: Massachusetts Institute of Technology Press.

Baron-Cohen S, Jolliffe T, Mortimer C (1997) Another advanced test of theory of mind: Evidence from very high functioning adults with autism or Asperger's syndrome. Journal of Child Psychology and Psychiatry and Allied Disciplines 38: 813–22.

Baron-Cohen S, Leslie AM, Frith U (1985) Does the autistic child have a 'theory of mind'? Cognition 21: 37–46.

Baron-Cohen S, Tager-Flusberg H, Cohen DJ (1993) Understanding Other Minds: Perspectives from autism. Oxford: Oxford University Press.

Bartlett FC (1932) Remembering. Cambridge: Cambridge University Press.

Berument SK, Rutter M, Lord C, Pickles A, Bailey A (1999) Autism Screening Questionnaire: Diagnostic validity. British Journal of Psychiatry 175: 444–51.

Brewer WF (1986) What is autobiographical memory? In: Rubin D (ed.) Autobiographical Memory. Cambridge: Cambridge University Press, pp. 25–49.

Brown R, Hobson RP, Lee A, Stevenson J (1997) Are there 'autistic-like' features in congenitally blind children? Journal of Child Psychology and Psychiatry 38: 693–703.

Chess S (1971) Autism in children with congenital rubella. Journal of Autism and Childhood Schizophrenia 1: 33–47.

Conway MA, Pleydell-Pearce CW, Whitecross S (2001) The neuroanatomy of autobiographical memory: A slow cortical potential study (SCP) of autobiographical memory retrieval. Journal of Memory and Language 45: 493–524.

Costa-Giomi E, Gilmour R, Siddell J, Lefebvre E (2001) Absolute pitch, early musical instruction, and spatial abilities. Annals of the New York Academy of Sciences 930(1): 394–6.

Dale N, Sonksen P (2002) Developmental outcome, including setback, in young children with severe visual impairment. Developmental Medicine and Child Neurology 44: 613–22.

Dowker A, Hermelin B, Pring L (1996) A savant poet. Psychological Medicine 26: 913–24.

Eastlund-Gromko J, Smith Poorman A (1998) The effect of music training on preschoolers' spatial-temporal task performance. Journal of Research in Music Education 46: 173–81.

Edmonds C, Pring L (1995) Inferences in blind and sighted children. Unpublished project.

Ericsson KA, Krampe R, Tesch-Romer C (1993) The role of deliberate practice in the acquisition of expert performance. Psychological Review 100: 363–406.

Fraiberg S (1977) Insights from the Blind. London: Souvenir Press.

Frith U (1989) Autism: Explaining the enigma. Oxford: Basil Blackwell.

Frith U, Snowling M (1983) Reading for meaning and reading for sound in autistic and dyslexic children. Journal of Developmental Psychology 1: 329–42.

Frith U, Happé F, Siddons F (1994) Autism and theory of mind in everyday life. Social Development 3: 108–24.

Gagné F (1998) Commentary. Innate talents: Reality or myth? Behavioural and Brain Science 21: 399–442.

Getzels JW, Csikszentmihalyi M (1976) The Creative Vision: A longitudinal study of problem finding in art. New York: John Wiley & Sons.

Goddard L, Pring L (2001) Autobiographical memory in the visually impaired: Initial findings and impressions. British Journal of Visual Impairment and Blindness September: 18–25.

Good WV (1993) Ophthalmology of visual impairment. In: Fielder AR, Best AB, Bax MCO (eds) The Management of Visual Impairment in Childhood. London: MacKeith Press.

Green AJK, Gilhooly KJ (1992) Empirical advances in expertise research. In: Keane MT, Gilhooly KJ (eds) Advances in the Psychology of Thinking. London: Harvester Wheatsheaf.

Green SA (2001) Social cognition in children with visual impairments. Unpublished PhD thesis, University of London.

Green SA, Pring L, Swettenham J (2004) An investigation of first-order false belief understanding of children with congenital profound visual impairment. British Journal of Developmental Psychology 22: 1–17.

Happé FGE (1993) Communicative competence and theory of mind in autism: A test of relevance theory. Cognition 48: 101–19.

Happé FGE (1994) An advanced test of theory of mind: understanding of story characters' thoughts and feelings by able autistic, mentally handicapped, and normal children and adults. Journal of Autism and Developmental Disorders 24: 129–54.

Happé FGE (1995) The role of age and verbal ability in the theory of mind task performance of subjects with autism. Child Development 66: 843–55.

Happé FGE (1999) Understanding assets and deficits in autism – why success is more interesting than failure. Psychologist 12: 540–6.

Heaton P (1998) Musical cognition of children with autism. Unpublished PhD thesis, University of London.

Heaton P, Hermelin B, Pring L (1998) Autism and pitch processing: a precursor for savant musical ability? Music Perception 15: 91–305.

Hermelin B (2001) Bright Splinters of the Mind: A personal story of research with autistic savants. London: Jessica Kingsley.

Hermelin B, O'Connor N (1986) Idiot savants calendrical calculators: Rules and regularities. Psychological Medicine 16: 885–93.

Hermelin B, O'Connor N, Lee S (1987) Musical inventiveness of five idiot-savants. Psychological Medicine 17: 685–94.

Hobson RP (1993) Autism and the Development of Mind. Hove: Erlbaum.

Hobson RP, Lee A, Brown R (1999) Autism and congenital blindness. Journal of Autism and Developmental Disorders 29: 45–56.

Howe JA, Davidson JW, Sloboda JA (1998) Innate talents: reality or myth? Behavioural and Brain Sciences 21: 399–442.

Landau B, Gleitman LR (1985) Language and Experience: Evidence from the blind child. Cambridge, MA: Harvard University Press.

Leekam S, Moore C (2001) The development of attention and joint attention in children with autism. In: Burack J, Charman T, Yirmiya N, Zelazo P (eds) The Development of Autism: Perspectives from theory and research. Mahwah, NJ: Lawrence Erlbaum Associates.

Mehegan C, Dreifuss F (1972) Hyperlexia: exceptional reading ability in brain damaged children. Neurology 22: 1105–11.

Meltzoff AN, Gopnik A (1993) The role of imitation in understanding persons and developing a theory of mind. In: Baron-Cohen S, Tager-Flusberg H, Cohen DJ (eds) Understanding Other Minds: Perspectives from autism. Oxford: Oxford University Press.

Miller L (1989) Musical Savants: Exceptional skill in the mentally retarded. Hillsdale, NJ: Lawrence Erlbaum Associates.

Minter M, Hobson RP, Bishop M (1998) Congenital visual impairment and 'theory of mind'. British Journal of Developmental Psychology 16: 183–96.

Minter ME, Hobson RP, Pring L (1991) Recognition of vocally expressed emotion by congenitally blind children. Journal of Visual Impairment and Blindness December: 411–15.

Oakes WF (1955) An experimental study of pitch naming and pitch discrimination reactions. Journal of Genetic Psychology 86: 237–59.

O'Connor N, Hermelin B (1978) Seeing and Hearing and Space and Time. London: Academic Press.

Perner J, Leekam SR, Wimmer H (1987) Three-year olds' difficulty with false belief: the case for a conceptual deficit. British Journal of Developmental Psychology 5: 125–37.

Peterson CC, Peterson JL, Webb J (2000) Factors influencing the development of a theory of mind in blind children. British Journal of Developmental Psychology 18: 431–47.

Pring L (1988) The 'reverse-generation' effect: A comparison of memory performance between blind and sighted children. British Journal of Psychology 79: 387–400.

Pring L, Hermelin B (2002) Numbers and letters: Exploring and autistic savant's unpractised ability. Neurocase 8: 330–7.

Pring L, Painter J (2002) Recollective experience in the visually impaired: The role of sensory and conceptual processing. British Journal of Visual Impairment and Blindness 20: 24–32.

Pring L, Dewart H, Brockbank M (1999) Social cognition in children with visual impairments. Journal of Visual Impairment and Blindness November: 754–68.

Pring L, Hermelin B, Heavey L (1995) Savants, segments, art and autism. Journal of Child Psychology and Psychiatry 36: 1065–76.

Pring L, Woolf K, Tadic V (accepted, subject to revision) Melody and pitch processing in five musical savants with congenital blindness. Music Perception.

Rogers SJ, Puchalski CB (1986) Social smiles of visually impaired infants. Journal of Visual Impairment and Blindness 80: 863–5.

Ryder N (2003) The creative and generative capacity of savant artists with autism. Unpublished PhD, University of London.

Ryder N, Pring L, Hermelin B (1999) The puzzle of the artistic savant: Generativity in autism. British Psychological Society Meeting, London, December.

Ryder N, Pring L, Hermelin B (2002) Lack of coherence and divergent thinking: Two sides of the same coin in artistic talent? Current Psychology 21: 168–75.

Schlaug G, Jncke L, Huang Y, Steinmetz H (1995) In-vivo evidence of structural brain asymmetry in musicians. Science 267: 699–701.

Schopler E, Reichler RJ, Renner BR (1988) The Childhood Autism Rating Scale (CARS). Los Angeles, CA: Western Psychological.

Selfe L (1978) Nadia's Case. The New York Review of Books 25(18; 23 November).

Shah A, Frith U (1993) Why do autistic individuals show superior performance on the Block Design task? Journal of Child Psychology and Psychiatry 34: 1351–64.

Sherman M, Shapiro T, Glassman M (1983) Play and Language in developmentally disordered preschoolers: A new approach to classification. Journal of the American Academy of Child Psychiatry 22: 511–24.

Smits BWGM, Mommers MJC (1976) Differences between blind and sighted children on WISC verbal subtests. New Outlook for the Blind 70: 240–6.

Sparrow SS, Balla DA, Cicchetti DV (1984) Vineland Adaptive Behaviour Scales. Circle Pines, MN: American Guidance Service.

Takeuchi A, Hulse S (1993) Absolute pitch. Psychological Bulletin 113: 345–61.

Treffert D (1989) Extraordinary People. London: Academic Press.

Tsimpli IM, Smith NV (1998) Modules and quasi-modules: language and theory of mind in a polyglot savant. Learning and Individual Differences 10: 193–215.

Webster A, Roe J (1998) Children with Visual Impairments: Social interaction, language and learning. London: Routledge.

Wechsler D (1967) The Wechsler Preschool and Primary Scale of Intelligence. Cleveland, OH: Psychological Corporation.

Wechsler D (1976) The Weschler Intelligence Scale for Children – Revised. Windsor: NFER-Nelson.

Williams JMG, Healy HG, Ellis NC (1999) The effect of imageability and predictability of cues in autobiographical memory. Quarterly Journal of Experimental Psychology 52A: 555–79.

Wills DM (1981) Some notes on the application of the diagnostic profile to young blind children. Psychoanalytic Study of the Child 36: 217–37.

Wimmer H, Perner J (1983) Beliefs about beliefs: Representation and constraining function of wrong beliefs in young children's understanding of deception. Cognition 14: 103–28.

CHAPTER 5

Early signs of developmental setback and autism in infants with severe visual impairment

NAOMI DALE

A substantial minority of infants with severe visual impairment (SVI) are at risk of a developmental setback or regression which has long-term consequences for their behaviour and development. Understanding of this early developmental crisis is still far from complete. The aims of this chapter are to consider current insights into developmental setback and to propose directions for future research and intervention. The question of whether setback is an early manifestation of an autistic spectrum disorder in the visually impaired child is also discussed.

Early delay – constraints and intervention

Impaired vision has complex far-reaching effects on early development. Constraints have been found in the integration and interpretation of input from the other senses, the development of emotional bonding, personality and self-concept, social interaction skills, sound and tactile localization skills, fine motor and locomotor competence, concept of object permanence, and the formation of language and other cognitive concepts (Norris, Spaulding and Brodie, 1957; Fraiberg and Freedman, 1964; Reynell and Zinkin, 1975; Fraiberg, 1977; Sonksen, 1979, 1983a; Sonksen, Levitt and Kitzinger, 1984; Dunlea, 1989). The constraints on any target skills are often cumulative, acting directly upon it but also on one or more of the skills that underpin its acquisition (Sonksen, 1983b). Infants with visual impairment show 1–2 years' delay in most areas of learning throughout the preschool years, compared with sighted infants. The only exception is the syntactical structure of expressive language, where the difference is less marked (Reynell, 1978; Landau and Gleitman, 1985). Comparisons, however, may be misleading; the cognitive demands on any sensorimotor and preschool cognitive tasks may far exceed those required for comparable tasks undertaken by the sighted child.

Atypical social behaviours have been reported particularly in children who are blind or profoundly visually impaired (Keeler, 1958; Fraiberg and Freedman, 1964; Rogers and Newhart-Larson, 1989; Brown et al., 1997). Infants may be socially withdrawn, self-absorbed and mute. Speech, if present, is often echolalic and repetitive. Infants may lack exploratory, functional or imaginative play and resort to repetitive behaviour stereo-typies like rocking, banging and eye poking. The behaviours share many of the characteristics of autistic spectrum disorders in the sighted (accord-ing to DSM-IV or ICD-10), raising the question of whether some infants with visual impairment also have a form of autism. Previously referred to as 'blindisms', these behaviours were until recently assumed to be the sec-ondary consequences of severe sensory deprivation caused by lack of vision.

By the late 1970s, various clinical teams were advocating early inter-vention to counter the developmental disadvantages of visual impairment (Fraiberg, 1977; Jan, Freeman and Scott, 1977; Sonksen et al., 1984). Patricia Sonksen and colleagues designed and applied a sys-tematic developmental and visual intervention programme for babies and preschoolers with SVI (Sonksen, Petrie and Drew, 1991). The pro-gramme continues to be delivered in our Developmental Vision Clinic at Great Ormond Street Hospital. The clinical and associated research team is multidisciplinary from neurodevelopmental paediatrics, psychology, speech and language therapy, occupational therapy and optometry. Babies and infants are referred to the clinic for specialist management of their development and include children with a wide variety of visual dis-orders. A database recording the findings of each clinic visit was established in 1977; it supports our research initiatives and currently contains data on more than 1300 young children, with information on most children spanning their early years.

The programme aims to achieve optimal progress in babies and young children with severe and profound visual impairment. Parents are assist-ed in developing an emotionally rewarding relationship with their baby and achieving the insights, skills and sensitivity to help their baby progress favourably. An integrated scheme of assessment and manage-ment for a range of areas of development including visual development and functional vision is arranged for the infant. Tests of functional vision (Sonksen, 1983a, 1983b) explore the infant's vision for the everyday environment and visual materials; the findings form the basis of guidance to promote visual development and to ensure optimal use of vision for development and learning. Development is assessed using the Reynell–Zinkin Scales for infants and preschoolers with a visual impair-ment (Reynell and Zinkin, 1975; Reynell, 1978), and the test results underpin the guidance to promote general development and to circum-vent the constraints arising from the visual impairment. The programme starts from the earliest stage of diagnosis of a visual impairment and continues, with 4- to 6-monthly updates, until the late preschool years. The developmental programme is published as a developmental guide for parents and professionals in four different languages, which is now in widespread use nationally and internationally (Sonksen and Stiff, 1991).

Early signs of developmental setback

Despite this intensive intervention, the clinical impression of our team was that a worryingly high proportion of infants with SVI were still failing to progress or were even regressing and losing skills. This included babies who were alert and responsive and who seemed to be doing very well in their first year of life, reaching appropriate motor and developmental milestones on the Reynell–Zinkin Scales. Cass, Sonksen and colleagues reviewed the developmental trajectories of infants who had attended our clinic in their first 16 months and had shown normal development during this time according to visual impairment (VI) norms (Cass, Sonksen and McConachie, 1994). One hundred and two infants met the inclusion criteria; the aetiology of their visual impairment covered a wide variety of visual disorders. The clinical records were analysed and developmental progress across the early years was plotted. Setback was defined as stasis or regression of raw scores, on one or more subscales of the Reynell–Zinkin Scales sustained over at least two consecutive assessments over a period of one or more years and/or increasing disorder of social communication. Eleven children (11%), equivalent to 1100 per 10 000, showed this severe setback, with plateauing or loss of cognitive and language skills followed by an extremely slow rate of learning. Almost all these children had profound visual impairment (PVI). The incidence of setback in the group with PVI was 10 out of 32 children, equivalent to 3100 per 10 000, compared with only one out of 72 children with severe visual impairment (SVI), i.e. children who had perception of more than light-reflecting objects and therefore had some 'form' vision. The seriousness of this problem for infants with PVI is apparent when contrasted with the much lower incidence of autistic regression in sighted children – 0.05–2 per 10 000 (Gillberg, Steffenburg and Schaumann, 1991) and is more in keeping with the incidence of autism in children with definitive medical conditions like tuberous sclerosis – 11–31% (Gillberg and Coleman, 1996).

According to the charted trajectories, the behavioural onset of the setback occurred between 15 and 27 months. Two broad patterns were identified, with varying degrees of change in social accessibility and behaviour being central features of both. In pattern A, developmental stasis or regression occurred in association with a loss of explorative and manipulative play. In pattern B, there was increasingly disordered social communication with continuing acquisition of non-verbal cognitive skills. Stereotypies including eye poking, rocking, flapping and face tapping were features of both patterns of deterioration, with the examiner often noting that the stereotypies appeared to be blocking learning. Apart from plateauing or loss of skills in cognition and language, the infants were reported to show severe difficulties in social behaviour, including becoming more withdrawn, self-directed and resistant to social approach. Marked difficulties in language and behaviour were noted including a high level of echolalia, repetitive language or mutism and severe tantrums.

Our group and others found that the setback phenomenon occurred in children with diverse congenital visual disorders including Norrie's disease, anophthalmia, optic nerve hypoplasia, Leber's amaurosis, microphthalmia, coloboma, retinopathy of prematurity and cerebral visual impairment (Norris et al., 1957; Keeler, 1958; Fraiberg and Freedman, 1964). This contrasts with the finding of Rogers and Newhart-Larson (1989), who reported a higher concentration of autistic features in Leber's amaurosis than in other visual disorder conditions.

Designing a research framework

In view of the seriousness of setback for infants with visual impairment, our team has subsequently worked to increase understanding of its aetiology and causative mechanisms. A main methodological obstacle, however, is the problem of additional learning difficulties and physical or other sensory disabilities in this population. At least 40–50% of children with visual impairment have additional impairments (Hirst, Poole and Snelling, 1993); one in three has damage of the posterior visual pathway (cerebral visual impairment). Relatively 'pure' research samples are needed to forward understanding of the specific consequences of *impaired vision* on development; otherwise it is impossible to separate the effects of learning difficulties, which compromise much of the existing literature.

Categorizing congenital visual disorders

Therefore in our most recent research studies, we have worked on achieving a sample of children with impaired vision without the confounding factor of additional disabilities. A new taxonomy for classifying children with visual impairment, according to the origin of their visual disorder, has been developed (Waugh, Chong and Sonksen, 1998; Dale and Sonksen, 2002; Sonksen and Dale, 2002). Congenital visual disorders are classified according to the site of origin of the visual impairment: (1) cerebral, that is arising in the posterior visual pathways or in the brain substance, and (2) peripheral, that is arising in the globe, retina or anterior pathway of the optic nerve. The peripheral disorders are referred to as 'congenital disorders of the peripheral visual system' (CDPVS). The CDPVS group is subdivided into (1) potentially simple CDPVS ('simple' CDPVS) and (2) potentially complicated ('complicated' CDPVS). In the latter group, the CDPVS is part of a neuro-ophthalmic condition, e.g. retinal dystrophy in peroxisomal disorder, a brain malformation syndrome, e.g. retinal dystrophy in Joubert's syndrome, or a neurosystemic dysmorphic syndrome, e.g. cataracts in Down syndrome. Central nervous system involvement is one of the diagnostic criteria of the 'complicated' CDPVS subgroup. The children excluded from our research programme, though not our clinical programme which is open to all who are clinically eligible, are those in the cerebral and the 'complicated' CDPVS groups. In both these groups the children have been exposed to potentially brain-damaging events, which greatly raise the likelihood of learning difficulties.

The remaining group of children with potentially 'simple' congenital disorders of the peripheral visual system ('simple' CDPVS) is expected to be relatively 'pure', even though some may have additional brain damage and neuropathology. Our research samples are therefore drawn from this group. Examples of visual disorders in this group include Leber's amaurosis, Norrie's disease, cone dystrophy, anophthalmia, microphthalmia, optic nerve hypoplasia, aniridia, glaucoma, coloboma, cataract, and anterior chamber defects and albinism.

Subsequent research supports our choice of this group for investigation of developmental issues in infants with visual impairment. In contrast to reported levels of 40–50% in population surveys (Hirst et al., 1993), we found that only 17% of infants in our study of 69 children with 'simple' CDPVS showed global learning difficulties at 27–54 months (Dale and Sonksen, 2002).

Categorizing visual level/degree of visual impairment

On the basis of clinical observation, our team has postulated that there are major group differences in terms of infant development between those with and those without 'form' vision. 'Form' (spatial) vision is defined as awareness of visual targets that do not reflect light (Cass et al., 1994; Waugh et al., 1998; Sonksen and Dale, 2002). The Near Detection Vision (NDV) scale, developed by Sonksen (Sonksen, 1983a; Sonksen et al., 1991), is used to categorize children into visual level groups for developmental studies. The terms SVI and PVI are used to distinguish between children with and without 'form' vision. On the NDV scale, SVI status implies that the child shows visual awareness of the 12.5-cm woolly ball spinning at 30 cm distance (point 2 or higher); PVI status implies the child shows no visual awareness of a 12.5-cm spinning woolly ball at 30 cm distance (point 0 or 1) and thus has no 'form' vision. Highly significant differences have been found between the PVI and SVI groups in all our recent developmental studies (Cass et al., 1994; Moore and McConachie, 1994; Waugh et al., 1998; Dale and Sonksen, 2002; Dale and Sonksen, submitted for publication), supporting our selection criteria for visual level.

Establishing risk factors

This section examines the empirical knowledge of factors that are associated with an infant developing setback and may function as 'risk' factors. Research might also inform on the factors that increase resilience and protection in young children with visual impairment; evidence that the majority of the infants with profound visual impairment in the study by Cass et al. (1994) did not show severe setback during the period of the study suggests that there is a resilience factor(s) that requires greater understanding.

Level of vision

Our group and others have already highlighted the importance of distinguishing *visual level* in the visually impaired population for understanding early developmental issues. Infants with PVI have been shown to be at greater developmental risk than those with SVI in language and cognitive studies (Bigelow, 1990; Preisler, 1991; Hatton et al., 1997).

Severity of visual level was shown to be a major risk factor for setback in the Cass et al. (1994) study. Almost all the children with setback (10 out of 11) had PVI and showed light perception only at best. Only one out of 72 children with SVI showed setback; even those who were very severely visually impaired and had only minimal 'form' vision, enabling them at best to detect dense coloured objects without vision for detail, seemed 'protected' from developing setback.

This finding was replicated in two of our later retrospective studies on neurological and developmental outcome in infants with 'simple' CDPVS (Waugh et al., 1998; Dale and Sonksen, 2002). All seven children with setback had PVI in Waugh et al.'s study. Using a different definition of setback – normal on two or more subscales of the Reynell–Zinkin Scales (including Sensorimotor Understanding) between 10 and 16 months (time 1) and deceleration of 30 or more Developmental Quotient (DQ) points to a DQ of less than 70 on one or more subscales by 27–54 months (time 2) – Dale and Sonksen (2002) found that 33% of the infants with PVI (n = 27) showed setback, in contrast to only 3% of those with SVI (n = 37).

As all visual diagnoses were represented in both the PVI and SVI groups, with only two or three exceptions, *visual level* rather than diagnosis appeared to exert the greater influence on outcome. The incidence of setback (22%) in the 'simple' CDPVS sample (n = 69) was even higher than that in the Cass et al. study (1994) using different sampling methods (note that the samples overlapped in 34 cases), establishing that setback is a serious risk of 'simple' CDPVS (Dale and Sonksen, 2002). The estimate of setback in this study was probably conservative because four children (all with PVI) whose first signs of setback in the Cass et al. cohort were in the domain of social communication were not classified as 'setback' children in our later study because of higher DQs at time 2 (Dale and Sonksen, 2002).

Age

The initial behavioural signs of setback were evident by 15–27 months of age (Cass et al., 1994). This age specificity suggests either a critical period or 'window of vulnerability' when infants with visual impairment are susceptible to setback or the age when the infant's neurobiology is manifested behaviourally. Our research programme has established signs of behavioural change only from about 15 months onwards. This does not discount the possibility of earlier behavioural signs or 'silent' precursors on the neurological level being operative (Sonksen and Dale, 2002). Qualitative analysis of the behavioural signs preceding the onset of setback might be illuminating and is planned by our team.

Of further relevance is the development of the visual system in the early years. Vision changes and improves for significant numbers of infants and young children with SVI. In our retrospective study of 'simple' CDPVS, we found that five children out of 69 had no 'form' vision at 10–16 months but had developed some by 27–54 months (Dale and Sonksen, 2002). Nevertheless all five had developed setback by the later age period. Although the numbers were very small, a tentative conclusion is that 'form' vision developed during the first year of life is 'protective', but not that developed at a later age. The contributory factors of visual level and age appear to interact and *lack of 'form' vision during the first year of life* may add a 'window of vulnerability' in early development.

Cognitive and language development

Global learning difficulties are almost absent at the end of the first year in infants with 'simple' CDPVS in our retrospective study (Dale and Sonksen,

2002). This low level of global learning difficulties not only justifies our taxonomy but also lowers the expectation of autism in the 'simple' CDPVS population, since autism is associated with severity of learning difficulties in the sighted (8.9–11.7% of children with mental handicap; Nordin and Gillberg, 1996). Nevertheless 15 (22%) of the sample (n = 69) developed a severe setback by 27–54 months (Dale and Sonksen, 2002).

Although more detailed insight into the cognitive and language patterns underlying the emergence of setback is still forthcoming, our retrospective study of infants with 'simple' CDPVS showed that deceleration was most marked in verbal comprehension (73% of the 15 children with setback) and sensorimotor understanding (80% of those with setback) (Dale and Sonksen, 2002). The syntactical and structural aspects of expressive language could, however, be superficially preserved. This led to a markedly uneven developmental profile in some children, with an apparent facility in language expression but lack of comparable understandings of language or the physical world. Although some infants chatted incessantly, their verbal expressions tended to be repetitive and lacking in semantic meaning and understandings that related to the 'here and now'. This was particularly pertinent to object vocabulary and referential language (see next section).

By 27–54 months, 80% of those children showing setback had developed global developmental delay, with DQs of less than 70 in sensori-motor understanding, verbal comprehension and expressive language (Dale and Sonksen, 2002). Severe learning difficulties generally appear to be part of the longer-term prognosis of young children suffering severe setback since only a minority of children showed partial recovery (Cass et al., 1994); this agrees with Brown et al.'s finding (1997) of significant cognitive deficits in their older blind children who also exhibited autism. At present we do not know whether the setback group has learning difficulties in the first year of life that the Reynell–Zinkin Scales were insufficiently sensitive to detect, or whether the promising early cognitive and language development is halted abruptly by a regressive mechanism in the second year.

Although the majority of children with PVI did not show setback, deceleration in the rate of progress is a marked feature of cognitive and language development across the second and third year of life; 70–74% of those with PVI (n = 27) decelerated in their sensorimotor/cognitive and receptive language development (Dale and Sonksen, 2002). Severe deceleration occurred in all vision level groups, on all subscales and across the full developmental spectrum, but at much lower levels in the severely visually impaired (24–30%). Hypothetically, the cognitive skills to be acquired in the second and third year are becoming more challenging for the profoundly visually impaired child (see Bigelow, 1990) or the effects of earlier constraints from PVI are accumulating negatively.

Joint attention

Social–communicative development is a vulnerable process in the visually impaired infant, as shown in our earlier study (Cass et al., 1994) and other studies. Disruption has been recorded at the behavioural level, but the neuropsychological correlates are yet to be charted and may be revealing in the future. Investigation at the behavioural level is hampered by lack of knowledge of the normative sequence and range of social–communicative development in the visually impaired infant who is progressing well (Cass et al., 1994; Perez-Pereira and Conti-Ramsden, 1999). Currently available infant scales draw heavily on vision-dependent behaviours such as eye gaze, facial expression and gesture, and have norms for the sighted population. Without knowing more about adaptive development in infants with visual impairment, it is impossible to detect deviation from the norm that signals early signs of concern.

Other reports have suggested that at the end of the first year social reciprocity and responsiveness might be a domain that remains intact in infants with visual impairment (Rowland, 1983; Urwin, 1983; Preisler, 1991); our findings agree with this. In a recent cross-sectional study by our team, 74 infants aged 10–40 months with 'simple' CDPVS or normal sight were investigated. The visually impaired group were divided into those with SVI and those with PVI. An independent researcher interviewed the mothers of the infants at home, using a structured interview method with a Questionnaire of Social Communication in Young Children with Visual Impairment (SCYVI) which was designed by our team. The questionnaire included 40 questions to investigate the child's current social and communicative behaviour without using wording that referred to vision-dependent behaviours. Mothers were asked to consider the previous 4 weeks and report whether the infant had shown the particular behaviour (incidence), how often (frequency) and in what form (mode).

The social–communicative behaviours of the visually impaired infants were found to be very similar to those of the sighted in the first to second year and there were no apparent signs of emerging setback. Others have demonstrated that parent–infant interactions in the early months of life can be successfully organized through alternative tactile, kinaesthetic and auditory channels, thus enabling their development without vision (Rowland, 1983; Urwin, 1983; Preisler, 1991). Nevertheless by the third year, the profoundly visually impaired group started to differ significantly from the severely visually impaired and sighted groups, particularly in areas of 'joint attention' and 'referential communication' (i.e. the sharing of interests and attention to objects with an interacting adult). Joint referential attention requires the infant initially to coordinate his attention and interaction with the object and with the interacting adult and, as the infant matures, to secure the adult's attention to his actions with the object. This set of competences was reported to be absent or suboptimal in frequency in the group with PVI, in contrast to the frequent incidence in the other two groups in our study.

The considerable problem for the visually impaired infant in achieving joint attention with objects has been discussed by others (Preisler, 1991; Cass et al., 1994; Hobson et al., 1997; Perez-Pereira and Conti-Ramsden, 1999). Bigelow (2003) demonstrates that joint attention, though delayed, can be achieved in two blind children of normal intelligence. Hobson et al. (1997) and Bigelow (2003) speculate on the possible mechanisms of joint referential attention in the sighted and the problems that can arise for the visually impaired infant. Although the reasons for delay or deficit in the infant with PVI are not yet apparent, aspects of the process such as preverbal communication using gaze monitoring, switching of attention from object to interacting adult and gesture may be particularly dependent on vision. There may also be environmental impoverishment arising from the failure on the parent's part to interpret the infant's non-visual communicative signs (Moore and McConachie, 1994). Bigelow (2003) reports that parallel delays in cognitive attainments may be associated. Difficulty in switching attention from non-social to social objects has also been recorded in sighted children with autism (Swettenham et al., 1998).

Profound visual impairment appears to have a seriously disruptive effect on joint referential attention in the second to third year of life. This raises the intriguing question of whether joint referential attention is temporarily disrupted for all or most infants with PVI – at least during the preverbal stage of communication. If this is so, what is the relationship between this temporary disruption and the setback phenomenon? In the children showing setback in our earlier research, difficulties in social communication showed continuing disorder rather than delay (Cass et al., 1994). Moreover, does disorder persist in some children who do not show the setback phenomenon – and what are the longer-term implications for social–communicative and referential language development? There is particular reason for concern because joint attention has been shown to be an important precursor to language development in the sighted child and deficiency in this area is one of the diagnostic criteria for autism in the young (Baron-Cohen, 1995).

The interrelationship of joint attention, social–communicative and cognitive and language development in infants with visual impairment has still to be clarified though promising investigations have begun (Bigelow, 2003).

Familial and psychosocial environment

Visual impairment has a disruptive effect potentially on the early parent–baby relationship (Fraiberg and Freedman, 1964). Whilst dealing with the stress reactions, distress and depression that are common during the post-diagnostic period, parents have to adjust to a baby who responds very differently to a normally sighted baby. The baby may lack eye contact, facial expression and behavioural responses that indicate positive affect and responsiveness. The parent may find it hard to interpret the baby's non-visual responses and consider the baby unresponsive (Fraiberg, 1977). The parent may fail to find alternative sensory substitutes for interacting with the baby, potentially compounding the sensory deprivation for the baby (Fraiberg, 1977). The risk is increased in depressed parents who may withdraw further from the baby.

Other groups have observed variability in the quality of interaction between parents of children with VI (Norris et al., 1957; Urwin, 1983; Preisler, 1991) and variability in the personality and developmental attributes between children with VI (Preisler, 1991). The experience of our team suggests that, until the infant has acquired sound/object concept and sound localization skills, parents frequently lack techniques for motivating their interest and mobility (Sonksen et al., 1984). They are also reported to use different speech styles with 2- to 3-year-old children with VI compared with sighted peers (Kekelis and Andersen, 1984). Parents of young children with PVI use a high rate of reference to objects or activities that are not the immediate focus of the child's attention (Moore and McConachie, 1994). These parents also made frequent requests for information from the child and referred to the environment using non-specific labels – both patterns of parental speech that are associated with slower language development in the sighted child. An over-reliance on repetitive social rhymes observed in some parent–child dyads is also associated with poor cognitive and language functioning in the second to third year (Norgate, Collis and Lewis, 1998). The evidence is growing for considerable variation in the patterns of parent–child interaction in families with visually impaired babies; some of these differences appear to seriously disadvantage the child with PVI and present a considerable challenge for future clinical intervention and research.

Although a link between features of the psychosocial environment and the genesis of setback has been speculated, the evidence and direction of effects are not clear. In the Cass et al. (1994) study, it was noted that a significantly higher number of psychosocial adversity factors, including hospitalization of the child, marital discord or breakdown, maternal depression, parental drug addiction, major financial or housing problems, were recorded for the families than for the families without setback children. Nevertheless, focus on the psychosocial environment was not one of the original objectives of the study nor was it prospectively studied. Since children causing concern were more likely to be investigated and recorded extensively, the recording may be clinically biased.

Moreover, children who were failing to prosper may in turn have contributed to increased parental depression and marital discord. Perplexing behaviours and symptoms may have intensified professional concerns and led to increased hospitalization and investigations. One hypothesis is that variations in parental reactions and quality of the psychosocial environment might interact with susceptibility to setback and act to increase or reduce risk.

Brain lesions

Brain structure and functioning can now be investigated with modern neuroimaging techniques and new information is continually emerging. The nature and role of brain lesions of developmental origin in autistic spectrum and pervasive developmental disorders that feature regression in the sighted are being actively explored by several teams (e.g. Courchesne, Townsend and Saitoh, 1994). The neuroimaging literature with reference to normal development, setback and autistic spectrum disorders for VI children with 'simple' CDPVS is, however, still sparse. Findings have been correlated with developmental outcome in optic nerve hypoplasia (e.g. Brodsky and Glasier, 1993) but not in retinal and globe conditions.

Our research group has carried out a retrospective review of 254 children with a wide variety of conditions within the 'simple' CDPVS spectrum; 79 had neuroimaging of the brain – 51 with computed tomography (CT) and 28 with magnetic resonance imaging (MRI) (Waugh et al., 1998). Although this sample did not have central nervous system involvement as part of their diagnostic criteria, 51% of the children ($n = 79$) (38% of those who had CT and 86% of those who had MRI) were found to have brain lesions of a developmental nature. These included deficient myelination (in the MR scans only), cerebellar abnormalities, midline defects and abnormalities of the optic pathways. The brain lesions were found in a wide variety of diagnostic conditions and there were no specific patterns to the site of lesion or to the diagnostic condition, the only exception being pituitary lesions and cortical clefting which occurred only in optic nerve hypoplasia. The incidence of lesions was higher in this sample with 'simple' CDPVS than in the sighted autistic population (level of 5–10%, Courchesne et al., 1994), suggesting that 'simple' CDPVS disorders might be considered as neurodevelopmental disorders that target the brain as well as the eye (Sonksen and Dale, 2002). The variability in nature and site of discrete focal lesions was similar to that reported for sighted children with any of the developmental disorders of childhood including autistic regression (Filipek, 1999).

The *number of lesions* per child (range one to six) was significantly greater in the seven children who suffered developmental setback than in the 72 children who did not (Waugh et al., 1998). This finding parallels that demonstrated by Bolton and Griffiths (1997) in children with tuberous sclerosis. The high incidence of *multiple lesions* in the setback group strengthens the probability of a link between lesions and developmental outcome (Sonksen and Dale, 2002) although the mechanisms are unclear. Although grey matter lesions are uncommon in sighted children with autistic regression, all three children with cortical dysplasia in our study showed setback.

An association between number of lesions and severity of visual impairment was also found in our group's study. The number of brain lesions per child was significantly greater with PVI than with SVI. Embryological development may be significant here – the neural crest is the embryological precursor of most structures of both the eye and the brain. If the agent affecting the eye and the brain is common, it might be expected to influence the severity of expression in the same direction in both (Sonksen and Dale, 2002). Hence, if the brain is more severely affected, vision may also be more severely impaired. Genes are likely to be the common proactive agent in most cases, because most 'simple' CDPVS disorders have a genetic basis (Sonksen and Dale, 2002).

An additional or related mechanism linking the visual and developmental domains that contributes to poor developmental outcome in infants with 'simple' CDPVS may be that of failure of the myelination process. Myelination was delayed in nine out of 28 MRI studies in the cohort; the incidence of delayed myelination was higher with PVI than with SVI (Waugh et al., 1998). Severity of expression of vision loss might have a direct impact on the process of myelination and lead to deficient and deviant connectivity due to a deprivation of visual input.

The number of brain lesions and degree of abnormal connectivity are both likely to be greater in children with more PVI and might interact to increase vulnerability to setback and autism in children with congenital VI (Sonksen and Dale, 2002). Deprivation of visual input may also potentially affect the *functional* systems of the brain; new techniques of functional neuroimaging may elucidate this in the future.

Genetic factors and sex

Most 'simple' CDPVS disorders have a genetic basis and genetic factors probably operate to influence developmental outcome in children with VI via various routes. The finding of our group that developmental setback occurs throughout the 'simple' CDPVS spectrum (Waugh et al., 1998; Dale and Sonksen, 2002) shows that the problem is not disorder specific and linked to a single gene defect. Some gene defects responsible for 'simple' CDPVS conditions could theoretically influence the development of other structures and functions derived from the neural crest (Sonksen and Dale, 2002). The available literature gives some support to this hypothesis. In case series of specific disorders like Leber's amaurosis, Norrie's disease and optic nerve hypoplasia, learning disability shows varying incidence (Nickel and Hoyt, 1982; Goodyear, Sonksen and McConachie, 1989). For Leber's amaurosis, children with additional medical conditions like deafness, medullary sponge kidney, cardiomyopathy or neuromotor problems were at greater risk of learning disability than those with uncomplicated eye disease (Black and Sonksen, 1992). Other possible mechanisms include the involvement of genes flanking the gene segment responsible for the 'simple' CDPVS condition; this could extend the spectrum of expression to affect developmental functioning and/or additional systemic dysmorphology – such a contiguous gene syndrome has been demonstrated in some cases of Norrie's disease (Goodyear et al., 1989).

Developmental setback in children with 'simple' CDPVS conditions is likely to be a complex disorder that is genetically heterogeneous. Single and multigenic factors may exert their influence on neurobiological and neuropsychological processes via a variety of routes and mechanisms, as has been postulated for autism in the sighted (Bailey, Phillips and Rutter, 1996; Sonksen and Dale, 2002). Studies in molecular genetics are making rapid progress in determination of the genetic basis of many of the conditions in the 'simple' CDPVS spectrum. In future molecular genetic studies may lead to determination of differences in deletions and gene sequences between individuals with the same 'simple' CDPVS condition who have good and poor developmental trajectories. As suggested in Sonksen and Dale (2002), many of the research strategies reviewed by Bailey et al. (1996) that have and inform on genetic mechanisms in autism could effectively be applied to the visually impaired population.

In our recent retrospective study of cognitive and language outcome in infants with 'simple' CDPVS disorders, a sex difference in developmental outcome was found (Dale and Sonksen, 2002). Preschool boys were more delayed in language development, as has been shown frequently in sighted boys, but the effects of sex differences varied according to visual level. Boys with PVI were significantly more delayed in their verbal comprehension than girls with a similar visual level. Boys with SVI were significantly more delayed in their expressive language than girls. There was a significantly higher representation in the setback group – 12 (80%) out of the 15 children showing setback were boys, with a ratio of 4:1 to girls. The sex ratio is similar to that found for language disorders, dyslexia and autism (Volkmar, Szatmari and Sparrow, 1993), reinforcing our hypothesis that setback in 'simple' CDPVS disorders might constitute a distinct category of *neurodevelopmental disorder* (Sonksen and Dale, 2002).

Summary of risk factors

Current knowledge about the risk factors associated with setback is accumulating. As the previous section shows, evidence to date suggests that setback is associated with multiple factors which may operate on multiple levels – genetic, neurobiological, visual, psychological and psychosocial (Sonksen and Dale, 2002). The specific risk factors that may increase susceptibility to setback are starting to be identified, although we are still a long way from identifying their *modus operandi*, the ways that they combine and interact with each other, and their varying weighting to affect the developmental process. Moreover, any evidence of an association is insufficient to lay claim to a *causal* relationship to outcome. The risk factors that have been identified so far are listed in Table 5.1; the more tentative ones are marked with an asterisk.

Table 5.1 Risk factors for setback

- 0 to 2-year age period
- Profound visual impairment – lack of 'form' vision
- Profound visual impairment under 10–16 months
- Rapid deceleration and failure to advance in sensorimotor understanding and verbal comprehension
- Severe global learning difficulties*
- Lack of joint attention and referential communication*
- Multiple brain lesions
- Male sex
- Qualitative factors in the psychosocial and familial environment*

*Only preliminary evidence available.

Is setback an early sign of autism?

Our understanding of the relationship between setback and autism in the visually impaired young child is still preliminary. Regression has been reported in sighted children with autism, Landau–Kleffner syndrome and other epileptic syndromes, but Cass et al. (1994) and Perez-Pereira and Conti-Ramsden (1999) caution about making a diagnosis of autism in the visually impaired child. The evaluation of *impairments* in all the behaviours associated with autism can be performed only in relation to normally or adaptively developing visually impaired children rather than sighted normal subjects. None of our team's reported studies used measures of autism that are validated on the visually impaired population to test the hypothesis that setback is a form of autistic regression. But a number of strands of investigation are beginning to strengthen the case that setback may be an early sign of autism.

We and other investigators have described the autistic-like behaviours that are associated with stasis and developmental setback (Norris et al., 1957; Keeler, 1958; Fraiberg and Freedman, 1964; Cass et al., 1994). Similar incidence levels to our own study of infants with PVI (Cass et al., 1994) have been reported in other studies of the congenitally blind child population (26–40%) (Fraiberg, 1977; Brown et al., 1997). In Cass et al.'s study all children undergoing setback showed disorders in social interaction, communication and imagination in association with a restricted and repetitive repertoire of activities. Current work by our team is proceeding in designing and standardizing a new observational checklist for identifying social-communication difficulties and disorder in infants with visual impairment. The study will investigate concurrent validity of the checklist with the Childhood Autism Rating Scale (CARS; Schopler, Reichler and Renner, 1988) and explore differences in the scores of those showing setback and those who are not, to see if the checklist differentiates the two groups. Pilot evidence suggests a strong positive correlation between the checklist ratings and the CARS (N. Dale and A. Salt, unpublished data). Although we have not yet compared the setback versus the non-setback group, we have already established problems in social relating, language and communication, play and behaviour that reach the threshold criterion for autism on the CARS in sizeable numbers of children with 'simple' CDPVS disorders, even when vision-dependent items like gestural communication and visual behaviour are excluded from the scoring (Dale and Salt, unpublished data). This compares positively with Brown et al.'s (1997) finding of two out of 24 congenitally blind children in their study reaching a full diagnosis of autism and 10 out of 24 reaching a borderline diagnosis.

There are a number of important sets of issues to be clarified in the future: first, can the setback group be differentiated from the non-setback group in terms of social-communication difficulties? This would suggest that a developing social–communicative disorder is a specific diagnostic feature of setback as in autism in the sighted. Conversely, do these difficulties occur in varying degrees of severity across the visually impaired population, including those maintaining normal adaptive development in cognitive and language skills, with perhaps greater severity in the setback group. The latter position would indicate that social-communication difficulties are a more generalized feature of early development in the visually impaired population. Issues of varying severity of social–communicative difficulties and possible cognitive and language associations would need to be unravelled. Cass et al. (1994) have already reported on a minority of setback children (two out of a group of 11) who maintained relatively normal non-verbal development but showed an increasing social-communication disorder. Our new checklist on social–communication difficulties in the young visually impaired has led us to identify autistic-like difficulties in young visually impaired children across the spectrum of cognitive and language ability and visual level (Dale and Salt, unpublished data). Hopefully our investigation using our new checklist in conjunction with mapping the developmental trajectory across the early years will shed light on the relationship between these autistic-like difficulties and the cognitive and visual levels (Dale and Salt, unpublished data).

Secondly, is early 'autistic-like' behaviour a *transient* phenomenon that disappears with maturation and/or appropriate developmental and educational supports? Evidence of reversibility of the autistic signs in the blind child, unlike in the sighted child with autism or the child with learning difficulties, would challenge the conception of setback as a neurodevelopmental disorder (Perez-Pereira and Conti-Ramsden, 1999). In older blind children there is evidence that after considerable delays in development of social–communicative understanding – particularly 'theory of mind' – the majority will catch up (Cupples, Swettenham and Pring, 2000). In the Cass et al. study (1994), four out of the 11 children showing setback were reported to show a partial recovery, apparently in association with changes in the developmental environment such as additional developmental support in the home or appropriate nursery school placement. In three of these four children, however, the recovery in non-verbal cognition was more complete than the recovery in expressive language, with the children showing continuing disorder, rather than delay, in their communication skills. The rest of the setback group (seven children) did not show recovery and their development in all areas continued to be extremely slow and disordered. Subsequently our team has been requested to clinically assess at least eight school-aged children of continuing concern to their parents and educational team. All had shown setback in their earlier years according to our records. They were judged by our multidisciplinary team – who have expertise in visual impairment and in autism in the sighted – as reaching threshold diagnostic criteria for an autistic spectrum disorder (ICD-10), using our new social-communication difficulties checklist, reports from class teachers and school, clinic observations, and an adapted version of the CARS. From an educational stance, progress has been variable, but slow, in all the children. Some of the most effective teaching methods, according to anecdotal reports of teachers, have been those used with sighted autistic children but adapted for the visually impaired child. Learning difficulties and social-communication difficulties tend to persist, but progress in adaptive behaviour and language has been achieved. Further long-term follow-up of all children showing setback is required to elucidate outcome.

The evidence so far lends itself to the tentative conclusion that setback is an early behavioural manifestation of an autistic spectrum disorder that affects a subgroup of children with visual impairment, though further research is needed to confirm this. At present it is not proven whether it is a primary neurodevelopmental condition that occurs independently of the visual disorder (possibly with a common causal agent such as a genetic defect) or whether it is secondary to visual disorder and associated with the disruption of vision. The evidence of the heterogeneity of visual disorders involved in setback (Cass et al., 1994; Dale and Sonksen, 2002) adds support to the second hypothesis. The aetiological routes and mechanisms of the autistic spectrum disorder in the young visually impaired child are still unknown and are not necessarily the same as those in autism in the sighted.

One clinical priority is to develop a scientifically strong observational checklist for diagnosing social-communication difficulties and disorders in infants and preschoolers with visual impairment (Dale and Salt, unpublished data). We have argued that new assessment tools measuring (1) adaptive social–communicative development and (2) social-communication difficulties and disorder, which are validated on the 'simple' CDPVS population, are required to shed light on this. There is also suggestive evidence that setback is the severe end of a spectrum of potential difficulties and vulnerabilities in the social, communicative and behavioural domains of the visually impaired infant, with factors like visual and cognitive levels contributing and interacting to increase or decrease vulnerability or resilience.

Future direction for intervention

Whether setback can be prevented or improved in terms of outcome is not yet known. The apparent multifactorial and multilevel nature of the factors that may contribute to setback raises hope of 'windows of opportunity' for early intervention and even prevention. Not all infants with profound visual impairment show setback and protective factors may hopefully be strengthened to increase resilience and adaptive progress.

The most important finding from our research and that of others is the critical significance of *infancy* in the development of the visually impaired child, suggesting that the *0 to 2-year period* is the time when intervention may be imperative since this is the period preceding the emergence of setback. Although the timing of an effective infancy intervention programme is yet to be established, every month lost for support may potentially reduce its effectiveness. Early identification of visual impairment may be crucial. Although some babies are identified at an early age through perinatal screening or diagnosis of a condition associated with having a visual disorder, for others there may be considerable delay in referral to a specialist ophthalmological unit because parental concerns are not heeded by their general practitioner. Confirmation of early suspicions of visual impairment is not achieved on average until 11 months after birth for children who are congenitally blind in Scotland. Reaching a medical diagnosis takes on average another 3 months from this age. The average ages for partially sighted children are considerably later (Visual Impairment Scotland, 2003). UK figures are not available nationally but are likely to be similar. This extended period potentially delays the local authority stepping in to provide services and the infant may not be receiving any developmental or educational support during this time.

Even after the diagnosis, there may be long periods of delay or failure to refer the infant to a local specialist to support the child and family. Local professionals from generic childcare backgrounds generally lack the expertise and specialist training to assist infants with visual impairment and their families. Nevertheless there is a common mistaken tendency to view the visually impaired baby as 'developmentally well' if contented and medically well and therefore not requiring any specialist help. Our research and that of others highlights the 'hidden vulnerability' of the baby with visual impairment, however well they are progressing in the early months. In the UK qualified teachers of the visually impaired are probably the most appropriate and knowledgeable professionals to provide ongoing support to parents, to assist them with an intervention programme and to monitor its efficacy. They are also especially valued by parents among their network of professionals (Irani, 2000). Nevertheless the local availability of qualified specialist teachers, and even their training and expertise to work with the 0 to 2-year range, is still highly variable. A multi-tier health–education partnership between a supra-regional specialist developmental vision clinic and the local specialist teacher working closely with the child and parents is likely to be the most effective model of service delivery for the design, implementation and evaluation of early intervention.

Even if an infant does not yet have a definite visual diagnosis, she or he should be referred for specialist developmental support immediately a significant concern about vision has been notified. Parents and primary care workers can jointly assess whether the baby is showing normal visual responses or not (A. Salt, personal communication). The gateway to an early intervention service should be on screening evidence of a *functional visual problem* by the primary care worker and general medical practitioner even if the nature of the visual disorder is still undergoing investigation and diagnosis. Issues of screening surveillance of visual impairment in infancy are pertinent for consideration here.

Since establishing 'form' vision by the age of 10–16 months appears to exert a major protective effect on development (see earlier), the importance of a systematic visual promotion programme in the first year of life is underlined. Infants with severely degraded vision may fail to use their available vision functionally because the blurred images lack meaning for them (Sonksen, 1983a, 1983b). The vision promotion programme designed and applied by Sonksen and colleagues works systematically in helping babies with SVI differentiate and get meaning from suboptimal visual cues (Sonksen et al., 1991). This approach is different from a visual stimulation programme that bombards the baby with undifferentiated visual stimulus. Systematic evaluation using a randomized controlled trial demonstrated significant improvement in functional vision for infants on the full programme compared with a matched sample receiving only a programme for general development and general visual stimulus from the everyday environment (Sonksen et al., 1991).

A vision promotion programme should be provided for any baby with VI who may potentially develop some functional vision, however limited. With the exception of babies with bilateral anophthalmia, congenital disorders of the peripheral visual system cover the spectrum of visual impairment from profound to severe or moderate. The decision to join a vision promotion programme should not be made on the basis of the child's specific visual disorder since the prognosis for functional vision cannot be ascertained with certainty during infancy.

The risk of developing learning difficulties, particularly for the profoundly visually impaired, has been discussed earlier. In our own clinic we provide a comprehensive developmental promotion programme, in addition to vision promotion, to help support the infant's developmental advances and circumvent the constraints on development arising from visual impairment. This is done through regular developmental assessments, using the Reynell–Zinkin Scales, to establish developmental level and progress, to update the programme and to provide developmental guidance. In addition to our programme (Sonksen et al., 1984, 1991; Sonksen and Stiff, 1991), other groups have also proposed directions for early developmental intervention (Fraiberg, 1977; Rogers and Puchalski, 1988), though systematic evaluation with appropriate control groups is still lacking.

On the basis of current knowledge, the other focus for targeted intervention should be the development and precursors of joint attention and joint object-related communication and play. The evidence to date suggests that this is a very vulnerable developmental process in young children with visual impairment, especially those who are most severely impaired, and also that some of the children fail to overcome disruption and delays in this process and become disordered in social communication. The components of such a programme are still being considered and are in their early stages of development (Bigelow, 2003; Dale and Salt, unpublished data). At the neurobiological level the intervention might be required to induce formation of compensatory and functionally satisfactory precursor templates for referential communication (Sonksen and Dale, 2002). Strategies derived from recent studies of infant social communication and parent–child interaction and adapted for the visually impaired population will need consideration. Focused research and clinical resources should now be targeted on this potentially important area of intervention. Table 5.2 summarizes key factors for early intervention on the basis of current knowledge.

Table 5.2 Key factors for early intervention

- Introduced as early as possible from the earliest concern of significant visual impairment
- Rapid referral route to early intervention
- Intensive support during the 0 to 2-year period
- Design, delivery and evaluation through specialist developmental vision clinic (multidisciplinary staff specializing in visual impairment, child development and paediatrics), in partnership with local specialists
- Key worker to support delivery of programme at home, e.g. qualified teacher for the visually impaired with specialist expertise in visual impairment and the early years
- Regular, comprehensive, functional visual and developmental assessment to establish current levels, update programme and provide guidance
- Visual promotion programme in the first year of life to develop 'form' vision if possible and to use available vision optimally
- Developmental promotion programme to promote development and overcome constraints
- Programme focused on the development of joint attention, referential communication and joint object-based play

Future direction for research

Although children with 'simple' congenital disorders of the peripheral visual system ('simple' CDPVS) comprise the smallest group of visually impaired children, we advocate that research endeavour in this area be concentrated on this group with VI because the yield to behavioural neuroscience and the potential benefits for clinical developmental management of all categories of infants with VI are extremely high (Sonksen and Dale, 2002). A taxonomy for defining appropriate research samples has been proposed and areas of potentially rich research activity have been highlighted in this chapter. Multilevel, multifactorial and interventional research to establish the risk factors and causal mechanisms underlying setback, to identify and strengthen protective factors and to evaluate systematic intervention has been promoted. The theoretical understanding of developmental setback and unfavourable outcome in this population is still rudimentary but already stages and processes of particular vulnerability have been identified. Social communication has been identified as a priority for interventional research towards the possible prevention or modification of setback among 'simple' CDPVS infants, especially those with profound visual impairment. An increased understanding of the factors and multilevel interactions determining developmental outcome and setback could provide insight into the mechanisms underlying regressive developmental disorders and autism in the sighted (Sonksen and Dale, 2002) as well as brain development in the normal child. The question of whether the aetiology of autism in the visually impaired is different from that in the sighted remains to be answered.

Scientifically strong psychometric tools which are validated on the visually impaired population are essential for furthering the multifactorial and interventional research. To advance research in this area, our team plans to develop new developmental scales using a 'simple' CDPVS population and defining visual level groups using our criteria for PVI and SVI. The existing normative values of the Reynell–Zinkin Scales are no longer suitable for a 'simple' CDPVS population, yet this is the group that will provide the most realistic normative measures (Dale and Sonksen, 2002). New developmental scales will give a better clinical and research tool for assessment of all children with visual impairment because they will have been standardized on the least neurologically compromised group (Dale and Sonksen, 2002).

Promising lines of research and intervention are progressing for infants with visual impairment, but only with concerted effort and collaborative expertise from many different fields – paediatrics, psychology, education, ophthalmology, visual physiology, neurophysiology, neuroradiology, genetics – can we establish whether the special risks and difficulties can be overcome. The aim must be to increase the optimal life chances of all infants and young children with visual impairment.

Acknowledgements

Special thanks to Patricia Sonksen who led and inspired the practice and research of our team described in this chapter; this chapter is dedicated to her in gratitude. Thank you to Alison Salt who read and commented on this chapter, to past and present colleagues in the Developmental Vision

Team and to all the parents and children who have shared their experiences over the years.

References

Bailey A, Phillips W, Rutter M (1996) Autism: towards an integration of clinical, genetic, neuropsychological, and neurobiological perspectives. Journal of Child Psychology and Psychiatry 37: 89–126.

Baron-Cohen S (1995) Mindblindness: An essay on autism and theory of mind. Cambridge, MA: MIT Press.

Bigelow A (1990) Relationship between the development of language and thought in young blind children. Journal of Visual Impairment and Blindness 84: 414–19.

Bigelow A (2003) The development of joint attention in blind infants. Development and Psychopathology 15: 259–75.

Black MM, Sonksen PM (1992) Congenital retinal dystrophies: a study of early cognitive and visual development. Archives of Disease in Childhood 67: 262–5.

Bolton P, Griffiths PD (1997) Association of tuberous sclerosis of temporal lobes with autism and atypical autism. Lancet 349: 392–5.

Brodsky MC, Glasier CM (1993) Optic nerve hypoplasia. Clinical significance of associated central nervous system abnormalities on magnetic resonance imaging. Archives of Ophthalmology 111: 66–74.

Brown R, Hobson RP, Lee A, Stevenson J (1997) Are there 'autistic-like' features in congenitally blind children? Journal of Child Psychology and Psychiatry 38: 693–703.

Cass H, Sonksen PM, McConachie HR (1994) Developmental setback in severe visual impairment. Archives of Disease in Childhood 70: 192–6.

Courchesne E, Townsend J, Saitoh O (1994) The brain in infantile autism: posterior fossa structures are abnormal. Neurology 44: 214–23.

Cupples S, Swettenham J, Pring L (2000) Theory of mind development in children with congenital profound visual impairments. Poster presented at the Third International Mary Kitzinger Symposium on Visual Impairment at University of Warwick, September 2000.

Dale N, Sonksen P (2002) Developmental outcome, including setback, in young children with severe visual impairment. Developmental Medicine and Child Neurology 44: 613–22.

Dunlea A (1989) Vision and the Emergence of Meaning: Blind and sighted children's early language. Cambridge: Cambridge University Press.

Filipek PA (1999) Neuroimaging in the developmental disorders: the status of the science. Journal of Child Psychology and Psychiatry 40: 113–28.

Fraiberg S (1977) Insights from the Blind. London: Souvenir Press.

Fraiberg S, Freedman D (1964) Studies in the ego development of the congenitally blind. Psychoanalytic Study of the Child 19: 113–69.

Gillberg C, Coleman M (1996) Autism and medical disorders: a review of the literature. Developmental Medicine and Child Neurology 38: 191–202.

Gillberg C, Steffenburg S, Schaumann H (1991) Is autism more common now than ten years ago? British Journal of Psychiatry 158: 403–9.

Goodyear HM, Sonksen PM, McConachie H (1989) Norrie's disease: a prospective study of development. Archives of Disease in Childhood 64: 1587–92.

Hatton DD, Bailey DB, Burchinal MR, Ferrell KA (1997) Developmental curves of preschool children with visual impairment. Child Development 68: 788–806.

Hirst C, Poole JJ, Snelling GS (1993) Liverpool Visual Assessment Team 1985–1989: 5 years on. Child: Care, Health and Development 19: 185–95.

Hobson RP, Brown R, Minter ME, Lee A (1997) Autism. In: Lewis V, Collis GM (eds) Blindness and Psychological Development in Young Children. Leicester, UK: British Psychological Society Books, pp. 99–115.

Irani M (2000) Parental perception of local services and service needs in a sample of parents of school-age children with visual impairment. Unpublished MSc dissertation, Institute of Child Health/University College London.

Jan JE, Freeman RD, Scott EP (1977) Visual Impairment in Children and Adolescents. New York: Grune & Stratton.

Keeler WR (1958) Autistic patterns and defective communication in blind children with retrolental fibroplasia. In: Hoch PH, Zubin J (eds) Psychopathology of Communication. New York: Grune & Stratton.

Kekelis LS, Andersen ES (1984) Family communication styles and language development. Journal of Visual Impairment and Blindness 78: 54–65.

Landau B, Gleitman LR (1985) Language and Experience: Evidence from the blind child. Cambridge, MA: Harvard University Press.

Moore V, McConachie HR (1994) Communication between blind children and severely visually impaired children and their parents. British Journal of Developmental Psychology 12: 491–502.

Nickel B, Hoyt CS (1982) Leber's congenital amaurosis: is mental retardation a frequent associated defect? Archives of Ophthalmology 100: 1089–92.

Nordin V, Gillberg C (1996) Autism spectrum disorders in children with physical or mental disability or both: 1. Clinical and epidemiological aspects. Developmental Medicine and Child Neurology 38: 297–313.

Norgate S, Collis GM, Lewis V (1998) The developmental role of rhymes and routines for congenitally blind children. Current Psychology of Cognition 17: 451–77.

Norris M, Spaulding PJ, Brodie FH (1957) Blindness in Children. Chicago: University of Chicago Press.

Perez-Pereira M, Conti-Ramsden G (1999) Language Development and Social Interaction in Blind Children. Hove: Psychology Press.

Preisler GM (1991) Early patterns of interaction between blind infants and their sighted mothers. Child: Care, Health and Development 17: 65–90.

Reynell J (1978) Developmental patterns of visually handicapped children. Child: Care, Health and Development 4: 291–303.

Reynell J, Zinkin PM (1975) New procedures for developmental assessment of young children with severe visual handicaps. Child: Care, Health and Development 1:61–9.

Rogers SJ, Newhart-Larson S (1989) Characteristics of infantile autism in five children with Leber's congenital amaurosis. Developmental Medicine and Child Neurology 31: 598–608.

Rowland C (1983) Patterns of interaction between three blind infants and their mothers. In: Mills AE (ed.) Language Acquisition in the Blind Child: Normal and deficient. London: Croom Helm, pp. 114–32.

Schopler E, Reichler RJ, Renner BR (1988) The Childhood Autism Rating Scale (CARS). Los Angeles, CA: Western Psychological.

Sonksen PM (1979) Sound and the visually handicapped baby. Child: Care, Health and Development 5: 413–20.

Sonksen PM (1983a) The assessment of 'vision for development' in severely visually handicapped babies. Acta Ophthalmologica Supplementum 157: 82–90.

Sonksen PM (1983b) Vision and early development. In: Wybar R, Taylor D (eds) Paediatric Ophthalmology: Current aspects. New York: Marcel Dekker, pp. 85–95.

Sonksen PM, Dale N (2002) Visual impairment in infancy: impact on neurodevelopmental and neurobiological processes. Developmental Medicine and Child Neurology 44: 782–91.

Sonksen PM, Stiff B (1991) Show Me What My Friends Can See: A developmental guide for parents of babies with severely impaired sight and their professional advisors. London: The Wolfson Centre.

Sonksen PM, Levitt SL, Kitzinger M (1984) Identification of constraints acting on motor development in young visually disabled children and principles of remediation. Child: Care, Health and Development 10: 273–86.

Sonksen PM, Petrie A, Drew KJ (1991) Promotion of visual development of severely visually impaired babies: evaluation of a developmentally based programme. Developmental Medicine and Child Neurology 33: 320–35.

Swettenham J, Baron Cohen S, Charman T, Cox A, Baird G, Drew A, Rees L, Wheelwright S (1998) The frequency and distribution of spontaneous attention shifts between social and nonsocial stimuli in autistic, typically developing, and nonautistic developmentally delayed infants. Journal of Child Psychology and Psychiatry 39: 747–53.

Urwin C (1983) Dialogue and cognitive functioning in the early language development of three blind children. In: Mills AE (ed.) Language Acquisition in the Blind Child. London: Croom Helm.

Visual Impairment Scotland (VIS) (2003) A New System of Notification of Childhood Visual Impairment and the Information it has Provided on Services for Scottish Children. Scotland: Visual Impairment Scotland.

Volkmar FR, Szatmari P, Sparrow SS (1993) Sex differences in pervasive developmental disorders. Journal of Autism and Developmental Disorders 23: 579–91.

Waugh MC, Chong WK, Sonksen PM (1998) Neuroimaging in children with congenital disorders of the peripheral visual system. Developmental Medicine and Child Neurology 40: 812–19.

CHAPTER 6

Do blind children show autistic features?

MIGUEL PÉREZ-PEREIRA AND GINA CONTI-RAMSDEN

Introduction

The idea that congenitally blind children show autistic features goes back to the time when a series of studies were published by psychoanalytically oriented researchers. Keeler (1957) firstly suggested that blind children show behaviours, such as social isolation, non-functional play with toys, frequent use of imitations and formulaic speech or stereotyped behaviours, which were similar to those shown by autistic children. Other psychoanalytically oriented authors (Burlingham, 1964, 1965; Nagera and Colonna, 1965; Fraiberg, 1968, 1977; Fay, 1973; Wills, 1979) suggested, in the 1960s and 1970s, that certain features of autistic children's behaviours could also be observed in blind children. Among those features were delayed and reversed use of personal pronouns, high rate of imitative speech or echolalia, frequent use of verbal routines and formulaic speech, abundance of egocentric speech, scarcity or absence of initiations of conversations, and difficulties with the use of symbolic play. A few of these authors (Burlingham, 1965; Nagera and Colonna, 1965; Wills, 1979) related the autistic-like behaviours of blind children to the problems that lack of vision produces in personal relationships between congenitally blind children and their mothers, which, in turn, may produce difficulties in blind children's personal development. Probably, the version of this view that had most influence was Selma Fraiberg's version. Fraiberg (Fraiberg and Adelson, 1973; Fraiberg, 1977) considered that lack of vision had an effect on blind children's self-image and self-representation, and this had consequences on blind children's ego (personality) development. Fraiberg formulated her theory based on Zazzó's theory of self-consciousness. This French psychologist stated that body image of self that infants observed as reflected in a mirror had important effects on the development of their personality (self-consciousness, Zazzó, 1948). Logically, congenitally blind infants are deprived of this experience, as Fraiberg

(1977) argued, and this lack of experience has cascading negative effects on the personality development of blind children.

Recently Hobson and colleagues have claimed that 'there is indeed something special about congenital blindness that predisposes to a full or partial syndrome of autism' (Brown et al., 1997, p. 701). Very succinctly, Hobson (1993) has suggested that two conditions are needed for an adequate development of mind and personality. In the first place children need to perceive other people's emotional reactions and attitudes towards the external world. In the second place, children need the ability to establish empathy or identification with other people's emotional reactions and attitudes. By observing the emotional attitudes of other people towards the external world, children can identify with them and show similar attitudes, which is of essential importance for the development of self and other selves. This, in turn, makes up the psychological basis for understanding minds and for acquiring a theory of mind. Blind children, because of their lack of vision, are thought to have difficulties in understanding and identifying themselves with other people's attitudes and emotional reactions towards objects, persons and events. Hobson and colleagues (Hobson, 1993; Brown et al., 1997; Hobson et al., 1997; Minter, Hobson and Bishop, 1998; Hobson, Lee and Brown, 1999) suggest that deprivation of this kind of socio-emotional experience may contribute to a range of social, cognitive and linguistic delays and abnormalities in blind children, resulting in an overlap in the developmental psychopathology of congenitally blind and autistic children. This overlap includes behaviours already mentioned such as high rate of echolalia, pronoun reversals, frequent use of verbal routines and formulaic speech among others. It is important to note, nevertheless, that, although both blind children and children with autism may show similar psychopathological (autistic-like) features, the underlying reasons for similarities in behaviour may in fact be quite different. While congenitally blind children are deprived of an essential socio-emotional experience for the development of a theory of mind, since they cannot see the expression of emotional attitudes of other people directed to a shared world, children with autism cannot identify with others' attitudes, that is to say they show a substantial deficit in their capacity for empathy (Brown et al., 1997).[1]

It is important to note that other theory of mind (ToM) theories do not relate blindness and autism. For instance, Baron-Cohen (1994, 1995) has proposed the existence in human beings of a mindreading system with four modular components: (1) an intentionality detector (ID), whose function is to represent behaviour in terms of volitional states; (2) an eye direction detector (EDD), whose function is to detect the presence of eye-like stimuli, and to represent gaze direction (agent seeing something); (3) a shared attention mechanism (SAM), whose function is to represent if the self and another agent are paying attention to the same object or event, such as in protodeclaratives; and (4) a theory of mind mechanism (ToMM), whose function is to represent the full range of mental states, and to integrate mental state knowledge into a coherent and usable theory for interpreting action. These mechanisms emerge at different points in development, SAM appearing at 9–12 months of age approximately, and ToMM around 4 years of age.

SAM generates triadic representations from EDD's output or from ID's output, which are dyadic. SAM's triadic representations integrate self, agent and object in a unified triadic representation, such as in the case of protodeclaratives or social referencing. ID and EDD build dyadic representations which specify the relation between an agent and something or someone else in a volitional or visual relationship, respectively. SAM's triadic representations trigger ToMM, and SAM is a necessary (though not sufficient) condition for the development of ToMM.

In the Baron-Cohen theory SAM is considered to be amodal; thus, although congenitally blind children cannot build EDD representations that feed SAM, they can build triadic representations from ID's output, in order to establish joint tactile or joint auditory attention (Baron-Cohen, 1994, 1995). However, building triadic representations from ID's representations may be considerably more difficult than for those derived from EDD. This would suggest that there may be additional difficulties for blind children in constructing SAM representation. Baron-Cohen explicitly draws implications from his theory to congenitally blind children and children with autism. According to him, in congenitally blind infants since SAM is intact, ToMM should develop, 'although a slight delay in this would not be surprising given the need for SAM to use ID instead of EDD' (Baron-Cohen, 1994, p. 539). In contrast, as is well known, children with autism do not activate ToMM. However, Baron-Cohen differentiates two subgroups of children with autism. Children with autism in subgroup A, which forms the largest group, have both SAM and ToMM impaired; children with autism in subgroup B have SAM intact, whilst ToMM is impaired in its own right. Baron-Cohen suggests that the children of subgroup B might correspond to those few and not fully investigated children who are reported to have a period of normal development up to the age of 18 months, and show signs of autism after this point. Therefore, the case of blind children is interesting as they may provide evidence that may be crucial in contrasting between Hobson's and Baron-Cohen's theories concerning the development of a theory of mind.

Blind children: the points in question

The purpose of this chapter is to analyse the empirical basis for claiming that blind children show autistic-like features. In doing this we will concentrate our efforts on three of the autistic-like features described by other authors engaged in this debate, which are listed in Table 6.1. These are (1) deficiencies in the development of a theory of mind, (2) difficulties in the capacity for participating in conversations, and (3) frequent use of formulas, imitations and routines in the speech of blind children.

Table 6.1 Autistic-like features of blind children

Mannerisms and stereotyped behaviours

Difficulties in social interaction and prelinguistic communication

Egocentric and not externally oriented use of language

Delayed and reversed use of personal pronouns

Frequent use of stereotyped speech, routines and formulaic speech

Frequent use of imitations and echolalic speech

Difficulties in communicative conversation: initiations, breakdowns and inadequacy

Delayed and restricted symbolic play

Difficulties in developing a theory of mind

Those topics that are discussed in depth are in italics.

Stereotyped behaviours and mannerisms, a form of non-functional and repetitive motor behaviour, are well documented in blind children (Brambring and Tröster, 1992) and children with autism (Frith, 1989). However, other children with developmental disorders, such as children with Down syndrome (Hanson, 1987; Pary and Hurley, 2002), also show stereotyped behaviours, such as body rocking, head nodding and sucking thumbs. But researchers are not inclined to characterize blind children as being 'Down syndrome-like' or presenting with Down syndrome features. In the same vein, it seems to us unhelpful to characterize blind children as showing autistic-like features because they show stereotyped behaviours that are also evident in children with autism. Stereotyped behaviours are quite common in many children with different developmental disorders. In addition, blind children show some unique stereotyped behaviours, such as eye poking, which are characteristic of blind children and, to our knowledge, no other disorder.

Congenitally blind children and their mothers have additional difficulties in social interactions and relationships (see Pérez-Pereira and Conti-Ramsden, 1999, for a review) due to blind children's inability to perceive their mothers' gestures and facial expressions and to blind children's atypical reactions to their mothers' intent to interact with them (silence and stillness). Thus, cycles of interaction involving alternate emotional expressions between the blind infant and his or her caregiver may be compromised or may not occur often enough. Furthermore, blind infants' vocalizations and smiles are not contingently produced to maternal reactions (Rowland, 1983, 1984). Blind infants and their caregivers are not able to easily establish face-to-face interactive routines. This makes it difficult for the blind infant to experience the regularity and turn-taking nature of parental contingent behaviours. This, in turn, makes it hard for the blind infant to anticipate and predict what is about to happen, and later to participate in conventional social games and routines. Young blind infants do not appear to use protoimperative or protodeclarative gestures, or use conventional communicative gestures, such as pointing or offering (Als, Tronick and Brazelton, 1980; Rowland, 1984; Urwin, 1984; Preisler, 1991). However, blind children and their mothers are able to use alternative ways of interaction that avoid use of the visual channel, and make use of shared movement and body contact, touch, noise and vocalizations, as several studies have reported (Als et al., 1980; Urwin, 1984). For example, they will play pat-a-cake, clap hands or this piggy went to market, they will engage in vocal imitation, and they will have tickling or kissing games which have strong physical contact and a predictable sequence. During these social interchanges and games the ability of caregivers to adequately interpret the reactions of blind infants and their bodily and facial expressions appears to be crucial. Caregivers' language can also play an enormously important compensatory role. Oral language makes it possible for caregivers to sustain contact with their infants and to express and share emotion with them (Peters, 1994; Lewis and Collis, 1997; Webster and Roe, 1998). Therefore, blind children have opportunities to develop socially and communicatively within the context of interactions where sensory modalities other than vision, as well as maternal language, are used and explored.

Fraiberg and Adelson (Fraiberg and Adelson, 1973; Fraiberg, 1977) were the first authors who claimed that symbolic play appeared very late in blind children (at nearly 4 years of age), and that its use by these children was very restricted. However, this observation came from the study of clinical cases. Other studies which have adopted a more systematic approach to controlled observational conditions (Rogers and Puchalski, 1984; Ferguson and Buultjiens, 1995; Lewis et al., 2000) have suggested that although blind children participated in situations of symbolic play less frequently, and showed less variety in symbolic play than sighted children, they participated in situations of symbolic play at a similar age to sighted children, with the exception of those blind children with pervasive impairments. Therefore, the strong claim that blind children show clear deficits in symbolic play needs to be revised, particularly if we take into consideration the fact that blind children's opportunities to establish links and similarities between two different objects are significantly reduced due to the lack of vision.

Furthermore, the delayed and reversed use of pronouns by children with autism is considered a key sign of autism by Kanner (Kanner, 1948; Fay and Schuler, 1980). Different researchers interested in blind children's development have reported that blind children use personal pronouns in a productive way very late (after 3;6 years of age, according to Fraiberg, 1977), and produce a high percentage of reversals in first and second person personal pronouns (up to 75% in some children, according to Dunlea, 1989). One problem with these studies is that there appears to be no detailed quantitative treatment of the data. For instance, Dunlea reports that 'almost all' of Lisa's self-references occur as *you* or proper name, and that 'approximately 75 per cent' of Teddy's self-references involve pronominal errors (Dunlea, 1989, pp. 83–4).

Other studies have been carried out which have attempted to overcome some of the above-mentioned difficulties. These studies (Pérez-Pereira, 1999; Peters, 1999) point out that not all blind children show problems with the use of personal pronouns and other self-reference terms (possessive pronouns and adjective pronouns). For instance, only one blind child longitudinally studied by Pérez-Pereira (1999) between the ages of 2;4 and 3;5 produced a significant percentage of errors (41.4%) in his use of first and second self-reference terms. However, the other two blind children produced very low rates of reversals (4.4% for one girl studied between 1;10 and 2;10 years, and 1.5% for another girl studied between 2;5 and 3;6 years of age), and one young partially sighted child studied between 1;2 and 2;1 years produced no reversal error at all. The results obtained by Pérez-Pereira (1999) also indicate that blind children use personal reference terms very frequently, and that they start to use them at similar ages to sighted children. Finally, the data reported by Peters (1999) and Pérez-Pereira (1999) show that imitation of the interlocutor's forms cannot fully explain why blind children produce reversal errors, and that these phenomena require more complex and multicausal explanations, which should involve the ability to adopt a distinctive perspective, different from the interlocutor's perspective, the ability to see an event from different points of view, or the ability to adapt formulas and expressions to conversational context. Therefore, the claim that blind children, in general, have problems with personal reference terms must be questioned.

Finally, different authors have claimed that blind children use a large proportion of egocentric, not externally oriented language (Burlingham,

1965; Nagera and Colonna, 1965; Wills, 1979). Probably the most serious claim for this characteristic of blind children's language comes from Dunlea's research (Dunlea, 1989). According to this author, the two blind children she studied used their first words only in reference to their own actions and to fulfil their own needs, but not in relation to actions performed by other people. Taking into account that the children were studied at very early ages (during their second year of life, approximately), this may be an expected outcome. Very young children without visual impairment also tend to use highly self-centred speech in relation to their needs and their ongoing activities (Barrett, 1981; Hoff, 2001). However, the crucial point is that blind children cannot gain access to the activities other people are performing unless these activities can be perceived through touch or hearing. An example given by Dunlea (1989) goes in this direction. One of the blind children studied by her (Teddy) produced the expression 'Linda burp(ed)' (Dunlea, 1989, p. 100). Interestingly, the action performed by Linda was an audible one, and, thus, could be reported by Teddy (blind). Therefore, although blind children make fewer references to other people's activities than sighted children, this does not imply that blind children have an inability to do so (see Pérez-Pereira and Conti-Ramsden, 1999, for a thorough discussion of this point).

Having discussed some of the claims in Table 6.1 in brief, in what follows we will analyse in detail the empirical basis for claiming that blind children show autistic-like features in relation to the main points of our interest, that is to say difficulties in the development of a theory of mind, difficulties in communicative capacity, and the frequent use of stereotyped speech, imitations and verbal routines.

Development of a theory of mind in congenitally blind children

As generally described, blind children show delays in the appearance of certain behaviours which are considered to be a precursor of the theory of mind, such as the use of conventional protodeclaratives or symbolic play (see above). Moreover, according to Hobson's theory (Hobson, 1993), blind children should present serious difficulties in the development of self and other selves. All these facts predict possible difficulties with blind children in solving what is thought to be the conventional test of the acquisition of the theory of mind: the false belief task (Wimmer and Perner, 1983). McAlpine and Moore (1995) carried out an experiment using an adaptation of the conventional false belief task (appearance/reality). They used containers with tactile familiarity, a McDonald's Styrofoam container and a cardboard milk container. Each child was presented with the container and asked to guess what was inside it. Once the child answered that it contained a hamburger or the like, the child was asked to open the container where a sock of the approximate weight of a hamburger was located. Next, a friend or parent or teacher was called to the experimental area; as the person approached, the child was asked what he or she thought the other person would answer when asked what was inside the container. The second task repeated the same procedure with a milk container which was in reality filled with water. McAlpine and Moore (1995) tested 15 blind subjects aged 4;0–9;0 years of average to above average intelligence. These authors found that the majority of blind children passed both tasks (10 out of 15 children), one child passed one task but not the other, and four children failed both tasks. The four children who failed both tasks had worse visual acuity and they were also in the younger age range in the sample (5;0–6;0 years). Unfortunately, these authors did not use a control group of sighted children; nevertheless, it has been found in other studies that sighted children are able to succeed in this type of task around the age of 4;6 years. Figure 6.1 shows the percentage of children who succeeded in the tasks of the McAlpine and Moore study.

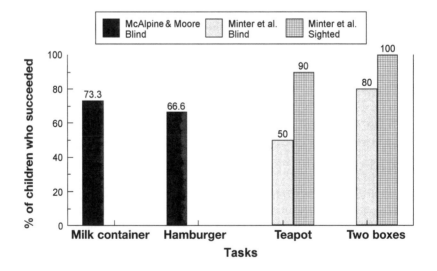

Figure 6.1 Results obtained by McAlpine and Moore (1995) and Minter et al. (1998): percentage of children who succeeded.

Hobson and his colleagues (Minter, Hobson and Bishop, 1998) also carried out a study of false belief with congenitally blind children. They studied 21 blind children and 21 sighted control children of similar chronological (5;0–9;0 years) and mental ages (mean verbal mental age for each group 6;10 years). Two different tasks were presented to the children. In the first task the children were asked to feel a warm teapot and to guess its contents. After that they were then shown that it contained sand, not tea. The children were then asked two questions: (1) what they first thought was in the teapot, and (2) what a peer (who had not seen the demonstration) would think was in the teapot. Interestingly, not all the sighted children passed the false belief question; 10% did not in this task, despite the fact that the youngest sighted child was 4;7 years. The blind children performed worse, with only about half the blind children passing the false belief question. In the second task two boxes were covered with different material, which differentiated a rough box from a soft-covered box. A person could see that a pencil was inside one of the boxes. When the person was not present, the pencil was displaced to the other box. The children were then asked to predict in which box this person would look for the pencil. The blind children did much better in this task this time, with 80% of the children passing the false belief question. All the sighted children could pass this task. Figure 6.1 shows the percentage of children who succeeded in these tasks.

More recently, Peterson, Peterson and Webb (2000) conducted a study which aimed to investigate blind children's ability to solve false belief tasks. This time the authors used two different types of false belief tasks (change of placement versus beliefs about content tasks). The children were 23 blind or severely visually impaired children from 5 to 12 years of age, who were in different age groups: eight children in the 6-year-old group, five children in the 8-year-old group and 10 children in the 12-year-old group. The children were tested with four different tasks. For the first task an egg box with squash balls instead of eggs was used. For the second task a cardboard milk container filled with water instead of milk was used (the same task as that used by McAlpine and Moore, 1995). In both cases the procedure was the same. Every child was asked what he or she thought was inside, and after his or her response the child was asked again what a classmate who was due to come would say was inside. The third task was a narrative similar to the classic Ann and Sally story (Baron-Cohen, Leslie and Frith, 1985), although this time the characters' names were Sally and Bill. As is well known, when the owner of a marble (Sally) goes out of the scene, the other character (Bill) changes the marble to a different placement. The critical question is, where will Sally look for the marble when she comes back? The adaptation of the classic false belief task did not use drawings, as is logical for investigations involving blind children, its content being entirely narrative. Finally, for the fourth task a basket, a box, a coin purse and one coin were used. The children could explore these objects in advance. The procedure was as follows: experimenter 1 puts a coin in the box and then goes out of the room. Experimenter 2 hides the coin with the child in the coin purse. Then, the child is asked, when experimenter 1 comes back, where he or she will look for the coin. The results obtained by the three age groups of children in Peterson et al.'s tasks are shown in Figure 6.2.

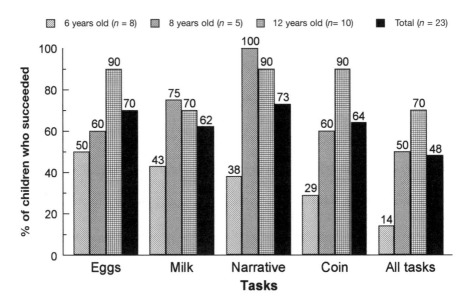

Figure 6.2 Results obtained by Peterson et al. (2000): percentage of children who succeeded.

The authors did not find differences related to degree of vision (contrary to McAlpine and Moore's results), or to the type of task (change of placement versus beliefs about content tasks).

Peterson et al. (2000) also applied a task of visual perspective-taking to test theory of mind level 2 construction of a non-egocentric visual perspective. The child had to place a toy puppy and a shoe in such a way that experimenter 1 or experimenter 2, who were sat at different sides of a table (opposite and at right angles) could see the dog's tail, etc. Blind children scored 3.77 over a maximum of 4 on average, and 87% of them obtained the maximum score. This result indicates that the blind children seem to be able to understand perspective, which is thought to develop prior to the acquisition of a theory of mind.

Taking into account the results of the three related studies, what surprises us is the high variability and inconsistency in the results obtained. In Minter et al.'s (1998) study, the same participants have discrepant results in tasks that are supposed to measure the same ability. Recall that the percentage of blind children who succeeded in the teapot task was only 50%, while in the two boxes task the number went up to 80%. This indicates a significant difference between tasks, which strongly suggests that they do not involve the same difficulty level. Differences among Peterson et al.'s (2000) results are also noticeable. For instance, 100% of 8-year-old children passed the narrative task (marble), but only 60% answered appropriately regarding the eggs task as well as the coin task. There is also a difference between the participants of different studies in their performance on the same task. This is the case with the milk task in the studies of McAlpine and Moore (1995) and Peterson et al. (2000).

We believe this indicates that it is difficult to find an adequate, valid and reliable task for blind children, equivalent to the tasks of false belief for sighted children. As Peterson et al. (2000) point out, it is complex to ascertain which are the cues that provide critical information to blind children. For instance, if we compare the results obtained by the blind children in Minter and others' tasks (Minter et al., 1998), it seems that the two boxes task provides a more adequate level of information for blind children than the teapot task. It is reasonable to think that the exploration of teapots is not a familiar experience for blind children. It may even be a dangerous situation for them which is necessarily avoided for safety reasons (the child may burn his or her hands). On the other hand, a teapot provides not only tactile information but also olfactory information, which is not provided in the task. The two boxes task, in contrast, provides the children with familiar materials. Educational techniques used with blind children usually enhance their sensibility to different surfaces and the education of touch is emphasized as a tool of exploration of external reality. The hamburger task in McAlpine and Moore's experiment (McAlpine and Moore, 1995) is another example of an artificial and unfamiliar situation to blind children, not because they do not eat hamburgers, but because in this experience they also feel the heat of the Styrofoam cover which contains the hamburger, and the smell of the meat. These sensorial experiences are absent in the situation created by McAlpine and Moore. Noticeably, the blind children tested in Minter et al.'s study and in McAlpine and Moore's study performed worse in both the teapot and the hamburger tasks than in the two boxes and the milk tasks, respectively, which seems to give support to our suggestion that these tasks are not appropriate for blind children.

If one is looking for tasks that facilitate the comprehension of the false belief test for blind children, it seems clear from the results obtained by Peterson et al. (2000) that the verbal task (marble) appears to be the most facilitative. This suggestion is reinforced by what happens in cognitive tasks that are verbally presented. Blind children solve logical thinking problems presented in a linguistic form, such as inductive reasoning problems and logical classification problems, at the same age as sighted children do (7 years), but 2 years later than they solve similar problems with figurative material (Hatwell, 1966; Dimcovic and Tobin, 1995). These results give support to those explanations that point to the fact that processing through touch and hearing gives fragmentary and sequential and not immediate (instant) information, which requires cognitive reorganization. In contrast, visual processing gives immediate, integrated and global information (Rosa and Ochaíta, 1993). In the case of linguistic information, we would suggest that both sighted and blind children are on a more level playing field. For this reason, the existence of a control group of sighted children who are in an equivalent condition to that of blind children is necessary in order to draw firm conclusions. The lack of such a control group of sighted blindfolded children is common to all the studies conducted on the development of the theory of mind in blind children, and this fact is a methodological weakness that needs to be surmounted in future research. Recall that in Minter's study (Minter et al., 1998) blind children have only language and touch information to work with to make their decision while the sighted peers have vision to provide them with cues as well. Thus, we would suggest that a third control group is necessary: sighted children who perform the task under blindfolded conditions.

In addition to these methodological problems, Hobson et al. (1997) acknowledge that, when undertaking the above tasks, the experimenters had to be extremely careful in communicating with the blind children through language and touch. They also found it difficult to interpret some of the blind children's responses. The authors also acknowledge the possible detrimental effect on communication if the experimenter is a stranger to the blind child.

What can we conclude from these studies on the development of theory of mind in blind children?

In the first place, informational access in these ToM tasks is impoverished for blind children in comparison to sighted children. Probably blind children need additional experience to solve false belief tests, although in due course they develop this capacity. As Peterson and others recognize, 'delayed development of theory of mind cannot be viewed as synonymous with autism' (Peterson et al., 2000, p. 444). The fact that blind children can solve ToM problems at an earlier age when they are presented with a narrative task indicates that we need to look for alternative ways in which blind children can show us what they know, otherwise we may reach the wrong conclusions. If the difficulties that blind children show are surmountable with time and/or relevant experience, then we have to concede that we are faced with something that is crucially different developmentally from what is observed in children with autism.

The above review provides support for Baron-Cohen's predictions about the development of a theory of mind in blind children. According to Baron-Cohen (1994, 1995) a slight delay in the development of ToM would not be surprising given the need for SAM to use ID instead of EDD. Up until now there appears to be little evidence available to support the position that blind children show a deficit similar to children with autism in the development of a theory of mind (Hobson, 1993).

Conversational capacity of blind children

Different researchers have pointed out that blind children show difficulties in conversational initiations and in topic continuation as compared with children with normal vision (Kekelis and Andersen, 1984; Moore and McConachie, 1994; Kekelis and Prinz, 1996). Blind children's poor ability to participate in conversations is shown also in their production of conversational breakdowns and/or inadequate participation. These characteristics have led some authors to point out similarities between blind children and children with autism (Kekelis and Andersen, 1984; Moore and McConachie, 1994).

Kekelis and Andersen (1984) compared the communicative abilities of two congenitally blind children with those of two sighted children. The children were longitudinally studied from 16 to 22 months of age. During the entire period blind children initiated 24% of conversations with their mothers, and their mothers initiated 76% of conversations with them. Sighted children initiated 37% of conversations and their mothers 63%. Moore and McConachie (1994) studied eight blind children with a mean age of 18.2 months, and eight visually impaired children with a mean age of 16.5 months in conversational interaction with their mothers during a 15-minute observational period. They found that blind children initiated 50% of the conversations and their mothers another 50%. Visually impaired children initiated 62% of the conversations and their mother 38%. The results of these two studies are shown in Figure 6.3.

Thus, at first sight, blind children seem to initiate a lesser proportion of conversations than sighted and visually impaired children. However, we need to be cautious about these data. In addition to the other methodological problems of these studies,[2] both Kekelis and Andersen (1984) and Moore and McConachie (1994) present their results in terms of relative proportions of initiations, but not in terms of frequencies of initiations. Given that in dyadic situations the proportion of initiations of one of the participants in the conversation is relative to the proportion of initiations of the other participant, if one of the participants initiates significantly more conversations than the other, this may give us the

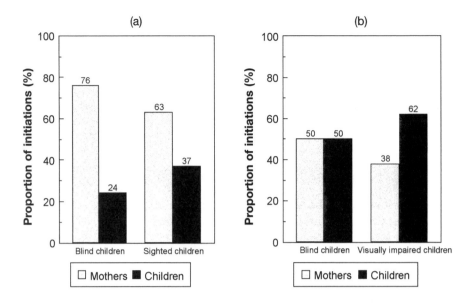

Figure 6.3 Proportion of initiations of conversation by mothers and children according to (a) Kekelis and Andersen (1984) and (b) Moore and McConachie (1994).

impression that the second participant hardly initiates conversations. In contrast, in a conversational situation in which a symmetry exists between the initiations of the participants (50% in cases of full symmetry), the impression will be of sharing of the conversational floor. However, data presented in these ways (proportions) may hide strengths and/or difficulties in the process of initiating conversations. If we want to understand the conversational abilities of dyads, we would need to have data presented in terms of frequency of initiations, at least in the first instance.

Pérez-Pereira and Conti-Ramsden (2001, 2003) compared the conversational initiations of three dyads: one blind girl, one visually impaired boy and one sighted girl and their corresponding mothers. The children were longitudinally studied from 22 to 25 months of age. Four one-hour sessions of observation were recorded. Transcriptions and analysis of verbal productions were carried out using the CHILDES system (MacWhinney, 2000). The children had a similar level of linguistic development at the beginning of the study as measured by mean length of utterance (MLU) scores: 1.21, 1.69 and 1.33, for the blind, the visually impaired, and the sighted children, respectively. Linguistic corpuses for the three children were equivalent, which facilitated comparisons between them. In addition, the children lived in similar family contexts (see Pérez-Pereira and Conti-Ramsden, 2001, 2003, for a full description). All these factors optimized comparisons between the participants.

The results obtained are presented in Figure 6.4 both in terms of proportion of initiations by every participant and in terms of the frequency of initiations. If comparisons between children are done in terms of proportions of initiations, the blind child seems to be at a disadvantage in relation to both the sighted and the visually impaired children. The blind child initiates only 33.1% of conversations, while the visually impaired and the sighted children initiate 44.4% and 48.1%, respectively. On the other hand, the mothers also show differences, with the blind child's mother showing a higher proportion of initiations than either the visually impaired child's mother or the sighted child's mother (66.9%, 55.6% and 51.9%, respectively). These results indicate that a higher asymmetry exists between the blind child and her mother than between the other children and their mothers in relation to the proportion of conversational initiations.

However, if we compare the children in terms of the number of initiations of conversations (frequency) differences disappear. The blind child produces 668 initiations, practically the same number as the visually impaired child (679) and the sighted child (639). In contrast, the mother of the blind child produces a greater number of initiations (1351) than the mother of the visually impaired child (850) and the mother of the sighted child (686).

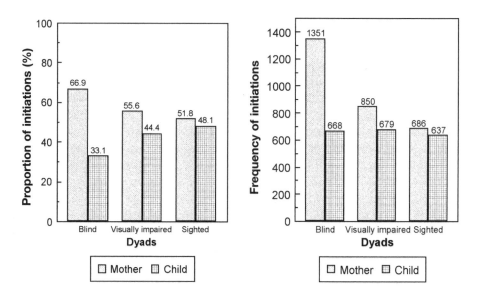

Figure 6.4 Proportion and frequency of initiations of conversation by mothers and children (Pérez-Pereira and Conti-Ramsden, 2003).

Taking the above into account, we would like to suggest that blind children do not produce fewer conversational initiations than sighted and visually impaired children. What we believe happens is that the mother of the blind child produces significantly more initiations than the mothers of visually impaired and sighted children. This then gives the impression that the blind child is poorer at initiation than the other children, if we base our comparisons on proportional data.

Interestingly, Kekelis and Prinz (1996) observed that the mean length of turn (MLT) scores per conversational episode of the two blind children they studied were lower than those of two children with normal vision (1.41 and 1.06 against 1.60 and 1.52, respectively). However they also point out that the blind children's mothers' MLTs were greater than those of the sighted children's mothers (3.99 and 4.21 versus 1.74 and 1.89, respectively). This resulted in highly asymmetrical conversations between blind children and their mothers.

Kekelis and Andersen (1984) also point out that blind children produce significantly more breakdowns than other children they studied: two visually impaired children and two sighted children. Those results, however, were not replicated by Kekelis and Prinz (1996). Kekelis and Prinz (1996) did not find differences in conversational breakdowns between the two blind children and the two sighted children they studied for 7 months. Within this context of conflicting results, Conti-Ramsden and Pérez-Pereira conducted a study looking specifically at conversational breakdowns (Conti-Ramsden and Pérez-Pereira, 1999; Pérez-Pereira and Conti-Ramsden, 2001, 2003). The same children and their mothers previously discussed in the section on conversational initiations were longitudinally studied between 22 and 25 months. In addition, three blind children (one of whom was a twin) and one sighted child (the twin of one of the blind children) in interaction with their mothers were studied between 28 and 40 months of age. The results indicate that the MLT scores of blind children were not lower than those of sighted children. One interesting result comes from the comparison of the MLT score of one of the mothers, who was the mother of the two twin girls, one of them blind and the other sighted. This mother produced a greater number of turns when she was interacting with her blind child than when she was interacting with her sighted child (3.97 versus 3.90 between 28 and 34 months of age, and 4.39 versus 2.88 between 35 and 40 months of age). We believe this result indicates that the mothers of blind children tend to produce more turns in conversations as an adaptive strategy which tries to promote the participation of their blind children. Blind children's mothers learn to be more insistent than sighted children's mothers as a strategy to make conversations longer.

In relation to conversational breakdowns neither blind nor sighted children produced many breakdowns. The percentage of breakdowns ranged from 0.4% to 6.3% of the total number of utterances (excluding initiations), which suggests that blind and sighted children participate in a positive communicative way most of the time during conversational interactions. Differences among children were not related to the degree of vision, and could probably be better explained by contextual situations and individual differences.

Overall, we would suggest that blind children's ability to initiate conversations is similar to that of sighted children and that they can participate contingently in conversations, which is shown by the MLT score blind children reach, and by the low frequency of breakdowns they produce. Mothers of blind children tend to produce a higher number of initiations and MLT scores than sighted children's mothers as a compensatory strategy with their blind children. In this way they probably try to provide more chances for their children to participate in conversations and to continue for a longer time engaging in conversational interaction.

Formulaic and imitative speech

Children with autism use highly imitative (echolalic) speech, as well as a speech full of verbal routines, frozen phrases, formulas and stereotypes (Fay and Schuler, 1980; Lord and Paul, 1997; Tager-Flusberg, 1999). Descriptions of blind children's language have also identified similar characteristics in blind children's language use (Andersen, Dunlea and Kekelis, 1984, 1993; Peters, 1987; Dunlea, 1989; Pérez-Pereira, 1994; Pérez-Pereira and Castro, 1997; Pérez-Pereira and Conti-Ramsden, 1999). For the sake of simplicity, we will name these behaviours modelled speech, since all these productions require the existence of a previous model which will be copied by the child. The model may be a deferred model, such as in many verbal routines, formulas or stereotypes, or a recently heard model (immediate model). At the same time, the model may be an utterance produced by another speaker or an utterance produced by the child him- or herself. The former is an *imitation* of another speaker's utterance, and the latter a *repetition* or self-repetition of an utterance produced by the child.

Nevertheless, the fact that apparently blind and autistic children show similar behaviours (modelled speech) does not imply that these behaviours have the same function. We will attempt to argue that modelled speech may play a very different role in development for blind children and children with autism. However, methodologically, one cannot investigate the function of a given behaviour if one observes only the presence or absence of that behaviour, or how frequently the behaviour is produced by the child (Hobson et al., 1999; Hobson and Bishop, 2003). There is a need to carry out functional analysis of the behaviour of interest.

Pérez-Pereira (1994) studied the language produced by dizygotic twin sisters, one blind and the other sighted, from 2;5 to 3;5 years, and compared the MLU of their utterances that were considered to be *modelled speech* because all of them had a previous model, to the MLU of the utterances that had no previous model and could be considered *spontaneous*. The results are shown in Figure 6.5.

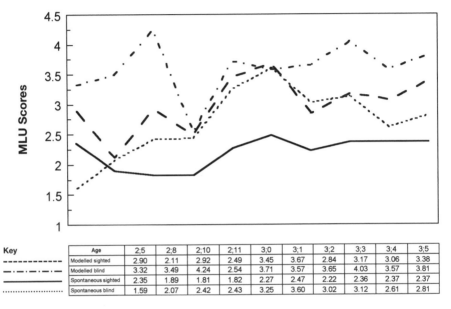

Key	Age	2;5	2;8	2;10	2;11	3;0	3;1	3;2	3;3	3;4	3;5
-----------	Modelled sighted	2.90	2.11	2.92	2.49	3.45	3.67	2.84	3.17	3.06	3.38
—·—·—·—·—	Modelled blind	3.32	3.49	4.24	2.54	3.71	3.57	3.65	4.03	3.57	3.81
———————	Spontaneous sighted	2.35	1.89	1.81	1.82	2.27	2.47	2.22	2.36	2.37	2.37
....	Spontaneous blind	1.59	2.07	2.42	2.43	3.25	3.60	3.02	3.12	2.61	2.81

Figure 6.5 MLU scores in modelled and spontaneous utterances (Pérez-Pereira, 1994).

Analysis of the results indicates that for both the blind and the sighted children the MLU scores of their modelled utterances were greater than the MLU scores of their spontaneous utterances. Wilcoxon's T tests confirm that these differences reached statistical significance ($T = 1$ for N = 10, two-tailed $p < 0.01$, for the blind girl; $T = 0$ for N = 10, two-tailed $p < 0.01$, for her sighted sister). This suggests that modelled speech facilitates language development, since the blind child as well as the sighted child produced utterances that were morphologically and syntactically more complex when a previous model was available than when no model was available (spontaneous utterances). The modelled utterance seems to have a scaffolding function for these children, since, with their help, they can build utterances that are further away from their actual level of development. Therefore modelled speech seems to have a positive, progressive function for the development of both sighted and blind children's language, in contrast to what happens in the case of children with autism.

Modelled speech of children with autism has been described as echolalia or echolalic speech, and this speech has been reported to be very frequent and persistent in autistic children (Fay and Schuler, 1980; Lord and Paul, 1997). Echolalic utterances produced by children with autism do not generally have greater complexity (MLU scores) than spontaneous utterances (Howlin, 1982), and are considered as lacking in meaning, non-communicative and not positively related to language development in children with autism (Fay, 1973; Fay and Schuler, 1980; Lord and Paul, 1997).

How can modelled speech work to help children in their attempts to learn language? Pérez-Pereira's research has some suggestions (Pérez-Pereira, 1994). Every utterance produced by the two twin sisters which were imitations or repetitions of a previous utterance were categorized according to their faithfulness to the model, i.e. whether they were exact, reduced, modified or expanded copies of a model. An *exact* repetition or imitation reproduces all the elements of the model utterance in the same order without any changes or additions (*give me the car* is copied by the child as *give me the car*). A *reduced* repetition or imitation involves omission of functor words, morphemes or content words from the utterance (based on the same model the child produces *the car*). A *modified* imitation or repetition uses part or all of a previous utterance as a model, but the child introduces changes in the person of the verb, the order of the elements, the pronoun, substitutes a noun predicate by a pronoun, etc. (the child utters *give me that*). Finally an *expanded* imitation or repetition takes place when one part of the utterance is imitated or repeated and another part is created by the child (in this case the child produces *give me the car which is on the floor*).

The results obtained by Pérez-Pereira (1994) are shown in Figure 6.6. Significant differences between the blind and the sighted child were found in relation to the use of these categories from 2;5 to 3;5 years of age χ^2 (3) = 82.78, p < 0.001). These differences were mainly due to the greater use of modified imitations and repetitions by the blind child as compared with the sighted child χ^2 (1) = 12.35, p < 0.001).

An interesting result was that both the blind child and the sighted child produced an important percentage of imitations and repetitions (40% and 30%, respectively) that were modified or expanded copies of the model. These types of utterances are more creative than exact or reduced imitations and repetitions. However, many studies on the use of imitations and repetitions by children with developmental disorders have excluded from the analysis utterances that are modified and expanded copies (for instance, Tager-Flusberg and Calkins, 1990). This approach does not allow researchers the opportunity to analyse possible functions of such repeated speech.

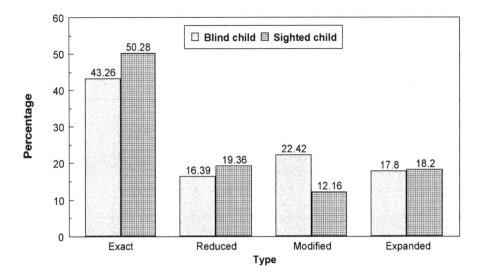

Figure 6.6 Percentage of exact, reduced, modified and expanded imitations and repetitions produced by the blind and sighted child (based on Pérez-Pereira, 1994).

The following examples of modified and expanded imitations and repetitions illustrate that blind, as well as sighted, children use this type of utterance to analyse language. They segment elements, and substitute one element for another in an analytical activity, which throws doubts on the suggestion that imitations and repetitions are only rote activities, and that blind children's language lacks creativity.

Example 1: Sandra (blind) and Andrea (sighted) are having tea with their mother. Sandra is 2;11 years old.

Mother: Sandra no se mastica, te lo acabo de decir. ('Sandra, you don't chew it, I've just told you.')
Andrea: ¿Que no se que? ('You don't what?')
Andrea: ¿No se que? ('you don't what?')

[They go on eating]

Sandra: Andrea no se tiran las cosas. ('Andrea you don't [mustn't] throw things.')

The blind child Sandra uses the Spanish scheme (proper name + *no se* + verbal predicate) as a formula to express forbidding. However, she substitutes the elements of the verbal predicate of her mother's modelled utterance. We suggest that she would not be able to do that unless she had previously analysed her mother's utterance.

Example 2: Sandra is playing with a board for fitting animal shapes in, together with Miguel and Andrea. Sandra wants to fit the camel in herself. Sandra is 2;11 years old.

Sandra: Poner el camello a mí. ('Me put the camel in.')
Sandra: Lo ponemos aquí. ('We put it in here.')
Sandra: Ponemos aquí el camello. ('We put the camel in here.')

The blind child substitutes the noun phrase for a pronoun and formulates her intention in a progressively clearer way after her first attempts.

What is noteworthy is the fact that the blind girl used modifications with a significantly higher frequency than her sighted sister. This suggests that she carried out a kind of self-scaffolding procedure, introducing successive modifications in a phrase or previous utterance which she thereby used as a frame for practising certain types of structures and pragmatic formulas. The successive modifications introduced, we believe, are a reflection of her analytical activity. The large number of modified and expanded imitations and repetitions used by both children is evidence of the potential of this self-scaffolding strategy.

Another type of production frequently used by blind children is formulas (also called frozen phrases, stereotyped speech or verbal routines). These are productions longer than a word associated with a particular context. Examples of formulas are routines linked to interpersonal routines, such as *good morning, thank you*, or to joint activities and games, such as *throw the ball* or *open your mouth*. Blind children show a greater tendency than sighted children to use this type of verbal production in contexts that they believe are similar to the original one where they heard the formula for the first time. However, we would like to suggest that their use is not mechanical or without meaning. As Peters (1994) has pointed out, the use of these formulas may be helpful for blind children to understand the context of where they are, to perform the appropriate action and also to interact with other people. For instance, if a child hears 'throw the ball', she knows that she is in a context of 'playing to throw the ball' to her father, because this is the expression associated with this game. This is important information for a child who does not have access to other types of clues, i.e. the objects involved and the gestures and activities of her father. At the same time, blind children can also easily convey their intention to their interlocutors through the use of formulas. When an adult hears an expression associated with a familiar situation of play or joint activity, he or she understands the child's intention. It is precisely the association of a formula with a particular event or activity that allows for this quick interpretation to take place. Formulas and imitations are particularly useful to young children with low levels of language development.

Pérez-Pereira (2001) suggests that blind children tend to use more frozen phrases, formulas and imitative speech than sighted and visually impaired children during the early stages of language development. The abundance of these types of productions has been considered to be a characteristic of those children who use a gestalt style or rote learning style. Following Lieven and colleagues' category system (Pine and Lieven, 1993; Lieven, Pine and Baldwin, 1997), Pérez-Pereira (2001) analysed all multiword utterances produced by one blind girl, one visually impaired boy and one sighted girl from 21–22 to 25 months of age (four recording sections one hour long). The children (described above) showed similar MLU scores at the beginning of the study (1.21 for the blind, 1.34 for the visually impaired and 1.33 for the sighted child), and came from very similar socio-cultural and linguistic environments. All multiword productions were classified as frozen phrases, intermediate utterances or constructed utterances. Table 6.2 summarizes the criteria for classifying multiword utterances into one of these categories.

Table 6.2 Categories used to classify multiword utterances – utterances consisting of more than one word (clitics included)

A *Frozen phrases*: utterances that contain two or more words which have not previously occurred alone in the child's vocabulary or which contain one such word, provided it has not occurred in the same position in a previous multiword utterance.

B *Intermediate utterances*: utterances in which (1) all the words or phrases have previously occurred independently in the child's vocabulary, provided none of them has occurred in the same position in two previous multiword utterances, and/or (2) one or more of the words or phrases have occurred in the same position as in one but only one other previous multiword utterance, provided the word or phrase that makes up the remainder of the utterance has already occurred independently in the child's vocabulary.

C *Constructed utterances*: utterances that (1) contain one or more words or phrases which have occurred independently in the child's vocabulary together with a word or phrase which has occurred in the same position in at least two other previous multiword utterances, the second of which must be classed as intermediate (B), or (2) conform to a positional pattern as in (C1) above which is already established in the child's vocabulary regardless of whether the variable word has occurred previously. Once a pattern is defined as constructed it forms a particular 'template or frame' consisting of a particular lexical item in a fixed position with a 'slot' on one or other side of it.

D *No relation*: novel combinations where there is no intrinsic relation between the words. These productions are usually uttered in situations such as answering a question during a conversation, exclamations or expressions of joy.

This category system makes it possible to study how an utterance of two (or more) words develops from a frozen construction to a constructed one. First, use of a combination of two words does not imply abstract knowledge of the combinatorial characteristics of the grammatical classes to which these elements belong. Children start to learn combinations of particular lexical items in a usage-based way (Lieven, 1997; Tomasello, 2003). That is to say, they associate a given expression with a given context of use. Little by little, children go on producing new combinations of elements belonging to these grammatical classes, up to a point at which children use this particular combination in a productive way. For instance, a child may say at 22 months 'a car', and this is the only example of the combination of the indefinite article with a common name. This expression is considered to be a frozen phrase. In this child's repertoire of expressions a new combination of the indefinite article plus common name appears at 23 months, when the child says 'a dog'. Now this is the second example of a combination of these elements, and we can say that this is an intermediate utterance. Finally, at 24 months the child produces two new instances of this type: 'a duck' and 'a book'. Now the child has produced two constructed utterances, and we can consider that this combinatorial type (indefinite article plus common noun) is productive in the child's speech.

The results of the analysis performed by Pérez-Pereira (2001) are shown in Figure 6.7.

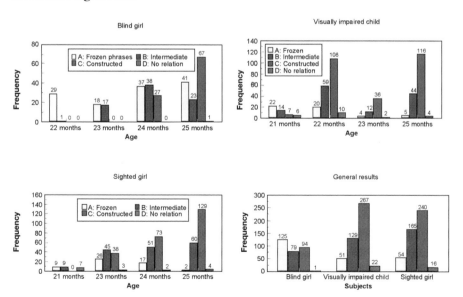

Figure 6.7 Types of multiword utterances produced by the blind, the visually impaired and the sighted child according to Pérez-Pereira (2001) – frequency of use at different ages.

The results indicate that in the early stages the blind child produces a large number of frozen phrases (29), and only one intermediate phrase. In contrast, the sighted and the visually impaired children have already produced a greater number of intermediate and constructed utterances. At the end of the period studied the blind child still produces many frozen phrases (41). Furthermore, the other two children hardly produce frozen phrases at 25 months of age. Taking into account the number of utterance types produced for the whole period of the study, the blind child shows a greater number of frozen phrases than intermediate or constructed utterances. In contrast, the sighted and the visually impaired children produce a greater number of constructed utterances.

Therefore, the results obtained by Pérez-Pereira (2001) indicate that the blind child seems to have a more pronounced gestalt style or rote learning style, while the other two children seem to be closer to an analytical style of learning language (Peters, 1987; Pérez-Pereira and Castro, 1997). It may be that such a style is particularly suitable to blind children's language learning as it captures 'whole intentions' and situations and may be a more effective communication strategy, particularly in the early stages of development.

In summary, the use of imitations, repetitions and routines by blind children, we would like to argue, may have an important function for the acquisition of language, and their use may be related to a rote learning style or gestalt style which seems to be characteristic of blind children. No doubt future research will investigate in more depth the issues involved in the possible advantages of such a style for blind children.

Concluding remarks

Generally, in the field, there are methodological pitfalls which not surprisingly have led to conflicting results and interpretations. There is also a lack of adequate techniques to assess blind children's abilities. Furthermore, the lack of desirable additional control groups and the reduced samples of blind children's behaviours have also limited the clarity of the findings in this field of research.

There is also a need for a more complex approach to the study of blind children. We have pointed out the need for a functional perspective on understanding particular behaviours. Here we would also like to argue that the approach to the study of blind children should be more sensitive to the blind children's situation, i.e. should be carried out within the perspective of the blind child.

Very often blind children do not have as many opportunities as sighted children to show a given ability, since visual experience may have a triggering function and may offer additional opportunities for a behaviour to appear. However, researchers should distinguish between frequency with which children produce a given behaviour and lack of ability. Blind children may show a behaviour, such as descriptions of others' actions, with a lesser frequency than sighted children; however, this does not mean that blind children lack the ability to produce this behaviour in adequate circumstances. Similarly, blind children may need additional time or additional experience for abilities to develop.

Furthermore, blind children show great individual differences (Warren, 1994; Pérez-Pereira and Conti-Ramsden, 1999), so it is difficult to make generalizations about them. For this reason, when we suggest that blind children do not show autistic features, we are aware that we are specifically talking about the majority of blind children and there may indeed be some blind children who show autistic-like features. In our experience, such blind children also exhibit significant cognitive delays or additional handicaps. However, if this is so, lack of vision is not a necessary or a sufficient cause for their autistic-like features.

Within the context of the above considerations, we want to argue that the evidence reviewed in this chapter does not give support to the hypothesis that blind children have autistic-like features (Hobson, 1993). The data seem to be more compatible with the theory proposed by Baron-Cohen (1994). The difficulties that blind children appear to have seem to be peripheral (lack of visual information which affects the EDD), not central. Therefore, they may need additional and/or compensatory experience to develop certain capacities, such as SAM and ToM, but the abilities eventually develop. This is markedly different from the developmental trajectories experienced by children with autism.

However, it is necessary for research to continue in order to understand in more detail the case of congenital blindness in its own right as well as in relation to autistic spectrum disorders.

Notes

1. More recently Hobson and Bishop (2003) seem to have limited the claim of similarity between children with autism and blind children to those blind children who are socially impaired, in contrast to those blind children who are not socially impaired. The former group of blind children showed autistic-like features in an observational study, while the latter did not. Hobson and Bishop (2003) classified both groups of blind children according to the results of the following question directed to their class teachers: 'on a scale of 1–5, how would you rate this child's ability to relate to adults and peers (rated separately), establishing normal mutual interpersonal contact with them?' Those children who were rated equal or less than 3 by their teachers were considered socially impaired (LS), while those blind children who rated higher than 3 on the same scale were classified as not socially impaired (MS).

2. For instance Moore and McConachie (1994) obtain their results with an extremely
   short sample of speech. Probably, this gives paradoxical results such as that children initiate conversations more frequently than mothers, contrary to what is usual
   in conversations between very young children and their mothers (Ninio and Snow,
   1996).

References

Als H, Tronick E, Brazelton B (1980) Affective reciprocity and the development of
   autonomy. The study of a blind infant. Journal of the American Academy of
   Child Psychology 19: 22–40.

Andersen ES, Dunlea A, Kekelis L (1984) Blind children's language: Resolving
   some differences. Journal of Child Language 11: 645–64.

Andersen ES, Dunlea A, Kekelis LS (1993) The impact of input: language acquisition in the visually impaired. First Language 13: 23–49.

Baron-Cohen S (1994) How to build a baby that can read minds: Cognitive mechanisms in mindreading. Cahiers de Psychologie Cognitive 13: 513–52.

Baron-Cohen S (1995) Mindblindness: An essay on autism and theory of mind.
   Cambridge, MA: MIT Press.

Baron-Cohen S, Leslie A, Frith U (1985) Does the autistic child have a theory of
   mind? Cognition 21: 37–46.

Barrett M (1981) The communicative functions of early child language.
   Linguistics 19: 273–305.

Brambring M, Tröster H (1992) On the stability of stereotyped behaviors in blind
   infants and preschoolers. Journal of Visual Impairment and Blindness 86:
   105–10.

Brown R, Hobson RP, Lee A, Stevenson J (1997) Are there 'autistic-like' features in
   congenitally blind children? Journal of Child Psychology and Psychiatry 38:
   693–703.

Burlingham D (1964) Hearing and its role in the development of the blind. The
   Psychoanalytic Study of the Child 19: 95–112.

Burlingham D (1965) Some problems of ego development in blind children. The
   Psychoanalytic Study of the Child 20: 194–208.

Conti-Ramsden G, Pérez-Pereira M (1999) Conversational interactions between
   mothers and their infants who are congenitally blind, have low vision, or are
   sighted. Journal of Visual Impairment and Blindness 93: 691–703.

Dimcovic N, Tobin MJ (1995) The use of language in simple classification tasks by
   children who are blind. Journal of Visual Impairment and Blindness 89:
   448–59.

Dunlea A (1989) Vision and the Emergence of Meaning: Blind and sighted children's early language. Cambridge: Cambridge University Press.

Fay WH (1973) On the echolalia of the blind and of the autistic child. Journal of
   Speech and Hearing Disorders 38: 478–89.

Fay WH, Schuler AL (1980) Emerging Language in Autistic Children. London:
   Edward Arnold.

Ferguson R, Buultjiens M (1995) The play behaviour of young blind children and its relationships to developmental stages. British Journal of Visual Impairment 13: 100–7.

Fraiberg S (1968) Parallel and divergent patterns in blind and sighted infants. The Psychoanalytic Study of the Child 23: 264–306.

Fraiberg S (1977) Insights from the Blind. London: Souvenir Press.

Fraiberg S, Adelson E (1973) Self-representation in language and play: Observations of blind children. Psychoanalysis Quarterly 42: 539–62.

Frith U (1989) Autism: Explaining the enigma. Oxford: Blackwell Science.

Hanson MJ (1987) Teaching the Infant with Down Syndrome: A guide for parents and professionals. Austin, TX: PRO-ED.

Hatwell Y (1966) Privation Sensorielle et Intelligence. Paris: Presses Universitaires de France.

Hobson RP (1993) Autism and the Development of Mind. Hillsdale, NJ: Lawrence Erlbaum Associates.

Hobson P, Bishop M (2003) The pathogenesis of autism: insights from congenital blindness. Philosophical Transactions of the Royal Society of London, Series B 358: 335–44.

Hobson P, Lee A, Brown R (1999) Autism and congenital blindness. Journal of Autism and Developmental Disorders 29: 45–56.

Hobson RP, Brown R, Minter ME, Lee A (1997) 'Autism' revisited: The case of congenital blindness. In: Lewis V, Collis GM (eds) Blindness and Psychological Development in Young Children. Leicester: British Psychological Society.

Hoff E (2001) Language Development. Belmont: Wadsworth/Thomson Learning.

Howlin P (1982) Echolalic and spontaneous phrase speech in autistic children. Journal of Child Psychology and Psychiatry 23: 281–93.

Kanner L (1948) Child Psychiatry, 2nd edn. Springfield, IL: Charles C Thomas.

Keeler WR (1957) Autistic patterns and defective communication in blind children with retrolental fibroplasia. In: Hoch PH, Zubin J (eds) Psychopathology of Communication. New York: Grune & Stratton.

Kekelis LS, Andersen E (1984) Family communication styles and language development. Journal of Visual Impairment and Blindness 78: 54–64.

Kekelis LS, Prinz PM (1996) Blind and sighted children with their mothers: The development of discourse skills. Journal of Visual Impairment and Blindness 90: 423–36.

Lewis V, Collis GM (1997) Methodological and theoretical issues associated with the study of children with visual impairment. In: Lewis V, Collis GM (eds) Blindness and Psychological Development in Young Children. Leicester: British Psychological Society.

Lewis V, Norgate S, Collis G, Reynolds R (2000) The consequences of visual impairment for children's symbolic and functional play. British Journal of Developmental Psychology 18: 449–64.

Lieven E (1997) Variation in a crosslinguistic context. In: Slobin DI (ed.) The Crosslinguistic Study of Language Acquisition, Vol. 5: Expanding the Contexts. Mahwah, NJ: Lawrence Erlbaum Associates, pp. 199–263.

Lieven EVM, Pine JM, Baldwin G (1997) Lexically based learning and early grammatical development. Journal of Child Language 24: 187–219.

Lord C, Paul R (1997) Language and communication in autism. In: Cohen DJ, Volkman FR (eds) Handbook of Autism and Pervasive Developmental Disorders, 2nd edn. New York: Wiley.

McAlpine LM, Moore CL (1995) The development of social understanding in children with visual impairments. Journal of Visual Impairment and Blindness 89: 349–58.

MacWhinney B (2000) The CHILDES Project: Tools for analyzing talk. Mahwah, NJ: Lawrence Erlbaum Associates.

Minter M, Hobson RP, Bishop M (1998) Congenital visual impairment and theory of mind. British Journal of Developmental Psychology 16: 183–96.

Moore V, McConachie HR (1994) Communication between blind children and severely visually impaired children and their parents. British Journal of Developmental Psychology 12: 491–502.

Nagera H, Colonna AB (1965) Aspects of the contribution of sight to ego and drive development. A comparison of the development of some blind and sighted children. The Psychoanalytic Study of the Child 20: 267–87.

Ninio A, Snow CE (1996) Pragmatic Development. Boulder, CO: Westview Press.

Pary R, Hurley A (2002) Down syndrome and autistic disorder. Mental Health Aspects of Developmental Disabilities 5(2): 64–5.

Pérez-Pereira M (1994) Imitations, repetitions, routines, and the child's analysis of language: Insights from the blind. Journal of Child Language 21: 317–37.

Pérez-Pereira M (1999) Deixis, personal reference, and the use of pronouns by blind children. Journal of Child Language 26: 655–80.

Pérez-Pereira M (2000) El lenguaje de los niños ciegos y la cuestión de los rasgos autistas. Revista de Psicología 17: 167–98.

Pérez-Pereira M (2001) First grammar in blind, visually impaired and sighted bilingual children: Do they follow a different route? In: Almgren M, Barreña A, Ezeizabarrena MJ, Idiazabal I, MacWhinney B (eds) Research on Child Language Acquisition. Proceedings of the VIIth International Congress for the Study of Child Language – IASCL. Somerville, MA: Cascadilla Press, pp. 1198–208.

Pérez-Pereira M, Castro J (1997) Language acquisition and the compensation of visual deficit: New comparative data on a controversial topic. British Journal of Developmental Psychology 15: 439–59.

Pérez-Pereira M, Conti-Ramsden G (1999) Language Development and Social Interaction in Blind Children. Hove: Psychology Press.

Pérez-Pereira M, Conti-Ramsden G (2001) The use of directives in verbal interactions between blind children and their mothers. Journal of Visual Impairment and Blindness 95: 133–49.

Pérez-Pereira M, Conti-Ramsden G (2003) Características generales de las interacciones verbales entre niños ciegos y sus madres. Infancia y Aprendizaje 26: 381–96.

Peters A (1987) The role of imitation in the developing syntax of a blind child. Text 7: 289–311.

Peters AM (1994) The interdependence of social, cognitive, and linguistic development: Evidence from a visually impaired child. In: Tager-Flusberg H (ed.) Constraints on Language Acquisition: Studies of atypical children. Hillsdale, NJ: Erlbaum.

Peters A (1999) The development of reference to self and other by one blind child. Paper presented at the 8th International Congress for the Study of Child Language (IASCL). San Sebastian, Spain.

Peterson CC, Peterson JL, Webb J (2000) Factors influencing the development of a theory of mind in blind children. British Journal of Developmental Psychology 18: 431–47.

Pine J, Lieven EVM (1993) Reanalysing rote-learned phrases: individual differences in the transition to multi-word speech. Journal of Child Language 20: 551–71.

Preisler GM (1991) Early patterns of interaction between blind infants and their sighted mothers. Child: Care, Health and Development 17: 65–90.

Rogers SJ, Puchalski CB (1984) Development of symbolic play in visually impaired young children. Topics in Early Childhood Special Education 3: 57–63.

Rosa A, Ochaíta E (eds) (1993) Psicología de la Ceguera. Madrid: Alianza.

Rowland C (1983) Patterns of interaction between three blind infants and their mothers. In: Mills AE (ed.) Language Acquisition in the Blind Child: Normal and deficient. London: Croom Helm.

Rowland C (1984) Preverbal communication of blind infants and their mothers. Journal of Visual Impairment and Blindness 78: 297–302.

Tager-Flusberg H (1999) Language development in atypical children. In: Barrett M (ed.) The Development of Language. Hove: Psychology Press, pp. 311–48.

Tager-Flusberg H, Calkins S (1990) Does imitation facilitate the acquisition of grammar? Evidence from a study of autistic, Down's syndrome and normal children. Journal of Child Language 17: 591–606.

Tomasello M (2003) Constructing a Language. A usage based theory of language acquisition. Boston, MA: Harvard University Press.

Urwin C (1984) Communication in infancy and the emergence of language in blind children. In: Schieffelbusch RL, Pickar J (eds) The Acquisition of Communicative Competence. Baltimore, MD: University of Park Press, pp. 479–520.

Warren DH (1994) Blindness and Children. An individual differences approach. New York: Cambridge University Press.

Webster A, Roe J (1998) Children with Visual Impairments: Social interaction, language and learning. London: Routledge.

Wills DM (1979) Early speech development in blind children. The Psychoanalytic Study of the Child 34: 85–117.

Wimmer H, Perner J (1983) Beliefs about beliefs: Representation and constraining function of wrong beliefs in young children's understanding of deception. Cognition 13: 103–28.

Zazzó R (1948) Images du corps et conscience de soi. Enfance 1: 29–43.

CHAPTER 7

Blind children and children with autism: research methods fit for purpose

VICKY LEWIS AND GLYN COLLIS

Introduction

The study of disabled children is important for both theoretical and practical reasons. As pointed out by Lewis (2003), among others, our theoretical understanding of developmental processes and the practical interventions that are offered to disabled children are dependent on our understanding of the processes underlying the development of both disabled children and typically developing children. However, this is very easy to say but much harder to achieve in reality. How do we know that our understanding of the implications of a particular disability is sound? It could be that we have interpreted the data in one way when in fact a different interpretation is closer to the truth. It may be that the data on which we are basing our interpretations are misleading in some way and do not reflect the underlying competence of particular children.

In this chapter we want to explore this latter possibility and in particular the question of how we should study the development of children with autism and blind children. This is a fundamental question since if the methods we employ are inappropriate given the nature of the disability then the data we collect are hardly going to be an accurate reflection of any child's competence. It is also fundamental because many research findings concerning disabled children focus on things that typically developing children can do but disabled children cannot. Indeed, the World Health Organization's (1980) definition of disability as 'any restriction or lack (resulting from an impairment) of ability to perform an activity in the manner or within the range considered normal for a human being' points to there needing to be differences between the abilities of typically developing children and those of disabled children. If there is no difference then the so-called disabled child is not disabled. So, definitions of disability emphasize 'restriction' or 'lack of ability' and indeed this is just what is reported. Such an approach has worrying implications with respect to physical abilities, but it seems to us that the problems have an extra layer of complexity with respect to psychological abilities, which is the issue that we are concerned with here.

The problem is that the conclusion of a lack of ability is based on children with a disability not doing the same things as children without the disability. But absence of some behavioural indicator of a psychological ability cannot be interpreted as evidence of a lack of the underlying ability since it may be that the conditions under which the behaviour have been studied are inappropriate. The problem of interpreting negative findings has been much aired when the abilities of very young infants are examined but seems to receive less attention when disabled children are considered. Perhaps, because of the terminology that is used, we have an expectation of disabled children not being able to do the same things as typically developing children and therefore we do not question negative findings to the same extent as we might with other populations.

In this chapter we seek to question negative findings. However, we are not questioning the existence of disability. Rather, we are concerned that the methods which are used to identify what a disabled child can and cannot do, and which ultimately assist in specifying the nature of the disability and subsequently contribute to theory and practice, do not produce spurious data. In other words, are the methods employed fit for purpose when the purpose is to identify the underlying competence of disabled children? In order to discuss this important issue we shall draw on four areas of research. In the first three areas – pretend play and young people with autism, pretend play and blind children, understanding of space and blind children – we shall argue that the competence of disabled children may have been underestimated as a result of the methods not being entirely fit for purpose. In the fourth area, drawing ability and children with autism, we shall consider the opposite situation where competence may have been overestimated, which is obviously as important as underestimating ability.

We have selected these four areas because they are areas that clearly illustrate our methodological concerns and are areas we have researched. There are many other areas that we could have chosen and in choosing areas that we have researched we are not intending to argue that we are the only researchers who are concerned with this issue. Indeed, many people carrying out research with children with autism and blind children have thought long and hard about this issue and have developed methods accordingly.

Pretend play and children and young people with autism

In 1988 Lewis and Boucher published a paper entitled 'Spontaneous, instructed and elicited play in relatively able autistic children'. This paper reported that, among other things, in a structured situation involving a doll or toy car plus non-representational objects such as a short length of a drinking straw, a Rawlplug or five small wooden sticks, children and young people with autism aged between 6 and 16 years of age produced as many examples of using these objects in symbolic ways, that is pretending that the objects were things that they were not, as children and young people with difficulties in learning and younger typically developing children of similar verbal ability. This was an important finding because many earlier accounts of autism had emphasized an impairment of symbolic ability. These previous accounts were based on observations of children with autism in free play situations and indeed Lewis and Boucher also reported that the children and young people with autism produced little spontaneous symbolic play. The important point is that the earlier observations of free play behaviour were generalized and interpreted as an overall impairment. But how can there be an impairment of symbolic functioning if, under different conditions, children and young people with autism use objects as if they are different objects, i.e. they use them in symbolic ways?

In response to this paper, Baron-Cohen (1990) argued that the findings could be interpreted in a different way. In particular, he argued that when the young people were given a car and a small box they did the only thing that could be done with a car and a small box and put the car inside the box. In other words they were not using the box 'as if' it was a garage and therefore there was nothing symbolic about their use of the box. In response to Baron-Cohen, Boucher and Lewis (1990) reported an example from every young person with autism who took part in the study using an object in a symbolic way. These examples provided good evidence that the children and young people were not simply doing the only thing that could be done with the objects that they were given. Thus, the following were among the examples reported from the children and young people with autism: when given a car and a short length of drinking straw a child rotated the straw under the car, saying 'I'm screwing . . . spannering the wheels'; with the doll and Rawlplug a child put the narrow end of the Rawlplug to the doll's mouth, saying 'trumpet'; with the doll and five sticks, a child stood the sticks up in a row, stood the doll a little distant and mimed the doll rolling a ball, saying 'skittles'.

In 1995 Lewis and Boucher reported some findings from another part of this study, in which the children and young people were handed either a doll or a toy car and asked, 'Show me what the car/doll can do', 'Can you make the car/doll do different things?'. These prompts were repeated until 12 different ideas for things that the car/doll could do had been suggested by the children and young people. As found elsewhere in this study, the children and young people with autism produced as many ideas that were symbolic as the typically developing children and children and young people with difficulties in learning. Examples of symbolic play with the car included. 'people getting out of the car', 'tow a caravan' and with the doll, 'waving Mummy goodbye' and the doll 'cries'.

So why are these examples important? It is clear that children and young people with autism do experience difficulties in areas involving symbolic representation. However, these difficulties are most evident when they are observed in unstructured situations. In other situations they show evidence of symbolic ability. This must mean that they have some underlying symbolic competence. Thus, while their everyday play may be 'devoid of symbolic representation', as Quinn and Rubin (1984) stated, this does not mean that they lack the competence to play symbolically.

What was different about Lewis and Boucher's study was that they structured the situation in which symbolic play was elicited. Subsequently, other researchers have confirmed that young people with autism can produce symbolic play in structured situations (for a review see Jarrold, 2003). This leads to two important implications. One is that free play settings are inappropriate for identifying whether or not young people with autism can play symbolically, unless, of course, you are specifically interested in play in unstructured settings. The second is that, as argued in the introduction to this chapter, negative findings, such as a lack of pretend play, are notoriously difficult to interpret. It may be very misleading to interpret them as evidence of a lack of ability. In the next section we shall stay with pretend play but move to consider the study of pretend play in blind children.

Pretend play and blind children and young people

Like children and young people with autism, a number of studies have reported that blind children seldom engage in symbolic play (e.g. Fraiberg, 1977; Rogers and Puchalski, 1984; Tröster and Brambring, 1994; Hughes, Dore-Kwan and Dolendo, 1998). Most of these studies have been based on direct observation of blind children, although some have been based on parental reports. But what does this paucity of symbolic play mean? Does it mean that blind children cannot play symbolically or that blind children seldom engage in symbolic play in the situations in which they have been observed? Again, it is important to consider whether or not the methods that have been used – observing blind children in their everyday settings or parental reports of such situations – are the most appropriate for demonstrating competence. Once again, it would be dangerous to conclude that blind children cannot play symbolically just because they do not do so in those situations in which typically developing children do play symbolically. Perhaps there is something about blindness that makes the situations that prompt symbolic play in typically developing children very different for blind children – perhaps even something as obvious as being unable to see what is available to play with.

The study by Lewis and Boucher discussed in the last section led to the development of a test that examines symbolic play in a structured way, the Test of Pretend Play or ToPP (Lewis and Boucher, 1997). This test was designed to help clinicians explore the underlying symbolic abilities of children with limited communication. It consists of four sections. Section I assesses the ability to refer to something that is absent, supported by everyday objects. Section II assesses the ability to substitute one, two, three and four pieces of non-representational materials for other objects in a related way. Sections III and IV assess the ability to substitute an object, refer to an absent object, attribute a non-existent property and act out a pretend scenario when either a teddy or the child is the subject of the play respectively. ToPP was not specifically designed for use with blind children. However, Lewis et al. (2000) administered ToPP to a group of 12 children with light perception or less, and six children with limited vision. The results were intriguing. Four of the children showed autistic-like behaviours and these children produced little or no symbolic play. One other child also chose not to play although she showed no signs of autistic-like behaviour. She was functioning at a level appropriate for her age but just disliked children's games, preferring to talk with people around her. However, the remaining children did not differ from the sighted children on whom the ToPP was standardized for sections I, III and IV. But on section II, which required substitution of varying numbers of objects for other things in a related way, the blind children produced much less symbolic play than the sighted children. Many of the blind children substituted one or two objects but, unlike the sighted children, seldom substituted three or four objects. Thus, although the average score of the blind children on ToPP did not differ from that of the sighted children, there was a marked difference on section II.

There are two important points to be made from this study for our current argument. The first is that, despite earlier studies concluding that the symbolic play skills of blind children are delayed, if they are assessed in a structured setting it becomes apparent that their play skills are not delayed unless they exhibit autistic-like behaviours. The second is that the nature of the structured setting is important. If the task requires blind children to incorporate a number of different objects into their play they do this to a lesser extent than sighted children, as was seen in section II of the ToPP. It is possible that in this part of the test, as in free play situations, because of their lack of vision blind children find it difficult to keep track of the objects and therefore tend to play with one object at a time.

Thus, their symbolic play appears to be less well developed than that of sighted children of a similar age.

A second explanation was also suggested to us by the observation that many of the blind children asked questions about the materials used in section II of the ToPP. These questions took the form of 'What is this?', 'Is this a . . . ?', 'Is this made of . . . ?'. The sighted children did not ask these sorts of questions. Perhaps the form and colour of the different materials prompted ideas for symbolic play in the sighted children whereas the tactual characteristics of the materials left the blind children wondering what the materials were supposed to be and this prompted their questions. Certainly, when the ToPP was designed, the visual similarity of the materials to everyday objects was uppermost in the minds of the developers, rather than the tactual similarity. As Lewis, Norgate and Collis (2002b) described, one child, on being given a doll, a round tub, a piece of grey felt and a plastic stick and asked 'Can you make the doll row the boat on the water?', responded with 'where is the boat?' and commented 'well there isn't any water'. Sighted children readily use the tub as a boat and the square of grey felt as water but the tactual impression of these objects is very different from the objects they are standing for. Perhaps if a piece of thin plastic had been provided to represent water, rather than a piece of grey felt, and a shallow rectangular box to represent a boat, rather than a round tub, the blind children might have been more likely to use the materials to stand for other things. As Lewis et al. (2000) indicated, the ToPP, and in particular section II, seems not to be well suited to assessing blind children's symbolic play.

Thus, once again we have an example of how the methods employed to study a particular behaviour affect the results and subsequent interpretations which might be drawn in terms of competence. In the next section we shall look at a further example of how using different methods may access previously unobserved competence in young blind children.

Understanding of space and blind children and young people

In the 1990s, two papers were published which seemed to demonstrate that blind children do not have an understanding of space in Euclidean terms until they reach their teens (Bigelow, 1991, 1996). In other words, blind children do not understand that different places can be related to one another in terms of the shortest straight line distance between them. Rather, the evidence suggested that blind children understand the relationship between different places in terms of the routes that they would take when moving from one place to another. This is in contrast to sighted children who demonstrate an understanding of space in Euclidean terms from about the age of 6 years.

Bigelow reached her conclusion about blind children's understanding on the basis of how two blind children responded in two different tasks which were administered in the children's homes. In the first task the children sat in one room of their own home and were asked to point to other locations in and around the house. The idea was that if the children had a Euclidean understanding of space they would point in a straight line direction toward the named room (typically through a wall or ceiling). Although they could point to objects in the same room as themselves, these two blind children found the task very difficult. Instead of pointing towards the named location, they tended to point in the direction of the route that they would take to get to the named location (typically towards a door). This error is interesting since it suggests that they are mapping their environment in terms of routes taken rather than in Euclidean terms.

In the second of her two tasks, Bigelow (1996) examined the possibility that the blind children did not interpret a request such as 'Point to your bedroom' as a request to point in a straight line direction. In this second paper, the two blind children were asked to imagine three magic ropes which could go through walls and ceilings from a specific starting point to each of three locations in or near to their home which were well known to the children. One location was closest to the starting point in straight line (Euclidean) terms; a second location was closest in terms of route but not straight line distance; the third location was furthest away by both route and straight line distance. The children had to compare the lengths of these imaginary magic ropes and say which of them was the shortest. Bigelow reasoned that this was a way of discovering whether they could appreciate straight line distances despite obstructions such as walls and ceilings. The blind children found this task difficult too, only succeeding by around the age of 13 years.

Apart from the problem that Bigelow's conclusions are based on data from only two blind children, this second task introduced the need for the children to imagine magic ropes which can pass through walls and to make judgements about relative lengths of these imagined devices. Both of these requirements are quite demanding. In addition, the children would have to understand the specific configuration of rope extended in large-scale space, which seems to be very similar to the understanding of space that is under examination.

In response to these concerns, Lewis et al. (2002a) developed and piloted a number of new tasks. Two tasks followed the same basic rationale as Bigelow's pointing task, but addressed the problem that some blind children do not point. The children were asked to look toward and make a teddy look toward selected locations in their own homes. In a further pointing task the child was asked to point to two different locations at the same time. This was to address the possibility that the route-oriented responses of the children in Bigelow's pointing task reflected not a lack of Euclidean understanding but an interpretation of the request to point at a particular room as 'Point in the direction of the route you would take to get to X'. Asking the child to point to two different locations simultaneously should reduce this problem since, if both points were based on routes, they would both be directed toward the exit from the room the child was in.

Two tasks were developed to explore the children's Euclidean understanding by asking them to identify rooms adjacent to the room they were in (but with no interconnecting door). One of these involved asking the child questions such as 'If I made a hole in this wall (or ceiling/floor) and we walked (climbed) through, which room would we be in?' and 'If I wanted to get into (an adjacent room with no interconnecting door) which wall would I need to make a hole/doorway in?' In a variation of this task, the child was taken to the (upstairs) bathroom and asked where the water would go if the bath overflowed – 'Which other rooms might get wet?'. Another task explored this understanding using large building blocks to represent the different rooms in the child's home. The child was handed a large building block which was identified as the room he or she was in, with an appropriately positioned window indicated tactually by a square of fabric attached to one side of the block. The 'room' was oriented correctly on the floor. Three further blocks were placed to represent another downstairs room and two upstairs rooms and, as each was positioned, the child was asked to name the additional 'room'.

The tasks were administered to three children who were blind from birth with at most limited light perception, and aged 7, 10 and 14 years. There were also two children with severe visual impairments aged 8 and 10 years, and 10 sighted children aged between 5 and 9 years of age. The sighted children had a near perfect performance from 8 years and the three blind children and two children with severe visual impairments performed at a level similar to the sighted children on all the tasks. In contrast, the blind children's performance on the tasks devised by Bigelow, particularly her magic rope task, was not as good. It seems that the blind children's competence was underestimated by Bigelow's methods and, notwithstanding the small number of blind children studied, it is reasonably certain that blindness does not preclude the early development of a Euclidean understanding of medium-scale space. More recently we have completed a longitudinal study involving a larger group of blind children and findings from an initial visit are reported in Lewis et al. (2004). These findings confirm our original pilot findings.

Of course, the robustness of these conclusions that blind children can readily develop a Euclidean understanding would be further supported if we better understood *how* this understanding developed. A start has been made in exploring this problem by Collis et al. (2004), who suggest that part of the answer may lie in the children's use of social information, especially when a child's understanding of the spatial layout of the family home is being considered. The family home is a social space inhabited by people, with spatially relevant information available from sounds of people moving about the house, their use of artefacts, the prevalence of known family routines and especially people's talk with one another (not just talk directed towards the blind child). We have argued that day-to-day exposure to such cues provides an important source of information for a blind child to construct a spatial representation of his or her home.

Some progress has been made in examining the implications of this model empirically. In order effectively to use social information, especially incidental talk, to construct a spatial representation of the family home, a blind child would need to be able to discriminate the scale of the space that is being talked about, and whether spatial talk they overhear relates to the home rather than somewhere else. To test scale discrimination, Collis et al. presented blind children with tape recordings of everyday speech and asked them to decide whether *big movements* or *small movements* were being talked about. Children were asked to respond with gestures – either arms stretched out sideways so their hands were as far apart as possible, or hands just a few centimetres apart. Examples of utterances were: 'I need somewhere to sit – I'll get one from over there' (big movement) and 'Open it – I think it's a birthday card' accompanied by sound of tearing paper (small movement). The children were also presented with utterances some of which could refer to the child's own home, and some that probably would not. The distinguishing characteristics were features (e.g. back door, the lift), activities (e.g. washing up, driving), reference to times (e.g. before bedtime, lunchtime – spoken by someone who was typically not home for lunch) and named people (a family member or a known work colleague). The children were presented with audio recordings of these utterances, which were individually recorded for each child, and they were asked to operate a bell or a hooter to indicate whether they were about their own home or elsewhere. For both the scale and the home/not-home discriminations, 5-year-old blind children performed well, with instances of greater than 80% correct responding and, from 7 years of age, they performed very well. It is thus clear that blind children can readily apply two basic abilities for making sense of spatial talk about their own home.

So far we have examined three areas of research: symbolic play and young people with autism, symbolic play and blind children, and blind children's appreciation of the Euclidean properties of space. In each case we have examined research which has questioned previous findings suggesting that these children and young people lack certain abilities. In all three examples we have illustrated how different tasks and methods have demonstrated that these children and young people may have the underlying competence which was previously argued to be absent. Such findings should be a salutary lesson to us all particularly when interpreting negative findings. When data seem to suggest that a disabled child or young person cannot do something, we need to examine the method used very carefully and convince ourselves that it is not some feature of the method that has prevented the child or young person from demonstrating his or her true competence.

While there is a real danger of misinterpreting negative findings and thereby underestimating ability, the converse can also present problems. In other words, there can be a danger of overestimating abilities in a population by generalizing observations of surprising competence identified in a limited number of cases. We consider this related problem in the next section.

Drawing ability and children with autism

In his original observations, Kanner (1943) noted that children with autism were often particularly good at something, at least in relation to their other abilities. Over the years since Kanner's seminal paper there have been a number of reports of children and young people demonstrating exceptional abilities. Many of these abilities involve visual–spatial skills. One of the areas that has received attention is that of drawing. Several young people with autism have been described as exceptionally gifted artists. These include the well-known examples of Nadia, studied by Selfe (1977, 1983), and Stephen Wiltshire (1987), studied by Pring and Hermelin, with Buhler and Walker (1997). There is no question that some children and young people with autism are able to produce drawings that very accurately reflect what they actually see when they look at an object, person or view. Nevertheless, one of the problems with positive findings such as these is that they may lead researchers to focus on the few individuals who have these exceptional abilities rather than the majority of children and young people with autism who do not. Because of this it is possible that a particular disability, in this case autism, becomes misleadingly associated with a particular competence, in this case artistic ability. The generality of this association is not borne out by the literature. Parallels could perhaps be drawn here with the view, now largely discounted, that blind people benefit from a *sixth sense*. In other words, there is a danger in reading too much into findings because of the way in which the data have been collected.

While it is obviously important to document areas of competence, even if only evident in a minority, it is also important to explore the nature of such developments in all individuals with a particular disability. This was the motivation behind a study by Lewis and Boucher (1991) of the drawings of a group of young people with autism. What was important was that the participants were not selected because they had any special talent in this area. Also, the study did not focus just on their artistic ability but also on other aspects of their drawings which might reflect characteristics of autism, such as what they included in their drawings and their ability to generate different ideas for drawings. To this end, the young people produced 20 drawings over the course of a year, with a maximum of three drawings per session. The drawings of the young people with autism were examined alongside drawings collected under similar conditions from a group of children with learning difficulties who had similar verbal and non-verbal ability. Interestingly, what this comparison showed was that, although the content of the drawings and the skill with which they were drawn were similar in the two groups, the drawings of the young people with autism were more similar in terms of the ideas represented than those of the young people with learning difficulties.

Discussion

The question that dominates the literature on the psychology of autism is: what is the nature of the disability (antecedent) that produces the behaviours which characterize the condition? In contrast, in research with blind children the antecedent (lack of vision) tends to be taken as given, and the dominant question is: what are the consequences? Nevertheless, with respect to how methods map onto conclusions, the examples we have described from children with autism have much in common with our examples from blind children.

Our first example, on pretend play in children with autism, was connected with the idea that a particular limitation in representational functioning lay at the heart of autism (e.g. Leslie, 1987), and that an early manifestation of this limitation was a lack of pretend play. The logic is that, if children with autism could exhibit pretence under suitable conditions, as was indicated by Lewis and Boucher (1988; Boucher and Lewis 1990), then it could not be true that a deficit in an ability necessary for pretence was also the core deficit in autism. This points to the more subtle and probably more interesting question as to why children with autism show pretence only rarely and in particular circumstances.

This example has obvious parallels with the logic of the debate about whether children who have been without sight since birth develop a

Euclidean understanding of space in the same way as sighted children. What is at issue is whether vision has a unique role in the typical development of visual representation. It is not difficult to understand why sighted investigators might presume that it does, and Bigelow's finding that blind children were markedly delayed (until their teens) in achieving success on her tasks seemed to be consistent with that assumption. Again, the logic of the situation is that a demonstration of Euclidean understanding of space in young children who are completely without sight leads us to conclude that vision is not a necessary condition for the early development of Euclidean spatial representations. This in turn leads to more interesting questions about how non-visual information contributes to spatial representation. An understanding of this issue seems likely to be very relevant to mobility training for blind people.

Another of our examples concerned observations that blind children engage in pretend play less than typically developing children. Here, it was less clear that there was a plausible hypothesis that a lack of vision led to a representational deficit in blind children. Although Fraiberg (1977) rather strongly suggested that there was such a link, this was based on evidence from only a minority of the children whom she studied. Hobson et al. (1997) made a similar case that a lack of vision led to a deficit in the kind of representational processes underlying pretend play, using assumptions strikingly distinct from those made by Leslie (1987). The idea was that vision is the sensory modality *par excellence* for appreciating that different people have different attitudes to the same object and that the same objects can have multiple meanings, so that a lack of vision prevents or delays the emergence of this crucial aspect of subjectivity, with deleterious consequences for representational functioning.

Like Fraiberg, Hobson et al.'s findings indicated that only a minority of congenitally blind children showed the developmental sequences they were describing and trying to understand. In other words, vision could not be seen as a necessary condition for the emergence of the kind of representational functioning that they conjectured to be impaired in some blind children. In our own sample, some blind children with clear autistic-like features failed to engage in symbolic play in a manner that suggested that they may have been simply unable to do so. However, the style of play by other blind children in our sample strongly suggested that they could engage in pretence but also indicated that some of our ideas about how pretend play should be characterized were simply inappropriate for children without vision. The causal role of vision must have been quite different in determining the way that the play of children in these two subsets deviated from that of typically developing children.

In this short chapter we have sought to argue that researchers should continually question negative (and sometimes even positive) findings which suggest that the abilities of disabled children and young people differ from those who do not have the disabilities. It is important to avoid any tendency to accept evidence of lack of competence just because the children and young people we are researching have been selected on account of their having a disability. Rather, we need to ensure that the methodologies that we use optimize the likelihood of disabled children and young people demonstrating their competences. In other words, our methods should be fit for purpose.

References

Baron-Cohen S (1990) Instructed and elicited play in autism: A reply to Lewis & Boucher. British Journal of Developmental Psychology 8: 207.

Bigelow AE (1991) Spatial mapping of familiar locations in blind children. Journal of Visual Impairment and Blindness 85: 113–17.

Bigelow AE (1996) Blind and sighted children's spatial knowledge of their home environments. International Journal of Behavioral Development 19: 797–816.

Boucher J, Lewis V (1990) Guessing or creating? A reply to Baron-Cohen. British Journal of Developmental Psychology 8: 205–6.

Collis GM, Lewis V, Nock J, Burns J, Twiselton R (2004) How the social environment provides blind children with information about space. In: Ballesteros S, Heller M (eds) Touch, Blindness and Neuroscience. Madrid: UNED-Varia, pp. 127–34.

Fraiberg S (1977) Insights from the Blind. London: Souvenir Press.

Hobson RP, Brown R, Minter ME, Lee A (1997) 'Autism' revisited: the case of congenital blindness. In: Lewis V, Collis GM (eds) Blindness and Psychological Development in Young Children. Leicester: BPS Books.

Hughes M, Dote-Kwan J, Dolendo J (1998) A close look at the cognitive play of preschoolers with visual impairments in the home. Exceptional Children 64: 451–62.

Jarrold C (2003) A review of research into pretend play in autism. Autism 7: 379–90.

Kanner L (1943) Autistic disturbances of affective contact. Nervous Child 2: 217–50.

Leslie AM (1987) Pretence and representation: the origins of 'theory of mind'. Psychological Review 94: 412–26.

Lewis V (2003) Development and Disability. Oxford: Blackwell Publishing.

Lewis V, Boucher J (1988) Spontaneous, instructed and elicited play in relatively able autistic children. British Journal of Developmental Psychology 6: 325–39.

Lewis V, Boucher J (1991) Skill, content and generative strategies in autistic children's drawings. British Journal of Developmental Psychology 9: 393–416.

Lewis V, Boucher J (1995) Generativity in the play of young people with autism. Journal of Autism and Developmental Disorders 25: 105–21.

Lewis V, Boucher J (1997) The Test of Pretend Play. London: Harcourt Brace Jovanovich.

Lewis V, Norgate S, Collis G, Reynolds R (2000) The consequences of visual impairment for children's symbolic and functional play. British Journal of Developmental Psychology 18: 449–64.

Lewis V, Collis G, Shadlock R, Potts M, Norgate S (2002a) New methods for studying blind children's understanding of familiar space. British Journal of Visual Impairment 20: 17–23.

Lewis V, Norgate S, Collis G (2002b) Les capacités de représentation d'un enfant aveugle congénital entre un et sept ans. Enfance 54: 291–307.

Lewis V, Collis GM, Nock J, Burns J, Twiselton R (2004) Blind children's understanding of the euclidean properties of space. In: Ballesteros S, Heller M (eds) Touch, Blindness and Neuroscience. Madrid: UNED-Varia, pp. 119–27.

Pring L, Hermelin B, with Buhler M, Walker I (1997) Native savant talent and acquired skill. Autism 1: 199–214.

Quinn J, Rubin K (1984) The play of handicapped children. In: Yawkey TD, Pellegrini A (eds) Child's Play: Developmental and applied. Hillsdale, NJ: Erlbaum.

Rogers SJ, Puchalski CB (1984) Development of symbolic play in visually impaired young children. Topics in Early Childhood Special Education 3: 57–63.

Selfe L (1977) Nadia: A case of extraordinary drawing ability in an autistic child. London: Academic Press.

Selfe L (1983) Normal and Anomalous Representational Drawing Ability in Children. London: Academic Press.

Tröster H, Brambring M (1994) The play behavior and play materials of blind and sighted infants and preschoolers. Journal of Visual Impairment and Blindness 88: 421–32.

Wiltshire S (1987) Drawings. London: JM Dent.

World Health Organization (1980) International Classification of Impairments, Disabilities, and Handicaps: A Manual of Classification. Geneva: WHO.

CHAPTER 8

Educational implications of autism and visual impairment

RITA JORDAN

Introduction

I last wrote about this topic some 7 years ago (Jordan, 1996a) and coming back to it now it is distressing to see that, in spite of exponential growth of knowledge about autistic spectrum disorder (ASD) over this period, there has been very little systematic study of this rare, but particularly vulnerable group of children with visual impairment (VI) and ASD.

Visual impairment and ASD are both developmental disorders with varying behavioural symptomatology, varying aetiology, occurring at all levels of intelligence and with varying degrees of severity. They can occur as a single disorder, together, or as part of a multiple disability, often accompanying severe learning difficulties. They both have significant effects on processing information from the world around them, 80% of which in typical individuals comes from visual information. The behaviours found in infancy in both disorders vary over the lifespan and prognosis depends on a multiplicity of factors, including educational intervention. They are also disorders that can be misunderstood by others and both have transactional effects on those who live with and care for those with the disorders.

Visual impairment may not be fully understood, especially in forms arising from central brain dysfunction, but it gives rise to greater sympathy and empathy than autism, and educational and other systems are more able and willing to adapt to the needs of those with a VI than to those with ASD. The world (both within and outside of education) is designed for sighted people and yet children with a VI are seldom if ever told that their blindness is irrelevant and they will just have to learn to get on as best they can in an unadapted world; yet that is the message that is often conveyed to those with ASD, for whom the unadapted world is just as problematic. For those with a dual disability, it is not just a matter of adding the issues from one disability to the other; rather, the issues are multiplied through developmental processes. It is, therefore, even more important for this group to have effective education and support from as early an age as possible, to prevent secondary consequences of the disabilities and to teach key aspects of development upon which later learning and development depend.

Educational implications of a diagnostic category

The professional educational view of special needs is increasingly one of looking towards providing individual strategies for access to inclusive environments with a common curriculum. The rhetoric of entitlement and rights is replacing notions of assessing and meeting individual (and especially disability-focused) needs. Within this conceptual frame, sensory disorders hold a privileged position; their reality as 'within-child' variables cannot be denied and the need for expert understanding of those variables is recognized in the UK, as elsewhere, in mandatory specialist training for teachers working with the sensory impaired. Even there, however, there is uncertainty as increasing inclusion makes someone who is 'working with the sensory impaired' increasingly hard to define.

Douglas and McLinden (in press) and Jordan (in press) address the issue of what is meant by specialist pedagogy for visual impairment and ASD, respectively. In my chapter in that book, I make the case for the individualization of special needs in ASD (since individual differences make it impossible to make other than the broadest statements across the range of ASD), but also point out that knowledge of ASD is vital in determining those individual needs. One cannot use actual behaviour as anything other than a cue as to what is going on at the level at which we really need to understand and work: the level of psychological processing (Jordan and Powell, 1995). Otherwise, behaviour is interpreted intuitively in a common understanding (largely culturally determined) of how behaviour reflects underlying psychology, but that is misleading when it comes to ASD. It is necessary to understand ASD in order to suspend that intuitive interpretation and reconceptualize the significance of the behaviour that is seen. Jordan (2001, 2002) and Cumine, Stephenson and Leach (1997) give practical examples of the usefulness of applying what Cumine et al. refer to as an 'Asperger lens' to interpret and work with behaviour in children with ASD.

Visual impairment, especially when it involves central mechanisms rather than the ocular globe alone (Cass, 1996, 1998), also needs specialist understanding to interpret behaviour. Morse, Pawletko and Rocissano (2002) show that in ASD and VI it is important to use an understanding of what may underlie behaviours, in order to work effectively with either group. When considering those with VI and ASD, then, we need to understand the developmental effects of both disabilities when interpreting behaviour. As will be seen below, this is made somewhat less daunting because of the congruence of many of these developmental effects. Visual impairment in fact provides a useful analogy for ASD. It illustrates how development is affected by differences in processing information and how teaching approaches need to work with the children's strengths in helping them overcome any problems and developing their skills and understanding of the world, rather than trying to force them into forms of processing that are never going to be maximal for them. Most educationalists can recognize the futility of emphasizing visual instruction in the education of a blind child but find it harder to accept that orally presented information may (although not always) be as much of a barrier for children with ASD.

The problem with the dual disability is where some of the processing problems result in conflict over choice of approach. Most children with ASD, for example, will take in information more readily through visual channels and visual structure is the key to one of the most prevalent and accepted methods of educating such children: TEACCH (Treatment and Education of Autistic and Communication handicapped CHildren; Schopler, Mesibov and Hearsey, 1995; Mesibov, 1997; Peeters, 1997). Howley and Preece (2003) show how such an approach can be adapted to meet the needs of a child with both VI and ASD. However, vision may have such an advantage as an information channel for students with ASD that, unless they are totally blind, it may still be the best channel to use with students with dual impairments, albeit augmented and adapted to each child's particular VI (Pawletko, 2002).

In many cases, however, techniques of explicit teaching of what is commonly available (through vision and intuitive understanding) to others, of assisting in the development of self agency and awareness as a precursor to other awareness, and understanding behaviour through the 'lens' of the disability, are all common approaches, leading to common strategies. The dual disability emphasizes the point that is often made, but not always acted on, that each child's needs are different and have to be assessed on an individual basis, albeit through that lens. It prevents the application of teaching approaches as if they were recipes for action for particular groups and encourages teachers and others to look at the principles behind the teaching and adapt those principles to individual cases. That is an important ingredient of all good teaching.

Just as there are some aspects of teaching those with ASD that are problematic for those with VI, so there are approaches to VI teaching that may be difficult for those with ASD. Pawletko (2002) highlights some of these. Multisensory work may be particularly problematic, when it has been shown that children with ASD find it hard to integrate information from more than one sense (Grandin, 1995; Williams, 1996; Murray, Lawson and Lesser, 2004). Hand-over-hand prompting or guidance depends on the child's appreciation of its co-active intent but this is not likely in ASD. Such prompting does feature in some programmes for children with ASD (e.g. Lovaas, 1987), but it may also lead to problems with prompt dependence and lack of motivation, when the child has no control, as well as aversion in those with tactile defensiveness; there is certainly a case for working with, rather than against, the child's intent (Trevarthen, 2000).

The use of narrative commentary also has a role in those with ASD, but great care has to be taken that it is within the child's level of understanding and is not distracting from other relevant perceptions. Children with ASD have problems making sense of narrative forms (Bruner and Feldman, 1993) and their understanding of speech is often literal and idiosyncratic, below their expressive speech in most cases (Jordan, 1996b; Tager-Flusberg, 2003; Noens and Van Berckelaer-Onnes, 2004). Once more, it may be that such approaches have such value for the VI that they can be adapted for the dual disability, but the educator must be aware of the problems and limitations and use individual factors to assess their viability in each instance.

Autism and 'blindisms'

The papers by Cass (1996, 1998) illustrate the difficulties that can arise in differentiating the effects of autism from those of severe VI and the considerable overlap there might be in behaviour at certain points in development. She makes the case that one cannot use diagnostic instruments for ASD, when they have not been standardized on a blind or visually impaired population, since many of the behaviours that would indicate autism when compared with typical development are part of the normal development for a blind child. That is one of the reasons for the importance, raised above, of not viewing ASD as a collection of behaviours or symptoms. There is nothing that a child with an ASD does that cannot be found in other groups under other conditions and diagnosis is not a matter of checking off behaviours but of making a clinical judgement based on a developmental history and observation in at least two environments (Charman and Baird, 2002).

Educational definitions of need (Teacher Training Agency, 1999; DfES, 2001) that eschew categorical 'medical' descriptions in favour of behavioural descriptions miss the point, and thus the value, of diagnostic information in determining need. It is of minimal benefit to be told that a child has 'social and communication' difficulties, for example, since most teachers should be able to gain that knowledge for themselves after brief observation; what is important is to know whether those difficulties arise from an ASD, from a sensory impairment, from social and emotional neglect, and so on. It is not about the negative effects of labelling since the child already has a label and, without understanding of the true nature of the difficulties, will soon acquire more: 'stupid', 'inattentive', 'rude', and so on. It is important to have a label that leads to greater understanding, as opposed to one that merely stigmatizes.

Pawletko and Rocissano (2000) point out the very pertinent differences there are in the development of blind children without additional difficulties and the development of those who are blind and have autism. There may be some shared behaviours, albeit for different reasons, but there are also behaviours and dispositions that are found only in the former group. When there is no additional autism, blind children have non-visual ways of showing social interest, make attempts to communicate and orientate to the communication of others, show delayed imitative play but normal functional play with toys and can be redirected from stereotyped rocking or eye-poking. Children who have lacked visual input in the early months of development may develop prosopagnosia (failure of face recognition), yet still differ in their social responsiveness and communicative understanding from those who also have autism. This is confirmed by the experience of a mother with three children who have prosopagnosia but only one of whom also has an ASD (detailed in web chat group: Zusia, 2003).

It is not just that some behaviours in those with VI may be misleadingly assumed to be the result of an ASD, but that some behaviours in ASD may be better explained as a result of a VI. Kaplan (1996) discusses the fact that a far higher proportion of children with autism have some form of VI than in the population as a whole, and gives insights into how this may be affecting what are often regarded as 'typical' mannerisms in ASD. He reports that difficulties in the brainstem that have been identified in ASD may lead to problems in coordinating input from the two hemispheres, which in turn result in visual problems, especially related to ambient vision (depth perception, organizing space and orienting themselves), all features of visual perception that have to be learnt and require an intact system for this to occur. Using peripheral vision (instead of focal vision, which is the default, unlearned, visual identification process) may be a compensatory strategy for this – using monocular vision rather than risking a confused signal. If the visual identification system is stressed in this way (and personal reports suggest it may be: Grandin, 1995; Williams, 1996), then it can be very difficult to perceive and think at the same time or process visual and auditory information at the same time.

Hyperactivity often accompanies ASD, and this also may happen because the child is trying to gain the needed experience and rehearsal on which ambient vision depends, by using running around and touching, to replace the difficulties with vision. Kaplan suggests that many stereotypical behaviours such as toe walking are functional attempts to locate the body in space or result from not being able to process space and the self simultaneously. A person with autism, without a diagnosed VI, reports having to lean against tables when talking to a group, or else her concentration on what she is saying may mean that she will lose her balance and fall over, and making hand gestures in the middle of her talks to bring her hands back into her sense of herself. Kaplan further suggests that sideways rocking comes from orientation and visual attention problems, and rocking back and forth and flicking fingers in front of the eyes compensates for poor depth perception. Thus, even without a diagnosed VI impairment, there may be visual problems associated with ASD, which may lead to additional, or more severe, ASD symptoms.

Similarities and differences in development

Behaviours that have been reported to be common to both groups of children (those who are blind, and those with an ASD) have included problems in joint attention, understanding mental states, perceiving unified wholes, selecting attention to relevant information, imitating behaviours (except for echolalia), and reading and giving social signals. They also have similar difficulties in symbolizing, in adjusting concepts, schema or patterns of learnt behaviour to the context, and in imaginative play. In both children with an ASD and those who are blind, the extent of these difficulties depends to a large extent on the general cognitive and linguistic ability of the child. However, even where similar behaviours are shown, they may have different causes and different treatments may be effective, as will be explored below. A dual disability, then, provides no clear way of attacking the problem. Solutions will need to depend on individual factors, and neither disability should be forgotten.

Joint attention is a key developmental skill, essential for social and communicative development, and for conceptual understanding, and so an examination of its differential development in ASD and VI can illustrate the fact that similar difficulties may have different roots. Its development is affected in both ASD and VI, although in VI without autism the child will acquire joint attention eventually through other senses. Joint attention capability depends on acquiring two aspects of a sense of self and the capacity to coordinate these. Baron-Cohen (1995) suggested a mechanism for this (the shared attention mechanism: SAM), which was disrupted in ASD but would only be delayed in VI as non-preferred senses were used to activate it. Hobson (1990, 1993) has also addressed joint attention problems in these two groups, but attributes differences to the differential experience of social interaction and sees the sense of self as developing within the context of this interaction.

The problems in developing joint attention in VI appear to arise from difficulties in developing an 'ecological self' (Neisser, 1991) – a sense of self in relation to objects and events. This is difficult for the blind child to achieve without direct teaching. Bigelow (2003) traced the development of joint attention in two congenitally blind infants at Piagetian stage 4 in sensorimotor development, whereby object permanence is achieved. Behaviour that was judged preliminary to joint attention occurred throughout stage 4 (which was itself delayed in these infants); actual joint attention (broadly or tightly defined) did not become prevalent until the second half of that stage. The interpersonal self, on the other hand, may develop relatively normally in children with VI unless they have ASD, whereas difficulties with this are at the heart of an ASD (Hobson, 1993, 2002; Powell and Jordan, 1993; Jordan, 1999).

There are additional difficulties, however, for both groups, at the stage of coordinating these selves. Cass (1996), for example, points out that it is often sighted others who fail to recognize and respond to the child's ways of attending (leaning towards, rather than pointing) that leads to misidentification of the focus of joint attention and thus further problems. Bakeman and Adamson (1984) have shown the importance of coordinated visual attention to both object and partner in developing joint attention, which requires an awareness of the direction of attention of others. This is hard to achieve for the blind, since it must be done through other senses, such as touch (a personal sense) or hearing (non-directional). It is hard in ASD because of difficulties in reading intentions and monitoring eye gaze (Tomasello, 1995).

The example of joint attention illustrates why it is important to distinguish the difficulties of the child at the psychological developmental level, to understand the strategies that need to be adopted in teaching. Children with VI need an emphasis on developing their sense of agency with objects (their ecological selves), whereas for those with ASD the priority is the development of the interpersonal self through explicit structured forms of interaction with others. However, at the stage of coordination of these two selves into joint attention, similar teaching approaches may be effective. For the child with a dual disability, both forms of self need to be enabled, and then coordination assisted through drawing attention to others' focus of attention in ways that are meaningful to the individual. Language will be the easiest medium to effect this but for young children, or where there is an additional learning or language disability, it may be best to start with proximal joint attention, so that touch can be used to demonstrate, and then investigate, that focus of attention. McLinden and McCall (2002) make a useful distinction between interactive and non-interactive touch and it is this latter sense of touch, which is the one that can be used in exploration, that can be used by children with the dual disability.

Common difficulties in the two disabilities (mirroring the three areas of development through which ASD is diagnosed) have been found in the following:

- Communication: failing to pick up (or understand) non-verbal cues; missing (or misunderstanding) turn-taking signals; using speech as self-stimulation rather than communication; echolalia; delayed personal pronoun development; few gestures; odd intonation patterns.
- Socialization: failure or extreme delay in joint attention (as explored above), problems with second-order imitation (i.e. beyond echolalia, or echopraxia in ASD), abnormal eye contact, abnormal emotional contact, difficulty perceiving others' emotions, different play actions (although the nature of the difference will vary between the two groups).
- Inflexibilities of thinking and behaviour: resistant to changes in self-initiated routines; dependent on structures; self-stimulatory behaviour; liking to classify, sort and list; good rote but poor spontaneous memory, over-selectivity in attention, inattention to stimuli from the environment, good memory for music.

Effective educational strategies

The list of common difficulties (above) gives a clear focus for teaching strategies and priorities for this dually disabled group. Working with a child with an ASD means paying attention to all the areas that normally form part of the 'hidden' curriculum, the part that typical children just 'pick up' and which form common, intuitive assumptions about what things mean, what must be done and how. For a child with a VI one has to take the notion of 'hidden' more literally and examine how the particular visual impairment will lead to missing the cues for this normally intuitive understanding. With the dual disability one is denied the normal strategy for ASD of visually enhancing those cues to make them accessible, albeit through non-intuitive cognitive routes. However, the principle remains the same, with the enhancement having to take place through other senses.

These children will need stable surroundings (at least to begin their learning), predictable physical and social environments, repetition, time to process impressions and instructions, help to build sequential experiences into meaningful wholes, to appreciate the relevance (or otherwise) of the context, and to learn from positive experiences of social interaction. These will help the children develop the cognitive structures needed to compensate for their difficulties in learning intuitively and from direct appreciation of their environment, and, of course, there will also need to be physical structures and aids to help them move around and explore the environment for themselves.

Howley and Preece (2003) give components of structured teaching, designed to meet the needs of children with ASD, and explore the adaptations that can be made to meet the dual disability. The following is developed from those suggestions.

Physical structure

The aim is to make the purpose of different parts of the environment explicit. It implies that the learning environment can be physically divided in this way but, if that is not possible, then tactile or sound cues can be used to herald the different purposes (e.g. the addition of a cloth on a table to signal its switch from a work table to a snack table). Sobsey and Wolf-Schein (1996) have shown that it is just as important for the multiply sensory impaired child to have an environment that emphasizes its functionality and minimizes irrelevant distractions, as it is for children with ASD. Pease (2000) also discusses the value of having functional 'zones' in the physical environment, to meet the needs of children with multiple sensory impairments. In a classroom designed for a child with ASD and VI, a child can be given a tactile symbol to indicate that they are to go to the 'listening corner' (perhaps a piece of the soft carpet that covers the floor of that area) where there is tape equipment and headphones, which the child is being taught to use unaided. With this symbol in one hand, the child guides herself by means of the guiding rail round the classroom until she finds a matching symbol attached to the guiding rail by the entrance to the listening area. The child does the match and then turns (in a way she has been taught to do) to enter the correct area, already primed for the activity (or kind of activity) to take place there.

Schedules

These take varying forms (from objects of reference in stacked boxes to written agendas) and are of varying length, according to the ability and interests of the child. They are likely to include the symbols to the different activity areas in the learning environment (as above) that the child is taught to go through in a learnt sequence of left to right, top to bottom. For those with a dual disability, less visual modes will usually be preferred. The aim is to make the learning day (or part of the day) predictable and manageable. Van Dijk (1986, cited in MacFarland, 1995) has developed the idea of 'calendar boxes' for the deaf–blind and these seem very similar to the schedules developed for children with ASD in the TEACCH programme (Watson et al., 1989). The population with the dual disability need more attention than others to the meaning of the symbols used. For example, there is probably very little in the tactile or haptic qualities of a toy car that would relate in any iconic way to the experience of going out in a car for such a child. It may be possible to teach the connection eventually with massed learning trials but that may be tedious and destroy the meaning and value of going out in the car. Better then to use something like a seat belt buckle or the tactile feel of a car seat that might serve as a far more immediately perceptible signal (Jordan, 2001).

Work systems

The child with ASD and VI will need to develop systematic work habits and use spatial cues (usually, although some sound cues can be incorporated) to organize work and set up routines. Just as schedules work at the macro level of organization, so work systems help the child know what to do, when, what to do next and when to finish, within the work or activity areas. The same principles of left-to-right organization apply and tactile symbols are used to identify the next task to do or the nature of the task – especially for independent work. Smith's (2002) idea of 'activity calendars' is very similar to this TEACCH idea of work systems.

Routines

The establishment of work routines is an important aid to structuring and supporting learning in this group. Smith (2002) gives features for what constitutes a useful routine for a child with VI and these are just as useful where there is an additional ASD. The value of routines lies in the fact that they provide consistent expectations, predictability in terms of the support, anticipation of the activity and practice of new skills in familiar environments. There will be long-term need to gradually introduce variation and to develop routines that are child-initiated, but this is a good way to get learning started or to get new learning accepted. Smith identifies the following features:

- There is a clear signal to the student that the activity is starting.
- The steps of the activity occur in the same sequence.
- Each step is done is the same way each time (same materials, same person, same place).
- The minimum amount of assistance is given to allow the student to do as much as possible independently.
- Modifications and techniques provided by specialists are implemented exactly as directed.

- The pacing of instruction is precisely maintained until the activity is finished (no side conversations, no going off to get something forgotten, no spontaneously adding new or different steps that will not happen the next time the activity is done).
- There is a clear signal to the student that the activity is finished.

Additional structure

The purpose of this in ASD is to enhance relevance and reduce distraction and those aims are even more important with the dual disability. However, when there is VI, these additional structures need to be other than visual. Music may provide a structure that is appreciated by children with ASD, whereas use of a 'talking through' approach may be overwhelming and cause the child to 'switch off' entirely. Thus, individual needs will be paramount in deciding on necessary structures, but attention has to be paid to the particular constraints of ASD.

Students with ASD process one dimension at a time so multisensory approaches are not usually functional for them. Distractions are very disruptive and this might apply to verbal instructions, if the student does not recognize that they are directed at him and how they relate to the task in hand. Social rewards and a social context can be very helpful to the student with VI alone, but to the student with an ASD they are at best irrelevant and at worst disruptive of learning. The student will need to develop understanding of social stimulation and toleration of its presence, but it is unlikely ever to act as a facilitator of learning. All forms of irrelevant stimulation will disrupt the student's learning so steps need to be taken to minimize ambient noise (padding the bottoms – with half of a cut tennis ball, for example – of chairs and tables, hanging curtains and tapestries on walls to absorb sound, working in sound-proofed booths for new learning) and irrelevant tactile changes. It is important, for example, that, if tactile or sound 'symbols' are used in communication or as part of a schedule, they are not experienced in situations where that is not the meaning intended. For example, the carpet piece that 'means' listening area, should not have the same feel as the carpet in the child's bedroom at home, or in the shoe shop where she crawls around to avoid the painful business of having shoes fitted. Difficult behaviour is often triggered by such unwanted associations, either because they signify something unpleasant that is about to happen, or because they signal something pleasant, which when it does not happen, causes frustration.

Morse et al. (2000) discuss how strategies designed for those with VI alone need to be adapted to consider the needs of children with ASD and VI. Edland (2003) reports on a Nordic study of such a case where the principles and structures that were set up for children with VI seemed to work relatively well, although the teenager was far more responsive to non-social than social sounds, such as speech. Drissel (1997) reports on 'the Box Story' as a way of building narrative understanding and early literacy in students with VI and this should be applicable to those with the dual disability. Techniques of giving warning when approaching students with VI is a very useful discipline for those working with students with ASD also, as long as the signals used are clearly understood. Other aspects of VI education may be more problematic. The use of Braille involves clustering and separation of tactile stimulation in patterns with meaning. This may be harder for the student with an additional ASD because of problems with 'tunnel attention', in which stimulation points have to be closer together spatially (or in time) in order for meaningful connections to be made. Since many of those with the dual disability also have learning difficulties, there has been little practical experience of the optimal way of teaching Braille to dually disabled students, but possible difficulties should be noted.

Service models for students with VI and concomitant ASD

It is unlikely that the prevalence of the dual disability is such that it would merit separate specialist provision. The only feasible model, therefore, regardless of what is desirable, is for some form of additional support into other environments. As Jones (2002) points out, there is no single 'best' placement for a student with ASD and each case should be made on individual assessment of need and evaluation of available educational environments. Nevertheless, there are some general points to be made.

There are many strategies that are common to approaches in the two disability groups, but the balance of advantage would be in settings where there was expertise in VI, to which additional support in ASD could be added. The more severe the child's VI, the more this will be the case. The disadvantages of the reverse position (providing VI support to a specialist setting for children with ASD) is that most of those settings will be heavily reliant on visual structuring of the environment and teaching approach and will have students who are liable to be hyperactive, physically uncoordinated and not observant of others' space. They are also liable to be noisy, which is not good for other students with ASD but even less helpful where speech and other sounds may be used regularly to help the child focus and gain understanding of the environment. Nevertheless, as Howley and Preece (2003) show, it should be possible to adapt visual structures for other senses, and in certain cases this may be the most practical option.

There should always be a progression towards more inclusive environments but it is important that basic work in learning how to learn, and be comfortable in school environments, should happen in situations where there is maximal support from people who really understand the student's dual disability. Where typically developing children are nearby, this makes it possible to arrange 'reverse integration' and other forms of partial inclusion into lessons from which the student can benefit. Reverse integration is where typical children are introduced into the secure specialist environment until the student with ASD and VI has learnt to work and play with them, and then the student is taken back into more inclusive environments by the 'buddies' with whom he is already familiar. However, the learning needs of these children are extremely complex and variable, and it is not feasible to leave the management of their learning, and their integration opportunities, to untrained learning support assistants, as is often the case when 'inclusion' is a policy decision rather than a process based on the needs of the child (Jordan and Powell, 1994).

The actual mechanism in providing specialist input into other school settings is one that also needs to be carefully planned and monitored, as does the mechanism by which parents are to be consulted and involved. Smith (2002) makes a strong case for the 'trans-disciplinary model' of providing this form of consultancy. Its emphasis is on providing the expertise of specialists to the day-to-day instruction of students with severe multiple impairments. In this case that would be the VI specialist into an ASD setting, or the ASD specialist into a VI setting, or both into mainstream or generic needs settings.

These model specialists actually work in classrooms. They seldom provide direct instruction or therapy to the student, except to model, and their role is to coach and monitor the interventions implemented by others. Whenever possible, specialists, teachers from the host setting and family members collaborate by meeting together to design curriculum activities and adjustments and develop and review IEP (individual educational plan) goals. In less ideal, but still workable, situations, they collaborate by leaving each other notes, sharing video tapes and contacting by phone or even e-mail. True collaboration has the goal of consistency in programming across settings and people. Smith points out that the advantage of this collaboration is that specific information is shared, and input is frequent across all environments by all relevant people and in natural contexts. Accountability is also shared by all and measured by the direct benefits to the child and family. The disadvantage is that it takes more time than other models and so, where this involves highly skilled personnel, it is more expensive.

Summary

There are some similarities and some differences in the special educational needs arising from VI and from ASD and, when both disabilities co-occur, they can result in highly variable and complex patterns of need. Both developmental disorders are best understood at the level of psychological functioning and teachers need to consider the needs at an individual level, but taking account of the knowledge about the effects on development of both disabilities. Visual impairment provides a good model for understanding the difficulties associated with ASD, although the methods of compensation may be very different. Specialist techniques for the two developmental disorders also have some common features, but there are some important and relevant differences. It is possible to adjust teaching in either specialism to accommodate the needs of the dually disabled child, but this needs to be undertaken with a full understanding of both conditions and a full assessment of the student and the learning environment. Given the unlikelihood of finding sufficient dually qualified teachers in most settings, trans-disciplinary models of collaboration among teachers, parents and specialists are the most promising way of providing the education to which the student is entitled.

References

Bakeman R, Adamson LB (1984) Co-ordinating attention to people and objects in mother-infant and peer-infant interaction. Child Development 55: 1278–89.

Baron-Cohen S (1995) Mindblindness: An essay on autism and theory of mind. Cambridge, MA: MIT Press.

Bigelow AE (2003) The development of joint attention in blind infants. Development and Psychopathology 15: 259–75.

Bruner J, Feldman C (1993) Theories of mind and the problem of autism. In: Baron-Cohen S et al. (eds) Understanding Other Minds: Perspectives from autism. Oxford: Oxford University Press.

Cass H (1996) Visual impairment and autism: what we know about causation and early identification. In: Buultjens M, Tansley K (eds) Autism and Visual Impairment: Conference Report, Sensory Series No. 5. Edinburgh: Moray House Publications.

Cass H (1998) Visual impairment and autism. Autism: the International Journal of Research and Practice 2: 117–38.

Charman T, Baird G (2002) Practitioner review: diagnosis of autistic spectrum disorder in 2- and 3-year-old children. Journal of Child Psychology and Psychiatry 43: 289–306.

Cumine V, Stephenson G, Leach J (1997) Asperger Syndrome: A practical guide for teachers. London: David Fulton.

DfES (2001) The Special Educational Needs Code of Practice. Nottingham: DfES.

Douglas G, McLinden M (2004) Visual impairment. In: Norwich B, Lewis A (eds) Special Teaching for Special Children: A Pedagogy for Inclusion? Milton Keynes: Open University Press.

Drissel NM (1997) What is a story book? Do it yourself hands-on story-time experiences. Awareness: NAVPI Newsletter Summer: 24–5.

Edland V (2003) People with visual impairment and autism-related difficulties: a project description website: www.novir.net/NOVIR/autisme/visual_ impairment_autismrelated_project.htm (accessed, September 2003).

Grandin T (1995) How people with autism think. In: Schopler E, Mesibov GB (eds) Learning and Cognition in Autism. New York: Plenum Press.

Hobson RP (1990) On the origins of self and the case of autism. Developmental Psychopathology 2: 163–81.

Hobson RP (1993) Autism and the Development of Mind. London: Erlbaum.

Hobson P (2002) The Cradle of Thought: Exploring the origins of thinking. London: Macmillan.

Howley M, Preece D (2003) Structured teaching for individuals with visual impairments. British Journal of Visual Impairment 21: 78–83.

Jones GE (2002) Educational Provision for Children with Autism and Asperger Syndrome. London: David Fulton.

Jordan R (1996a) Educational implications of autism and visual impairment. In: Buultjens M, Tansley K (eds) Autism and Visual Impairment: Conference Report, Sensory Series No. 5. Edinburgh: Moray House Publications.

Jordan R (1996b) Teaching communication to individuals within the autistic spectrum. REACH – Journal of Special Needs Education in Ireland 9: 95–102.

Jordan R (1999) Autistic Spectrum Disorders: An introductory handbook for practitioners. London: David Fulton.

Jordan R (2001) Autism with Severe Learning Difficulties. London: Souvenir Press.

Jordan R (2002) Autistic Spectrum Disorders in the Early Years: A guide for practitioners. Lichfield: QED.

Jordan R (2004) Autistic spectrum disorders. In: Norwich B, Lewis A (eds) Special Teaching for Special Children: A pedagogy for inclusion? Milton Keynes: Open University Press.

Jordan R, Powell S (1994) Whose curriculum? Critical notes on integration and entitlement. European Journal of Special Needs Education 9: 27–39.

Jordan R, Powell S (1995) Understanding and Teaching Children with Autism. Chichester: Wiley.

Kaplan M (1996) Interview with Stephen Edelson on the web: www.autism.org/ interview/kaplan.html.

Lovaas OI (1987) Behavioural treatment and normal educational and intellectual functioning in young autistic children. Journal of Consulting and Clinical Psychology 55: 3–9.

MacFarland F (1995) The Van Dijk approach. Journal of Visual Impairment and Blindness May–June: 222.

McLinden M, McCall S (2002) Learning Through Touch: Supporting children with visual impairment and additional difficulties. London: David Fulton.

Mesibov G (1997) Formal and informal measures of the effectiveness of the TEACCH program. Autism: the International Journal of Research and Practice 1: 25–35.

Morse M, Pawletko T, Rocissano L (2002) Autistic spectrum disorders and cortical visual impairment: two worlds on parallel courses; website: www.tsbvi.edu/Education/vmi/autism-vi.htm.

Murray D, Lawson W, Lesser M (2004) Attention, monotropism and the diagnostic criteria for autism. Autism: the International Journal of Research and Practice 8: in press.

Neisser U (1991) Two perceptually-given aspects of the self and their role in development. Developmental Review 11: 197–209.

Noens I, Van Berckelaer-Onnes I (2004) Making sense in a fragmentary world: communication in people with autism and learning disability. Autism: the International Journal of Research and Practice 8: in press.

Pawletko T (2002) Autism and visual impairment. Focal Points 1(2): 35–42.

Pawletko T, Rocissano L (2000) (revised on web, 2003) Autism in the visually impaired child; website: www.tsbvi.edu/Education/vmi/autism-vi.htm.

Pease L (2000) Creating a communicative environment. In: Aitken S, Buultjens M, Clark C, Eyre J, Pease L (eds) Teaching Children who are Deaf-Blind: Contact, communication and learning. London: David Fulton.

Peeters T (1997) Autism: From theoretical understanding to educational intervention. London: Whurr.

Powell SD, Jordan RR (1993) Being subjective about autistic thinking and learning to learn. Educational Psychology 13: 359–70.

Schopler E, Mesibov GB, Hearsey K (1995) Structured teaching in the TEACCH system. In: Schopler E, Mesibov GB (eds) Learning and Cognition in Autism. New York: Plenum Press.

Smith M (2002) Joseph's coat: people teaming in transdisciplinary ways; website: www.tsbvi.edu/Outreach/seehear/spring98/joseph.htlm (Texas).

Sobsey D, Wolf-Schein E (1996) Children with sensory impairments. In: Orelove FP, Sobsey D (eds) Educating Children with Multiple Disabilities. London: Paul Brookes.

Tager-Flusberg H (2003) Effects of language and communication deficits on learning and behavior. In: Prior M (ed.) Learning and Behavior Problems in Asperger Syndrome. New York: Guilford Press.

Teacher Training Agency (1999) National Standards for SEN Specialist Teachers. London: Teacher Training Agency.

Tomasello M (1995) Joint attention as social cognition. In: Moore C, Dunham P (eds) Joint Attention: Its origins and role in development. Hillsdale, NJ: Erlbaum.

Trevarthen C (2000) Helping autism with knowledge of human nature. Foreword. In: Woodward B, Hogenboom M (eds) Autism: A holistic approach. Trowbridge: Cromwell Press.

Watson L, Lord C, Schaffer B, Schopler E (1989) Teaching Spontaneous Communication to Autistic and Developmentally Handicapped Children. New York: Irvington Press.

Williams D (1996) Autism: An inside-out approach. London: Jessica Kingsley.

Zusia (2003) zusia@a... (20/7/2003) web page: http://groups.yahoo.com/group/faceblind/messages/1301?viscount=100.

CHAPTER 9

Guidelines for teaching students with visual impairment and autistic spectrum disorders

ROS GIBBONS

Ben

Six-year-old Ben is having his functional visual assessment. He is registered blind and never appears to look at anything, but staff feel sure he must see something, because he can spot a door (his abiding passion) at 10 metres. Is he seeing the light from the door? Is he sensing the draught or hearing the noise of an opening door? Nobody can be sure, because Ben never speaks or communicates. The assessment team is trying to establish what Ben can see by presenting him with different visual stimuli and observing his responses.

Various brightly coloured sound toys are placed on the table in front of him. Ben appears to hear them, but does not touch or look at them, except to sweep them onto the floor. A large Smartie is placed on a contrasting background immediately in front of Ben. He ignores it and continues to flap his hands aimlessly. An experienced nursery nurse, who knows Ben well, suggests they try apple, Ben's favourite fruit. A peeled apple quarter is placed on a dark blue plate in front of Ben. He continues to gaze into the distance, flapping his hands, but suddenly reaches accurately for the apple and eats it. Progressively smaller pieces of apple are tried until a 1-cm piece on a white plate is placed just out of arm's reach. Again Ben shows no sign of registering it visually, but gets out of his chair to reach for the tiny piece of apple.

Ben has recently been diagnosed as having autistic spectrum disorder (ASD). It is still difficult to ascertain whether Ben uses peripheral vision in an unusual way or whether he is choosing not to use his functional vision. Teachers may question why this happens, but most faced with students like this are more concerned with 'How?'.

How can Ben see things without apparently looking?
How can Ben be taught to use the residual vision he obviously has?
How do they teach Ben as a tactile learner if he will not hold anything?
How do they teach him as a sighted learner if he 'refuses' to look?
How do they communicate with him if he will not engage with them?

Peter

Six-year-old Peter is definitely blind, as he was born without eyes. He is also difficult to engage, although he can understand simple instructional language. He rarely speaks and, if he does, it is usually a one-word echo of what someone else has said. The class group is playing a circle game, in which Peter is choosing not to participate. Suddenly he begins to intone a long monologue about the distribution of rainfall in Australia. The class stops in amazement; they have never really heard his voice. It transpires that a television programme about the climate of Australia had been playing in the background at home 2 weeks before. Nobody is able to ascertain the trigger that unleashed this monologue. Peter is strongly suspected of having ASD, because of the nature of his communication difficulties and his obsessive behaviours, but he has no diagnosis.

Again, the 'Why?' questions are not for present consideration. Teachers, however, must be concerned with the 'How?' questions:

How can this facility for speech be channelled into communication?
How can Peter be taught to listen to and absorb language which is useful for him?
How can such a prodigious 'memory' be harnessed to help Peter to learn?

This chapter concerns the 'How?' questions that teachers and carers must address when educating such children as Ben and Peter, who have complex needs involving a visual impairment (VI) and ASD. Teachers of students with multiple disability with visual impairment (MDVI) search for some kind of guidelines to help them in cases of suspected ASD. Of course, all children are highly individual, but many teachers feel disorientated by the impact of ASD on the child's visual impairment, because they find their usual programmes do not bring about the expected progress.

The similarities of behavioural patterns in many young children with severe visual impairment and those with autism have been well documented and analysed (compare Gense and Gense, 1994; Brown et al., 1997; Hobson, 2002). The subject of debate is the reason for these similarities and whether this makes a difference to the way the children should be educated. There may be some strategies for ASD that would benefit all or most children with MDVI. There may also be specific strategies that would be appropriate only to students with ASD. This chapter is not concerned with the causes of ASD or the reasons it may be linked to visual impairment. It will seek to suggest some teaching strategies to be tried when teachers suspect or know that a student has both VI and ASD (VI/ASD).

Planning teaching programmes for students with VI/ASD

As Jordan (1996) points out, it is not possible to teach children with ASD without understanding their needs related to autism. If a diagnosis of ASD is ignored, teaching programmes for students with VI may lead to failure. Conversely, if the ASD is over-emphasized, there may be a danger of attributing to autism behaviours that are 'normal' for children who are blind. To complicate matters further, these children are more likely to have multiple learning needs and may also be non-verbal.

Teachers may consider whether they should adapt their teaching programmes for students with VI to accommodate the ASD or adapt the normally accepted teaching programmes for students with ASD, in order to exclude the visual teaching elements. A further factor to consider is that virtually all the major teaching programmes for students with ASD advocate promoting the use of vision as the primary mode of learning.

To a certain extent, the procedures and teaching strategies chosen will depend on the educational setting. If a student with VI/ASD is in a special school or unit for students with VI, taking account of such needs as structure and clear communication will not be at odds with the needs of children with VI. If the child with VI is in a specialist setting for ASD, the teacher will need to adapt teaching strategies either to make full use of any residual vision or to find tactile or auditory alternatives. Interestingly, Bogdashina (2003) suggests that pupils with sensory impairment and ASD are likely to fare better in a special school for visual or hearing impairment, because their sensory difficulties will be addressed first. However, the number of these special schools has greatly reduced in recent years, whereas the number of diagnoses of VI/ASD has increased.

Students with VI/ASD in mainstream schools are more likely to have language to assist them in learning, but care must be taken not to over-estimate their true levels of communication. The case of Peter, discussed above, is maybe an extreme example. Nevertheless, there are many cases of students with ASD (particularly Asperger's syndrome) who appear to have sophisticated levels of language, but who in fact are not able to communicate effectively and understand only on a very literal level. Similarly, many teachers will recall students who read Braille fluently, but are quite unable to explain what they have read, because of communication difficulties.

There is an inherent anomaly in devising teaching strategies for students with ASD, which also exists to some extent when devising teaching strategies for students who are blind. Teachers may try to empathize with students, to view learning from their perspective, but they cannot ever truly understand what it means to be blind, any more than they can view things with an 'autistic' mind. The use of blindfolds or simulation spectacles can simulate only the immediate access difficulty, not the developmental learning one. In the same way, ASDs are pervasive developmental disorders, so it is difficult for teachers to view things from an 'autistic' perspective. This makes teaching programmes for VI/ASD more difficult to devise, because they need to be radically different from the conventional methods often adapted for students with other learning needs.

One way of attempting to see things from an autistic perspective is to question adults who have ASD. A further anomaly occurs when we use 'native experts' (Bogdashina, 2003) to help us to devise teaching programmes for ASD, because only the most able adults on the autistic spectrum are able to communicate their perceptions and difficulties to us. Yet two-thirds of those with ASD are estimated to have additional learning difficulties (Baron-Cohen and Bolton, 1993). Measures recommended by able adults with ASD may not be appropriate for those with severe learning difficulties and yet it is these students with complex difficulties that teachers are more likely to encounter. If students are non-verbal or have limited communication and display challenging behaviour, the temptation is to leave them to their own devices, in order not to provoke an outburst. However, it is precisely these students who need the most help. Children and adults with severe autism must constitute one of the most vulnerable sections of society. When the impact of visual impairment is added to the difficulties of autism, it is clear that devising appropriate learning materials will be a major challenge. It is also clear that the National Curriculum was not devised with these children in mind!

Sensory perceptions

Although it is not necessary to examine all the current theories for the causes of ASD in order to devise teaching programmes, there is one hypothesis that seems particularly pertinent to students with VI. This relates to the abnormal sensory perceptions of individuals with ASD. Temple Grandin (Grandin and Scariano, 1986) describes herself as 'cut off by over-reactions or inconsistent reactions from my five senses' and Donna Williams (1996) feels that her body is a disconnected enemy 'flooding' her with feelings beyond her control.

Many students with VI/ASD have hypersensitive reactions to different sensory inputs. One student with VI/ASD would become aggressive at the smell of glue. Another would scream every time he entered the visual enhancement room, although he loved the multisensory equipment inside the room. It was discovered that he was upset by a tiny buzz from the dimmer light that was inaudible to anyone else.

Nony (1993) describes both photosensitivity and her problem with eye contact:

> Eye contact was painful to me. It was not quite like a burn or broken bone, but it can only be described as pain. (Nony, 1993, p. 5)

Waterhouse (2000) points out one part of McInnes and Treffry's (1982) description of some children with MSI (multisensory impairment) which also appears relevant:

> They often appear to have useful vision: they will pick up a penny from a brown rug and then walk into a wall or coffee table without appearing to see the obstacle. (A description which prompted one *sighted* woman *with autism* to say 'That was me!') (Waterhouse, 2000, p. 44 – inserted words in italics)

This apparently arbitrary use of vision relates directly to Ben's functional vision assessment, described at the beginning of this chapter.

Rimland (1964) and Delacato (1974) first advanced the theory that these abnormal sensory perceptions could be the *cause* of autism, rather than the symptoms. According to this theory, the abnormal perceptions cause extreme anxiety and the reaction is to withdraw into oneself or to focus the mind on internal stimuli (hence self-stimulatory or self-abusive behaviours). The 'autistic behaviours' could thus be considered a normal reaction or defence mechanism to abnormal stimuli. People, who are the most unpredictable source of abnormal sensory perceptions, cause individuals with ASD further confusion and anxiety, which, in turn, results in further withdrawal. This leads to developmental delay, possibly regression to earlier developmental reflexes, such as the Moro reflex and the limbic system (Waterhouse, 2000). The brain then relies on sensory perception, rather than reasoned response, so that sensory perceptions are heightened, anxiety is increased and a 'vicious circle' is set up, which can be broken only by positive intervention.

Delacato, having observed the reactions of children with ASD over many years, proposed that the sensory 'problems' of children with ASD were caused by sensory channels being 'hyper' (too much stimulation, resulting in sensory overload), 'hypo' (sensory deprivation) or 'white noise'. This last does not apply only to sound: it refers to the reaction to any unwanted sensory input by substituting another, e.g. hand-flapping, twirling or staring at a detail, in order to avoid communication. Delacato pioneered the idea of identifying the sensory problems of each individual and seeking to 'normalize' the way they process sensory input, in order to normalize the responses.

It must be said that many individuals with ASD would not regard these heightened sensory experiences as a problem. For example, Donna Williams (1998) refers to them as 'the beautiful side of autism' and many able adults with ASD resent the intervention of 'neuro-typicals' to normalize their responses (Sinclair, 1992).

Delacato's ideas, largely disregarded for 30 years, have recently been reconsidered. Hinder (2003), using Delacato's perspective, lists observed examples of 'hyper', 'hypo' and 'white noise' sensory perceptions in children with ASD and suggests 'things to try', acknowledging that the measures will not help all students with these sensory–perceptual difficulties. In addition to the 'sensorisms' described by Delacato, Hinder indicates movement difficulties, related to proprioception and vestibular sensitivities. These suggestions form a useful starting point for teachers of students with ASD and many are suitable for those with VI/ASD.

Waterhouse (2000) suggests that the starting point should be investigation of stress levels. For example, some children with VI/ASD are regularly seen with their fingers in their ears, trying to avoid unwanted sounds. Some noises can be easily eliminated or avoided to decrease their stress levels. However, if the hypersensitivity is related to the sound of a child's voice in class or to the school signal for end of lessons, children with hypersensitive hearing may spend all lesson with fingers in both ears, worrying about when the unwanted sound *may* occur. In this case their attention is impossible to refocus and it is necessary to desensitize or acclimatize them to the sound, in order for learning to take place.

If abnormal perceptions are a *cause* rather than a symptom of ASD, this may help to explain why some children who are blind demonstrate certain behaviours associated with ASD, without a full diagnosis. Many able, blind adults have 'blindisms', closely related to the 'sensorisms' observed by Delacato and others. If input from one sense (the most important, coordinating sense of sight) is missing and the other senses cause abnormal perceptions, it is not difficult to imagine the resulting confusion and distress. This may cause the individual to become 'tactile defensive' or to cover their ears, to avoid painful hypersensitivities or sensory overload. If more than one sense is defective it is also easier to understand some students' inability to process more than one sensory input at a time (often called 'mono-processing'). This will be an essential factor in devising teaching programmes. Perhaps a 'multisensory approach', as is often advocated for children with complex difficulties, should in fact be a 'one-sense-at-a-time' approach.

Some measures used to teach deaf–blind children (sometimes called multisensorily deprived) may also be effective in teaching children with ASD. McInnes and Treffry describe two basic reactions in the deaf–blind child, which sound remarkably like descriptions of children with ASD:

> One approach is to become hypoactive . . . . Often they dislike being touched and spend most of their time in self-stimulating activities and ritualistic play . . . . The second group exhibit hyperactive-like behaviour . . . .

Often they don't like to be held or touched, avoid giving eye contact, and refuse to interact with peers or adults. (McInnes and Treffry, 1982, p. 19)

These similarities in behaviour between multisensory deprivation and autism have been noted many times. The question we need to consider is whether there is a similarity in cause, as well as in behaviour, and whether this should influence our teaching methods.

The most compelling fact for teachers of students with partial sight and a possible ASD is that it may be possible to improve the quality of life for these students by tackling their visual (and other sensory) difficulties. In other words, if abnormal visual perceptions are causing anxiety, which in turn triggers their challenging 'autistic' behaviour, improving functional use of vision will also help to address their ASD. The challenge to teachers of students with VI/ASD is to find visual programmes that encourage the development of functional vision without increasing levels of anxiety. For example, if eye contact is as painful as described by Nony (1993), programmes that encourage eye contact are not only fraught with difficulty, they can be viewed as a form of child abuse. This is particularly true if the child concerned cannot explain why it is painful. Imposing eye contact may also inhibit the use of other senses. Gerland (1997), for example, says that she is able to listen more effectively when she does not have to look at the person who is speaking. Care should therefore be taken when devising visual programmes for a child with partial sight if an ASD is suspected.

It appears that many of the teaching strategies for students with VI or MDVI may be suitable for students with ASD and vice versa. It will be helpful to teachers of students who have, or who are suspected to have, both conditions to consider established teaching programmes in both disciplines. Some strategies may be appropriate for both students who are blind and students who have autism. Other programmes may need considerable adaptation. Finally we should consider specific VI/ASD approaches to be tried for this complex group of children, whom Lilli Nielsen (1996) terms 'very special people'. An open, eclectic approach is likely to be the most successful.

What may be successful with one student with ASD/VI may not work at all for another. This may be because of different developmental or emotional levels, or different degrees of sight impairment, ASD or other distorted perceptions. Other variables include fluctuating functional vision or hearing, health and medication issues, and factors in the environment beyond the teacher's control, so that an individual teaching programme may work one day and not the other. It is important to remember that these students do not have the ability to vary their approach or be flexible, so this is the duty of the teacher. The key question should not be 'How do I make the student do this task?', but rather 'How do I present this task in a way that is accessible to this child?'. No one would present a sheet of printed material to a student without sight. Sometimes a task may be equally impossible for students because of their ASD.

Therapies for individuals with VI/ASD

We should first consider the best known therapies for people with ASDs, in order to consider which elements could be effective for students with little or no sight. Many therapies are not specific to either condition. These include aromatherapy, brushing and deep pressure massage, diet therapies, and music, art and play therapy, all of which may be helpful to some. Only those treatments that may have particular relevance to students with both VI and an ASD are briefly considered here.

Sensory integration therapy

Sensory integration therapy has been developed from Delacato's theories (1974) and is usually delivered by occupational therapists. One aim is to desensitize students to the sensory stimuli that cause them pain or anxiety, so that they become calmer and better able to cope with their environment. It has proved most successful with severely autistic children who display self-injurious behaviour. The other, as the name suggests, is to provide multisensory therapy to enable children with ASD to integrate their sensory intake and use more than one sense at a time (for example, looking at an object at the same time as reaching for it). This is more problematic, because many children with ASD are 'mono-processors', to avoid sensory overload. Students with cortical visual impairment also share this problem (Morse, Pawletko and Rocissano, 2000).

Auditory integration training (AIT)

If a student with VI/ASD has a problem with tolerating particular sounds, frequently putting fingers in both ears in an attempt to block them out, AIT could be considered.

> Controversy still surrounds Auditory Integration Training, as the method by which it actually works is still unclear. It is said to help by 'levelling out' the frequencies at which the person hears, so that they are no longer overwhelmed by particular sounds. (Waterhouse, 2000, p. 259)

AIT gained a great deal of interest after the publication of Annabel Stehli's *The Sound of a Miracle, A Child's Triumph over Autism*, which recounts the remarkable improvements in her severely autistic daughter, Georgiana, after AIT. Georgiana's main hypersensitivity was auditory, but she also had visual hypersensitivity, describing a single hair as looking like 'a piece of spaghetti'.

> AIT has enabled me to sleep better, be calmer while I am awake and understand what I hear more quickly and clearly. I can handle noises which had previously caused me to withdraw or panic .... I believe that it also reduced sensitivities in sight, smell, taste and tactile sensations. (Stehli, 1991, p. 186)

The treatment consists of half-hour sessions during which the person listens to a wide range of music in different frequencies. Some may feel it is unethical to inflict this treatment through headphones, if the child cannot communicate to refuse it. However, it would seem particularly relevant to those with VI/ASD, because they naturally have to rely heavily on their auditory channels for most of their information processing.

Touch therapy

It is well known that many individuals with severe visual impairment, with or without ASD, are 'tactile defensive' (Nielsen, 1996; McLinden and Hendrickson, 1997) and we have already considered why that might be. In the same way they dislike being 'handled' and anyone who has worked under blindfold will empathize with that. Yet children with severe visual impairment need more physical contact than is usual. For example, sighted guide technique requires trust in the person whose arm is being held and a reassuring hug or a touch on the arm may need to be used in place of a gesture or facial expression.

Individuals with ASD often dislike any physical contact that is not on their terms. In contrast, some young blind children cling to a preferred adult, often clasping them with their arms and legs in a kind of fetal position. When they are babies this closeness to parents/carers may be positively promoted, because touch is the primal sense and the best way for children who are blind to learn about movement. Children who demonstrate developmental setback resembling ASD (Cass, Sonksen and McConachie, 1994) often revert to this behaviour and refuse to walk. Some parents develop a reluctance to allow their child on the floor, perhaps seeking to protect them from being hurt. This can seriously impede a child's tactile responses and ability to explore their environment, so causing further withdrawal.

At first, some kind of touch therapy might appear to be a way of addressing this, but it would need to be sensitively delivered by carers or professionals who know the student well and understand visual impairment. Most forms of touch therapy either introduce physical contact gradually or allow the child to control the amount of pressure applied from inanimate objects, like Grandin's 'squeeze machine' (Grandin and

Scariano, 1986). She and others, such as Gunilla Gerland (1997), describe how light touch is physically painful and arousing (a fact that should be remembered if using 'Tac Pacs', commonly used for children with MDVI). Children with VI/ASD generally respond better to firm, positive touch: hesitation in physical contact usually provokes feelings of insecurity.

Holding therapy

Holding therapy, popular in the 1980s, is used rarely now, by parents rather than teachers. Proponents start with the premise that children with ASD are choosing to withhold their affection, speech, etc. and that it is necessary to force the bonding process on them. The 'treatment' consists of the parent or carer holding the child by force, provoking a tantrum or panic attack, and then continuing to hold until the child is exhausted and gives in. Claire Sainsbury (2000) describes her experience of holding therapy as a form of 'sensory rape'. The experience is even more horrific when the child is held to forcibly maintain eye contact (Welch, 1988). Holding therapy should not be confused with touch therapy.

Behaviour optometry

Behaviour optometrists claim to be able to retrain the brain and to eliminate 'visual dysfunction'. This is not the same as visual impairment: individuals may have 6/6 (normal) vision, but experience distortion when reading or simply when orientating themselves. These distortions are not usually identified in conventional eye tests and may resemble the visual hypersensitivities reported by able adults with ASD. There is a great deal of scepticism about the effectiveness of this therapy. However, the principle of vision training should be an inherent part of any teaching programme for students with residual vision. Care must be taken to allow for visual hypersensitivities: students should not be compelled to use their vision in a way that is painful or uncomfortable for them.

Tinted glasses

Many 'high-functioning' adults with ASD have found tinted 'Irlen' glasses helpful in eliminating their visual hypersensitivity. These have often been controversial, but some VI services now have weekly clinics to assess SS/IS (scotopic sensitivity/Irlen syndrome). The glasses were originally developed to help with dyslexia and visual perception problems unrelated to visual impairment (Irlen, 1991) and have also been developed by the Institute of Optometry and others. Proponents, such as Jordan (1998), claim that tinted lenses can also be effective in alleviating the symptoms of ASD. Donna Williams describes how, with the aid of her Irlen glasses, she was suddenly able to see other people's faces (Williams, 1996). Others with autism claim that the glasses enable them to conceptualize better, allowing them 'the freedom to see and hear at the same time' (Waterhouse, 2000).

Appropriate teaching programmes

There are practical interventions from established teaching programmes that can be utilized by classroom practitioners. Some programmes, not specific to ASD, can be appropriate for students with VI/ASD. These include Gentle Teaching, Intensive Interaction and various early intervention programmes. Most of them share the same premise, that communication can begin only when trust has been established and this is achieved by understanding and responding to the child's needs.

Behaviour modification programmes (e.g. Lovaas)

A large number of teaching approaches for use with students with ASD come under the umbrella of behaviour modification, but the methods of application and the outcomes expected are very different. Taken in its widest sense, all classroom teaching concerns behaviour modification, when it is considered that to sit at tables and listen to a teacher for several hours is not 'normal' behaviour for children! It is worth considering this factor in relation to children with ASD, for whom any kind of social conforming is alien.

Perhaps the most controversial prescribed programme of behaviour management is ABA (applied behaviour analysis), of which the Lovaas method is the most widely used (Lovaas, 1987). The basic principle of the Lovaas method is that the child is taught, by constant repetition, to imitate one action (e.g. to put a brick in a box) to the prompt of 'Do this'. Imitation is then extended to other skills and behaviour, including, hopefully, language.

Most practitioners only advocate ABA as a 'kick start' to initiate attention skills in children at the pre-communication stage. The drills would be difficult to teach children with severe VI, because they rely heavily on visual imitation. However, imitation and response to a verbal cue are useful skills to learn, which can be extended to all kinds of learning experiences. A child with partial sight may learn to copy some actions. A child without sight can sometimes learn to copy by sound. For example, one child who was blind with ASD learned to count by copying first the teacher's voice, as bricks were dropped into a metallic box and then by dropping the bricks in himself, while counting.

This strategy of imitation will work only when the teacher has already gained the child's attention and if there are no other distractions. Nielsen (1996) advocates playing alongside and imitating the child's play in order to introduce the concept of imitation.

Children with ASD have a strong compulsion for sameness, so it is possible to teach them a social rule to which they will always comply (for example, standing up when a teacher comes into the room). They will not, however, understand the social reason for this and may stand up when their teacher slips out of the room for a minute and returns. A child who is blind may make the same mistake, but will take their cue from others or accept an explanation.

For those with VI/ASD, social learning will be very impaired and behaviour modification more difficult. The first problem is that compliance is not understanding. Donna Williams sums up behaviour modification as allowing:

> little ownership over one's behaviour, except when it adheres to what is desired by the professional or carer and their definition of normal, 'non-autistic' behaviour .... In my view, compliance may teach people more about other people's power than about their own behaviour. (Williams, 1996, p. 52)

This is an interesting viewpoint from someone with ASD and raises some challenging ethical questions, perhaps even more relevant to people who are also blind.

TEACCH

TEACCH (Treatment and Education of Autistic and Communication handicapped CHildren) is perhaps the most widely used teaching programme for students with ASDs. Unlike most other autism-specific programmes, it is possible to use only those elements that are appropriate to each individual. Perhaps for this reason it is more adaptable for children who also have VI, although one of its precepts is that vision should be the main sensory channel. TEACCH principles are particularly effective with children who are mono-processors, as the workstation approach eliminates other distractions and focuses on one task at a time. Students who are blind are particularly prone to auditory distractions and the work booths also reduce extraneous noise as well as visual distractions. Unlike most programmes for MDVI, TEACCH advocates that new skills should not be learned in a group situation, because being part of a group is another learning experience for students with ASD.

Another vital element of the TEACCH system is the visual timetable. This enables the student to know what is going to happen next and how long it will last. A timetable in an accessible form alleviates anxieties and gives reassurance and structure to the day.

Summary of teaching guidelines for VI/ASD

Using an eclectic approach, it is possible to summarize specific guidelines which may be helpful for teaching students with VI/ASD.

First precepts

It is vital to make a thorough functional vision assessment. If the teacher is not experienced in doing this, he or she should seek support from the local advisory teacher for VI. The assessment should be carried out over a period of time, observing the student in a variety of settings, to allow for fluctuations in vision, the effects of different environments and other internal and external factors. Clinical information should be obtained first, but not necessarily relied upon (compare Ben's functional vision assessment).

If any residual vision is discovered it should be utilized as much as possible, remembering the precept that visual images are usually the most successful for children with ASD. Even light perception can be used for orientation and for cause/effect learning. If the student cannot access pictures or photographs (sometimes they can be taught to do so), objects or tactile symbols can be used, with the reinforcement of colour, if possible, for classification purposes. Visual programmes should be devised that encourage use of residual vision without causing anxieties.

It is also important to take into consideration the impact of photophobia, cortical vision impairment (CVI) and other visual processing difficulties, which are likely to occur with VI/ASD (Morse et al., 2000). Line drawings may not be appropriate, colours may be processed differently and all visual information is likely to take much longer to process.

It is equally important to assess the impact of other sensory perceptions, which are part of the student's ASD. Olga Bogdashina (2003) has devised a Sensory Profile Checklist, most of which is appropriate for children with VI. The aim is to attempt to 'normalize' all the sensory perceptions as much as possible, to eliminate anxieties and maximize learning potential.

Most problems for students with ASD concern communication. Those who are also blind are often non-verbal or have severe communication problems, resulting in challenging behaviour. The first priority for these students is to provide them with a means of communication (see below).

Most students with VI/ASD demonstrate behaviours that teachers would like to modify or eliminate. Having assessed the visual behaviours and the impact of other sensory impairments, it should be possible to understand the triggers for these behaviours, so that attempts can be made to eliminate or at least reduce them. Success in this is unlikely unless the reason for the behaviours is understood.

The 'golden rule' is to try to view things from the student's perspective. This can be difficult for a sighted, 'neuro-typical' teacher, especially if the students are unable to express their needs. With this perspective, the first area to tackle is the student's environment.

Adapting the environment

> My ideal educational environment would be one where the room had very little echo or reflective light . . . . It would be an environment where the educator's volume was soft . . . that took account of mono and sensory hypersensitivity and information overload . . . .
>
> Unfortunately most educational environments are all about the very things that are the strongest sources of aversion. (Williams, 1996, p. 284)

Many of the difficulties faced by people with ASD would be greatly reduced by changes in their environment, which are quite possible to effect. Unfortunately, the environment that suits the student with ASD/VI is not always appropriate to others. For example, the student with an ASD needs a simple, uncluttered, calm environment. If he or she is placed with other students who are visually impaired but without ASD, the classroom will probably be a riot of colour, textures and sound-making toys: a stimulating multisensory environment. In this case one corner or area of the room should be designated a quiet area, in which the student with ASD can feel comfortable and secure. If the student can be induced to allow others to share the space, this will be an added bonus, but it may prove beneficial to the whole class if they understand that this area is special to that one student.

If the student is partially sighted, the area can be designated by colour or pictures/symbols; if the student is blind, the area can be carpeted or designated by floor texture. Some students with visual perception difficulties benefit from a curtained area. If the other students in the class are naturally noisy, another quiet room may be needed. It must be remembered that sighted students with an ASD can have a large proportion of sensory input removed by removing visual distractions, whereas sensory perceptions are all concentrated in the other senses if they are blind.

It is essential that the student takes himself to this quiet area, *not* be sent or placed in there for 'punishment' or time out, because it must be regarded by the student as a secure refuge. The use of 'time out' should be used judiciously with students with ASD, because to be withdrawn from a group activity may be exactly what they seek. They may make their behaviour increasingly outrageous in order to achieve it!

Some sensory triggers are not easy to deduce. Darren, a partially sighted pupil with an ASD, appeared to hit out at people at random. He started to say 'Hands!' before lashing out and it was discovered that he could not tolerate anyone putting their hand up to their face. Any child near him who picked his nose or a passing teacher covering his mouth to cough was therefore the target of his punches. Most students cannot voice their anxieties. Ishmail, a non-verbal student with an ASD and no sight, suddenly started reacting violently to a favourite care worker. She thought long and hard about what she was doing differently and realized she had changed her perfume. The effect of ceasing to use it was immediate.

Some would argue that these students have to grow up in the 'real world' and unpleasant stimuli have to be tolerated. It may be true that part of their education is to become acclimatized, but no individual in a state of pain or panic is in a position to learn. School should be a safe and secure learning environment. Most teachers would agree that it is worth the small sacrifice of wearing muted colours and no perfume if peace reigns in the classroom. Moreover, removing specific triggers may be beneficial to all. For example, fluorescent lights are a frequent cause of anxiety for students with ASD; they are also detrimental to those with nystagmus or epilepsy. Many students with severe learning difficulties may be 'mono-processors', so they will also benefit from 'one-sense-at-a-time' stimulation, rather than multisensory bombardment.

Environmental noise is much harder to tackle. If the student with VI/ASD is in a mainstream classroom, the noise level is likely to be frequently unbearable. In a special school environment, the number of people will be fewer, but they are likely to make more unpredictable sounds and to demonstrate their distress vocally, which is often a trigger for panic attacks. A high staff–pupil ratio is needed, so that there is flexibility and one or other student can be removed to calm down.

There is a strong argument for students with VI/ASD, particularly if they are blind and non-verbal, to have an 'intervenor', in a similar way to deaf–blind children. Alex was 12 when he arrived in a special school for VI. Blind and with no means of communication, he naturally found it very difficult to sit still during 'news time' when the others reported what they had done at the weekend. A one-to-one support assistant was negotiated, who, among other tasks, sat next to Alex, reporting his news (gleaned from the home– school diary), whilst signing the news on Alex's body. Gradually Alex understood the purpose of this communication and tolerated it without spoiling the session for the others. He also learned to make a few spontaneous signs, so that he could sign yes or no to the teacher's questions.

Advisory teachers of the hearing impaired can be helpful in setting up a good acoustic listening environment. Some students with auditory hypersensitivity can hear sounds several rooms away or the digestive processes of a child the other side of the room. These sounds are virtually impossible to eliminate, but other background noises, imperceptible to most, can be reduced. For extreme cases of hearing sensitivity some would advocate earplugs, although others would regard this as abusive. If the student chooses to put them in himself it could be regarded as self-defence! An alternative is the use of a Walkman, with calming music, when the environment is particularly noisy, but care must be taken that this does not become obsessive. Most teachers find it useful as a reward for tasks finished, but the correct music for the student must be to hand, because the wrong one may have an adverse effect.

The most important factor in the sound environment is the human voice. Teachers are accustomed to projecting their voices and they are used to explaining things using a variety of descriptive words and inflections. This is especially true of teachers and support staff of children with VI. Minimum language and a soft, calm voice without much inflection is more effective with students with VI/ASD. Jamie, a 4-year-old boy with VI/ASD, only ever speaks to adults in a monotonous whisper. Gradually teachers have realized that this produces the desired effect. Everybody is reduced to whispering back!

Curriculum issues

The National Autistic Society (NAS) (2003) points out that neither it, nor any LEA, has made a commitment to any particular therapy or teaching approach, because there is no evidence to support claims of having 'cured' ASD. However, it summarizes its recommendations under five principles, which make the acronym SPELL:

Structure
Positive
Empathetic
Low arousal
Links

These principles apply to all students with ASD, including those with sight disabilities. For example, students with visual impairment respond well to an expected routine and clearly defined tasks. The *structure* needs to be apparent, like the visual timetables of TEACCH, and the best way of achieving this with children not able to access pictures or print is by the use of objects of reference (see 'Communication', page 176).

It is important to have a set routine for the beginning of the day, combining greetings songs and the opportunity for each class member to establish the order of the day ahead. The objects of reference can be used sequentially, in 'timetable boxes', moving from left to right. They can then be made smaller, using part of the object to represent the activity (stage 2 and 3) and be put into a book, maybe with Braille or Moon (a simpler tactile code based on print letters) attached. This establishes the routine of the day, as well as progressing to literacy.

All students respond well to *positive* reinforcement and to teachers being *empathetic*, but it must be acknowledged that empathy is harder to achieve with a person with VI/ASD, especially if they have no means of communication. *Low arousal* can be difficult to ensure. The main aim for conventional students with VI is to provide a stimulating learning environment, which may involve higher levels of arousal than students with ASD can cope with. *Links* are very important for students with VI/ASD, but are more difficult to achieve without the benefit of sight. Objects of reference are often the best method, because they can signify a whole situation, but care must be taken. One student with VI/ASD was introduced to the concept of a plastic ball signifying the ball pool, but it had been cleaned with antiseptic, the smell of which he associated with the toilet. Disastrous results ensued when he entered the ball pool!

Music is important to students with VI or an ASD, but for students with both conditions it is often a vital channel for learning. They seem to find it easier to attach meaning to new skills if these are accompanied by songs or rhythms. A sung phrase or a chord on the guitar will often attract the student's attention better than oral instruction and can be used to alert them to change of activity or to a new piece of information. This will serve as a *link*, so that they can remember what they have to do next time they hear the same phrase or chord. Generalization has to be undertaken later.

As well as the principles of SPELL, there are specific curriculum issues relating to sight impairment. Many teaching programmes advocate choice-making and this is vital when the student cannot go and choose independently. Sometimes this can be done by smell (e.g. 'Apple or orange juice?'), allowing time to sniff and choose. Sound references can also be used for activities, but in most cases the natural method of offering choice is to allow the student with VI/ASD to feel the two options. If they do not naturally explore tactually, the temptation is to place the hands on the first object, which may meet great resistance and they may not wish to explore the second 'choice'. As with all students with ASD, it is vital to adhere to the chosen option, otherwise the concept of choice cannot be learned.

As most students with VI/ASD are tactile defensive, a programme of desensitizing may be necessary, in which they can feel in control of what they are touching. Hard, plastic surfaces are usually preferable, because they hold fewer surprises. Many students can be encouraged to touch switches that produce a predictable effect, before they can face the challenge of 'messy play'. Another good introduction is water, dry pasta or beads: the rhythmic sound and tactile effect of running these through fingers is often soothing to a student with VI/ASD, as they give good sensory feedback.

The importance of physical exercise for students with ASD has often been emphasized and it is equally important for students with VI, who are frequently overweight because of lack of normal exercise. Students with VI/ASD often love exercise such as swimming or trampolining, but these are not always possible to provide on a frequent basis. It is worth ensuring that these students can have regular access to playground or exercise equipment, soft play or multisensory rooms or simply walks outside. Physical exercise releases endorphins, which promote calmness and concentration, but it must be made clear to the student, by a visual or tactile timetable, that these spells of physical exercise are limited, otherwise the transition to the next activity will be time-consuming and stressful. Some teachers use 5-minute physical activities as a bridge to the next activity, to facilitate transfer. Others alternate longer periods of exercise with regular classroom work. If only one or two students in the class have VI/ASD they will require an individual timetable and some imaginative use of support staff.

Behavioural issues

Bogdashina (2003) points out that, whereas the behavioural characteristics of the 'triad of impairments' (Wing and Gould, 1979) form a useful tool for diagnosis, they do not tell us why individuals exhibit the behaviours or how they experience the world. Teachers cannot hope to eliminate the behaviours they would wish to change in their students if they cannot understand the underlying causes and this must underpin any teaching strategy. Behaviour management issues, which often preoccupy teachers of students with VI/ASD, should be considered as part of the curricular and environmental adaptation. Students with VI/ASD cannot be 'naughty', because they lack the social communication skills, but they can be very manipulative, in order to achieve the desired response. For example, if they find that banging their head against a corner of the table produces an instant reaction from teachers, they will continue to do so, to produce the same reaction. The teacher must then decide whether to change the environmental factor (separate the child from the table) or change the curriculum on offer to something more interesting, so that the student loses interest in head-banging. This is not easy, when dealing with obsessive behaviour.

Students with VI/ASD cannot help their reactions to 'trigger stimuli' and they can neither see nor understand other people's reactions. If the obsessive behaviour is unacceptable (e.g. playing with globules of saliva), a more acceptable behaviour should be found (e.g. rolling beads or drops of water on a tray). Care must be taken that the substitute activity does not become more unacceptable than the original one. It is highly unlikely that all obsessive behaviours will be eliminated in a student with two conditions that are both apt to produce stereotypical behaviour.

In the same way, it must be accepted that there will always be occasions when all the strategies and avoidance tactics fail and behaviour will become challenging or unacceptable. There are no set measures for dealing with this: the British Institute of Learning Difficulties (BILD) recommend that a Reactive Plan be prepared, by the class team, for each individual in this situation. Reactive measures will be different for each student, but the plan should take account of the impact of visual impairment in cases of VI/ASD.

Communication

Communication is the key to understanding and learning. Interventions for encouraging communication in students with VI are often appropriate for students with ASD. For example, both sectors need to have their name spoken when they are addressed, or before they are approached and both need clear, specific language. Students with ASD also need a calm, uninflected voice and instructions using minimum language, to take account of their communication difficulties. For example, negatives and unnecessary adjectives should be avoided and humour must be judicious. Both students with VI and those with ASD tend to understand things literally, but blind children without an ASD can usually interpret meaning from the tone of voice.

For non-verbal students, or those with severe communication difficulties, many methods of augmentative communication may be tried, including some autism-specific interventions.

Picture Exchange Communication System (PECS)

PECS (Bondy and Frost, 1994) is widely used with children with ASD who use vision as the main learning channel. The principle is to encourage the child to *initiate* communication and offer independently a picture of the item wanted. The disadvantage for children with partial sight is that, while their vision may be sufficient to see the card when it is presented to them, it may be difficult to get them to look for the cards: offering the cards to them defeats the principle of PECS. PECS can be adapted to make best use of residual vision, e.g. the line drawing format may not be suitable for children with cortical VI, so photographs or simplified colour block drawings can be substituted. Objects of reference can be used instead of cards, but the principle of the student finding the object to initiate the communication must be retained, so they must learn where to look for the objects, which can present difficulties.

Signing

Most students with ASD have as much difficulty understanding signing as speech, because they do not understand communicative intent. However, there is evidence that some of these students come to speech through the additional use of signing and some retain a greater number of meaningful signs than they do words (Jordan and Powell, 1998). Signing is usually based on Makaton (a simplified version of British Sign Language) but is adapted to be used 'on the body' so that students without sight can use the signs both receptively and expressively.

Augmented speech

There is a wide range of speech synthesizers available, ranging from a simple Big Mack, which, when touched, simply repeats what has been pre-recorded in speech, to sophisticated Touch Talkers, with complex grammar sequences. A Big Mack is a good way to introduce students with VI/ASD to the basic concept of communication, because pressing the switch 'gives' them a voice and introduces them to the concept of turn taking. Touch Talkers normally have keyboards with picture symbols and these have to be adapted to tactile keyboards for students with severe VI. Use of augmentative speech devices normally encourages speech in students with VI/ASD, rather than replacing it.

Social stories

These were developed by Carol Gray (2002) to enable people with ASD to learn the correct sequences of social responses to cope in ordinary life. The principle is to make a simple story out of what the child has to do, for example when he or she arrives at school, with the child as the subject of the story. These can work well for students with VI, as they often memorize sequences of events subjectively. The story can be read, if the student can read, or listened to on tape, but it needs to be repeated many times, with the student repeating the sequence until the story prompts can be faded. The use of picture prompts is unlikely to be possible for VI/ASD.

Objects of reference

Objects of reference (see Ockelford, 2002; Donaldson, 2003) can be difficult to initiate if the child will not hold or handle objects, but it is well worth
persevering, because, used systematically, they are probably the most useful
tool for teaching students with ASD/VI. Each representative object should
be presented to the child systematically and consistently, immediately
before each activity. (The easiest object to introduce is usually a cup before
drinks time or a spoon before lunch.) If the student will not hold the object,
it should be attached to them in some way, using, for example, a money
belt, an apron with pockets or soap-tablet dispenser bags pinned to cloth-
ing. Immediately the activity is finished, it is important to say, 'finished',
signing on the student's body, and to remove the object. Remarkable results
have been achieved using this simple method, because, once the student
has grasped the principle, it is much easier to accomplish transition to a
new activity, which is always a problem for individuals with VI/ASD.

Some maintain that the objects chosen should be personal to the individual. This may seem more relevant to the child, but it could develop
into an attachment for the object, rather than an understanding of sym-
bolization or a communication system. In order for the child to
understand that the cup signifies a drink or the piece of towelling signifies swimming, the objects have to be formalized and used consistently by
all people in contact with the child. Otherwise the object will not be generalized to all situations and the student will not understand the principle
of communication.

For a student without speech, objects can be used both receptively
('You're going swimming now') and expressively ('Can I go swimming
now?'). They also introduce the child in a practical way to symbolic meaning. The object is more permanent than speech, which is transitory. The
important breakthrough occurs when the child grasps that the object has
a 'shared' meaning, which is the beginning of communication. More
advanced objects of reference, representing emotions, have been developed in the Texas School for the Blind and are at present being piloted in
the UK. This may be a way forward in promoting expression, particularly
with those who are non-verbal.

Conclusion

Individuals with ASD often depict themselves as 'aliens', as reflected in the
titles of their books (*Through the Eyes of Aliens* (O'Neill, 1999), *Freaks,
Geeks and Asperger Syndrome* (Jackson, 2002)). Moreover, many students
with ASD resent what they perceive as misconceived intervention:

My teachers think they know more about autism than me because they have been on a course. But I have been autistic all my life! (Matthew Stanton, in Bogdashina, 2003)

This quotation could be equally used by someone who is congenitally blind. When devising teaching strategies for students with VI/ASD it is important to listen to the individuals and when they cannot communicate their needs we can learn only by careful observation. In this way we can establish communication and devise teaching programmes that are helpful rather than intrusive.

References

Baron-Cohen S, Bolton P (1993) Autism: The facts. Oxford: Oxford University Press.

Bogdashina O (2003) Sensory Perceptual Issues in Autism and Asperger Syndrome. London: Jessica Kingsley.

Bondy AS, Frost LA (1994) Pre-school Education Programmes for Children with Autism. Austin, TX: Pro-Ed.

Brown R, Hobson RP, Lee A, Stevenson J (1997) Are there 'autistic-like' features in congenitally blind children? Journal of Child Psychology 38: 693–703.

Cass H, Sonksen P, McConachie H (1994) Developmental setback in severe visual impairment. Archives of Disease in Childhood 70: 192–6.

Delacato C (1974) The Ultimate Stranger. New York: Doubleday.

Donaldson M (2003) Objects of reference: An investigation into their development and use in schools with pupils who have MDVI. MEd Dissertation, University of Birmingham.

Gense MH, Gense DJ (1994) Identifying autism in children with blindness and visual impairments. RE: Views 26(2): 55–62.

Gerland G (1997) A Real Person – Life on the Outside. London: Souvenir Press.

Grandin T, Scariano MM (1986) Emergence Labelled Autism. Novato, CA: Arena Press.

Gray C (2002) My Social Stories Book. London: Jessica Kingsley.

Hinder S (2003) Sensory Motor Difficulties in People with Autistic Spectrum Disorder. BILD conference.

Hobson P (2002) The Cradle of Thought. London: Pan Macmillan.

Irlen H (1991) Reading By the Colors. New York: Avery Publishing Group.

Jackson L (2002) Freaks, Geeks and Asperger Syndrome. London: Jessica Kingsley.

Jordan I (1998) Visual Dyslexia. Scunthorpe: Desk Top Publications.

Jordan R (1996) Educational Implications of Autism and Visual Impairment (www.ssc.mhie.ac.uk/docs/jordan.html).

Jordan R, Powell S (1998) Understanding and Teaching Children with Autism. London: David Fulton.

Lovaas OI (1987) Behavioural treatment and normal educational and intellectual functioning in young autistic children. Journal of Consulting and Clinical Psychology 55: 3–9.

McInnes JA, Treffry JM (1982) Deaf-Blind Infants and Children. Buckingham: Open University Press.

McLinden MT, Hendrickson H (1997) Implications of a visual impairment for early communication development. SLD Experience 17: 2–5.

Morse MT, Pawletko T, Rocissano L (2000) Autistic Spectrum Disorders and Cortical Visual Impairment: Two worlds on parallel courses (www.tsbvi.edu/Education/vmi/autism-cvi.htm).

National Autistic Society (2003) Fact Sheet (www.nas.org.uk).

Nielsen L (1996) The Challenges of the Nineties Concerning Children with Visual and Multiple Impairments, from Scottish Education for the Nineties: Learning with Visual Impairment. Proceedings of 3-day conference, September 1990, Scottish Sensory Centre, updated 1998.

Nony (1993) Speculation on light sensitivity. Our Voice 3: 1.

Ockelford A (2002) Objects of Reference. London: RNIB.

O'Neill JL (1999) Through the Eyes of Aliens. London: Jessica Kingsley.

Rimland B (1964) Infantile Autism. New York: Appleton-Century-Crofts.

Sainsbury C (2000) Holding Therapy: An autistic perspective (www.nas.org.uk/pubs/archive/hold.html).

Sinclair J (1992) Bridging the gaps: an inside view of autism. In: Schopler E, Mesibov G (eds) High Functioning Individuals with Autism. New York: Plenum Press.

Stehli A (1991) The Sound of a Miracle, A Child's Triumph over Autism. New York: Doubleday.

Waterhouse S (2000) A Positive Approach to Autism. London: Jessica Kingsley.

Welch M (1988) Holding Time. London: Century.

Williams D (1996) Autism: An inside-out approach. London: Jessica Kingsley.

Williams D (1998) Like Colour to the Blind. London: Jessica Kingsley.

Wing L, Gould J (1979) Severe impairments of social interaction and associated abnormalities in children: Epidemiology and classification. Journal of Autism and Developmental Disorders 9: 11–30.

Reflections on the connections between autism and blindness

HELEN TAGER-FLUSBERG

Personal reflections

For over 25 years I have studied autism: children and adults, low-functioning and high-functioning individuals, cross-sectional studies and longitudinal studies, cognitive–linguistic and social–affective impairments. These studies have been designed from the perspective of an experimental psychologist, which was the focus of my undergraduate and postgraduate training. I have compared autism with many other neuro-developmental disorders: Down syndrome, mental handicap, specific language impairment, Williams syndrome, Prader–Willi syndrome, and, of course, non-disordered controls. Yet in all this time I have never studied children or adults with sensory impairment. Over the past decade I realized how much I have missed in excluding both deaf and blind people from my research programmes, especially since I have had the opportunity to meet blind children and adults in my everyday life, outside the laboratory.

I live less than three miles from the Perkins School for the Blind (made famous by its most illustrious alumna, Helen Keller), and the Carroll Center for the Blind is less than half a mile from my house. On a regular basis I get the chance to speak to students attending these institutions on walks in the neighbourhood, waiting at the bus stop or enjoying coffee at our local Starbucks. These informal meetings leave me with a singular reaction: blind people are both strikingly similar to people with autism, yet at the same time they are quite different. What are these similarities? What are the differences? How do the distinctive behavioural, social and communicative patterns of blind people impact on their experiences of others and their everyday life? The wonderful and original collection of chapters in this volume has helped to provide some answers to these questions, and has underscored how enriched my own research on autism would be if I could also study blind children and adults.

Reflections on the book

The chapters in this volume present a wide variety of research programmes on autism and blindness, as well as diverse perspectives and
opinions on how to conduct and interpret results of investigations that
compare or contrast these two conditions. To some authors there are
striking similarities between autistic and blind people, similarities that
reveal important insights into the development of communication and
social cognition. Other authors focus on important differences between
autism and blindness, cautioning against drawing strong conclusions
about one population from the other.

Explaining conflicting views

How might we reconcile these conflicting perspectives? Similar contro-
versies can be found in investigations of other neurodevelopmental
disorders or other special populations (Tager-Flusberg, 1999), for example Williams syndrome. Williams syndrome is a rare genetic disorder
caused by a small deletion on one copy of chromosome 7 that includes
about 20 genes. It has captured the interest of cognitive scientists because
of its striking and unusual behavioural profile and pattern of cognitive
strengths and weaknesses. In Williams syndrome there are huge dispari-
ties between the good performance on language and face processing tests
and the highly impaired performance on visual–spatial constructive tests.
Initially, researchers were captivated by the extreme loquaciousness and
linguistic sophistication of people with Williams syndrome. As more
detailed investigations have been published, researchers disagree regarding the language abilities of this unique and rare genetic syndrome. Some
continue to claim that language is relatively intact (e.g. Bellugi, Wang and
Jernigan, 1994; Clahsen and Almazan, 1998), while others argue that,
despite superficial linguistic fluency, morpho-grammatical deficits are evident across children of different ages (Karmiloff-Smith et al., 1997; Levy
and Hermon, 2003; Volterra et al., 2003).

One way of thinking about conflicting views of this sort is to consider
the difference between a clinical perspective and an experimental perspective. At a clinical level, a person with Williams syndrome presents as
a highly verbal and sophisticated communicator. It is only when given
quite challenging experimental tasks in a controlled research setting that
certain specific deficits become evident. Similarly, at the clinical level of
presentation some blind people exhibit many behavioural symptoms that
are characteristic of autism. On deeper empirical analysis fundamental
differences between blind and autistic individuals may be revealed, as
illustrated in several of the chapters in this volume.

A second issue concerns the variability found among blind people. One key aspect of this variability concerns the onset and degree of visual impairment. Autistic features, especially in social–communicative functioning, are found only among those individuals who are totally blind from birth. A minimal degree of visual input significantly reduces or eliminates autistic-like impairments in visually impaired children. It seems that social–affective developments can build on even the most limited access to information from the environment about moving entities, which may be all that is needed to trigger the infant's understanding that others are intentional beings. Interestingly, this is not the case among deaf children. Significant delays in the acquisition of spoken language are still evident when there is some residual hearing. The complex sound structure of language requires access to much more detailed acoustic information than may be available to moderately deaf children. There are other important aspects of variability among blind children that may account for some of the differences in findings across research programmes. These include variability in neurological status, intelligence, language skills, background variables such as socio-economic status, and perhaps most importantly intervention history. These factors, all of which are known to influence social–communicative development, are not always measured or incorporated into analyses and interpretation of findings.

Third, as noted by several contributors to this volume, methodological factors need to be taken into consideration. Developmental psychologists have designed many ingenious tasks to tap children's conceptual knowledge, such as false belief. Yet these tasks cannot simply be administered to either autistic or blind children without considerable creative adaptation. False belief tasks entail complex linguistic narratives and test questions. For some children with autism who also have language impairments, it is possible that the language of the task, rather than a lack of understanding of the concept of belief, leads to failure (Tager-Flusberg and Sullivan, 1994). Thus, care must be taken to redesign false belief tasks reducing the language demands for children with autism. The challenge of designing a false belief task for blind children is even greater since traditional tasks are so dependent on the child witnessing an event or having perceptual access to familiar objects. Different research teams have resolved this challenge in different ways but we do not know whether the modified tasks are genuinely equivalent to one another or to the standard false belief tasks used in studies of sighted children.

Finally, there is the thorny issue of choosing appropriate comparison groups and selecting variables for matching children in different groups. Autism researchers have included many different kinds of comparison groups and it is still not clear which variables are crucial for matching across different populations. There are pitfalls associated with different approaches, and none seems to eliminate all concerns (Tager-Flusberg, 2004). An alternative strategy is to explore within-group performance, especially to investigate the variability that is inherent in the population. Our recent research on language, cognitive profiles and theory of mind in autism has moved to this within-group design (Kjelgaard and Tager-Flusberg, 2001; Steele, Joseph and Tager-Flusberg, 2003; Tager-Flusberg and Joseph, 2003) in order to identify more homogeneous subtypes within the heterogeneity that characterizes autistic spectrum disorders. Similarly, as noted in his chapter, Hobson has also moved to explore within-group differences among blind children, which has led to a more complete understanding of similarities and differences between autistic and blind children. As research on both autism and blindness continues, we can expect to see more complementary methodological approaches that will provide further insight into how these populations compare with one another, and with normally developing children.

Autism and blindness

The central question that seems to lie at the heart of this volume is: *Do blind children have autism?* Worded in this way, the clear answer is *No!* Autism is a genetically based neurodevelopmental disorder. Evidence points to brain pathology beginning very early in fetal development (Bauman, 1999). Blind children do not suffer from brain pathology and thus, by definition at this level of analysis, do not have autism. There are fundamental differences between children who have a disorder affecting brain development and children who come into this world with essentially a normal brain, but with peripheral sensory impairment. These differences must be respected in considering the parallels between autistic and blind children. At the same time, we can reword the question to: *Do blind children exhibit the same constellation of atypical behaviours as autistic children?* Asked in this way, the answer is clearly *Yes!*

Within the field of autism we distinguish between idiopathic autism (with no known other causes) and non-idiopathic autism. The classic cases that Kanner (1943) described, and which are studied in most genetic and behavioural studies, involve idiopathic autism. But there are also other children who exhibit the symptoms of autism and meet DSM-IV criteria (American Psychiatric Association, 1994) for this disorder, including children with severe deprivation or children with other syndromes such as fragile-X syndrome or tuberous sclerosis. Blind children fall into this latter category of non-idiopathic autism. Some consider these non-idiopathic examples to be phenocopies of classic autism, suggesting that there may be subtle differences in the expression of certain symptoms (e.g. Feinstein and Reiss, 1998; Rutter et al., 1999). The significant

similarities between idiopathic autism and non-idiopathic autism, especially exemplified by blindness, provide an important theoretical window
onto our understanding of developmental trajectories in the domain of
social–communicative development. It is this level of similarity that is captured by our clinical intuition about congenitally blind children and which
is discussed so powerfully by Hobson in Chapter 2. Such similarities cannot and should not be ignored, even though there are subtle differences
in certain behavioural patterns, and in the developmental outcomes.

Lessons learned from investigating autism among blind children

One of the most intriguing lessons to be learned from the study of blind
children is the significance of the ability to perceive non-verbal social
cues, such as facial expressions and body gestures, in the development of
theory of mind and other aspects of social cognition. Deficits in
social–communicative functioning among blind children can be traced
more directly to their lack of access to social–perceptual information,
rather than to fundamental impairments in a computational theory of
mind module (Leslie and Roth, 1993). Studies of blind children highlight
the significance of a developmental approach to theory of mind, one that
emphasizes the fundamental significance of a social–affective component.
Interestingly, more recent theoretical and empirical approaches to theory
of mind impairment in autism have also moved in this direction, focusing
on what are now viewed as core deficits in social–perceptual abilities
rather than social cognitive aspects of theory of mind (e.g. Tager-Flusberg,
2001; Klin et al., 2003).

On reflection, given the developmental significance of visual information for other people, especially newborns and young infants, it is
perhaps not surprising that congenitally blind children suffer social and
communicative impairments that are parallel to those found among autistic children. Of greater significance are the *other* behavioural symptoms
that illustrate similarities between blind and autistic children, discussed in
the chapters by Hobson (Chapter 2) and Pring and Tadic (Chapter 4).
These include, for example, repetitive behaviours, stereotypies, symbolic
play deficits and unusual cognitive abilities such as absolute pitch. The
presence of these behavioural patterns alongside the social–communicative
impairments suggests strongly that this constellation of features represents a unitary phenomenon.

The key question is: Why do social, communicative, repetitive or
stereotyped behaviour, and atypical cognitive talents, co-occur whether in
autism or blind children? Our current conceptual and developmental

theories have not really provided a satisfactory answer – there is no single cognitive mechanism that seems to underlie these diverse behavioural characteristics. Among autism researchers these characteristics are interpreted as highlighting the *complexity* of the phenotype, especially as exemplified in the component traits that make up the broader phenotype of autism found among relatives of children with autism. Thus, one widely held current view in the field of autism is that we can dissect the phenotype into distinct components such as social affiliation, motor patterns and language ability (e.g. Dawson et al., 2002). These distinct components are hypothesized to come under the control of different neural mechanisms and genes. This perspective is used to explain why autism is not caused by a single gene, but rather by the interaction of several genes, each putatively responsible for these different facets of the phenotype. Indeed, this is the prevailing view among genetic researchers in the field of autism (e.g. Bailey, Phillips and Rutter, 1996; Santangelo and Folstein, 1999). The fact that in blind children we see these diverse behaviours cohere in the same constellation poses a significant challenge to this hypothesis.

There are no easy answers to the questions raised by investigations comparing parallel behaviour patterns among blind and autistic children. Whether or not we refer to blind children who exhibit the full range of autistic features as 'autism' and whether or not we decide that these parallels are merely superficial, we still need to develop models for understanding why we see these similar patterns, and what they may reveal about the mechanisms that underlie social, communicative and behavioural abilities. The most profound lesson I learned from reading this volume was eloquently stated by Peter Hobson in the conclusion to his chapter: 'The pathogenesis of autism in blind children may prove to be invaluable for our understanding of "autism" itself.'

Acknowledgements

Preparation of this contribution was supported by grants from the National Institutes of Health (U19 DC 03610 and U54 MH 66398).

References

American Psychiatric Association (1994) Diagnostic and Statistical Manual of Mental Disorders (DSM-IV), 4th edn. Washington, DC: APA.

Bailey A, Phillips W, Rutter R (1996) Autism: Toward an integration of clinical, genetic, neuropsychological, and neurobiological perspectives. Journal of Child Psychology and Psychiatry 37: 89–126.

Bauman M (1999) Autism: Clinical features and neurobiological observations. In: Tager-Flusberg H (ed.) Neurodevelopmental Disorders. Cambridge, MA: MIT Press/Bradford Books, pp. 383–99.

Bellugi U, Wang P, Jernigan T (1994) Williams syndrome: An unusual neuropsychological profile. In: Broman SH, Grafman J (eds) Atypical Cognitive Deficits in Developmental Disorders: Implications for brain function. Hillsdale, NJ: Lawrence Erlbaum Associates, pp. 23–56.

Clahsen H, Almazan M (1998) Syntax and morphology in Williams syndrome. Cognition 68: 167–98.

Dawson G, Webb S, Schellenberg G, Dager S, Friedman S, Aylward E, Richards T (2002) Defining the broader phenotype of autism: Genetic, brain, and behavioral perspectives. Development and Psychopathology 14: 581–611.

Feinstein C, Reiss AL (1998) Autism: The point of view from fragile X studies. Journal of Autism and Developmental Disorders 28: 393–405.

Kanner L (1943) Autistic disturbances of affective contact. Nervous Child 2:217–50.

Karmiloff-Smith A, Grant J, Berthoud I, Davies M, Howlin P, Udwin O (1997) Language and Williams syndrome: How intact is 'intact'? Child Development 68: 274–90.

Kjelgaard M, Tager-Flusberg H (2001) An investigation of language impairment in autism: Implications for genetic subgroups. Language and Cognitive Processes 16: 287–308.

Klin A, Jones W, Schultz R, Volkmar F (2003) The enactive mind, or from actions to cognition: Lessons from autism. Philosophical Transactions of the Royal Society, Series B 358: 345–60.

Leslie AM, Roth D (1993) What autism teaches us about metarepresentation. In: Baron-Cohen S, Tager-Flusberg H, Cohen DJ (eds) Understanding Other Minds: Perspectives from Autism. Oxford: Oxford University Press, pp. 83–111.

Levy Y, Hermon S (2003) Morphological abilities of Hebrew-speaking adolescents with Williams syndrome. Developmental Neuropsychology 23: 59–83.

Rutter M, Andersen-Wood L, Beckett C, Bredenkapm D, Castle J, Groothues C, Kreppner J, Keaveney L, Lord C, O'Connor TG (1999) Quasi-autistic patterns following severe early global deprivation. English and Romanian adoptees (ERA) study team. Journal of Child Psychology and Psychiatry 40: 537–49.

Santangelo SL, Folstein SE (1999) Autism: A genetic perspective. In: Tager-Flusberg H (ed.) Neurodevelopmental Disorders. Cambridge, MA: MIT Press, pp. 431–47.

Steele S, Joseph RM, Tager-Flusberg H (2003) Developmental change in theory of mind abilities in children with autism. Journal of Autism and Developmental Disorders 33: 461–7.

Tager-Flusberg H (1999) Introduction to research on neurodevelopmental disorders from a cognitive neuroscience perspective. In: Tager-Flusberg H (ed.) Neurodevelopmental Disorders. Cambridge, MA: MIT Press/Bradford Books, pp. 3–24.

Tager-Flusberg H (2001) A re-examination of the theory of mind hypothesis of autism. In: Burack J, Charman T, Yirmiya N, Zelazo P (eds) The Development of Autism: Perspectives from theory and research. Mahwah, NJ: Lawrence Erlbaum Associates, pp. 173–93.

Tager-Flusberg H (2004) Strategies for conducting research on language in autism. Journal of Autism and Developmental Disorders 34: 75–80.

Tager-Flusberg H, Joseph RM (2003) Identifying neurocognitive phenotypes in autism. Philosophical Transactions of the Royal Society, Series B 358: 303–14.

Tager-Flusberg H, Sullivan K (1994) Predicting and explaining behavior: A comparison of autistic, mentally retarded and normal children. Journal of Child Psychology and Psychiatry 35: 1059–75.

Volterra V, Caselli C, Capirci O, Tonucci F, Vicari S (2003) Early linguistic abilities of Italian children with Williams syndrome. Developmental Neuropsychology 23: 33–58.

Index